The Prentice-Hall Series in Personality

Richard S. Lazarus, editor

*This volume is one of a series of short textbooks
being developed for undergraduate instruction
in the fields of personality. There will be separate volumes
on personality theory, personality assessment,
abnormal personality, and special issues of
contemporary research.*

ROBERT HOGAN

The Johns Hopkins University

Personality Theory

The Personological Tradition

Prentice-Hall, Inc., Englewood Cliffs, New Jersey

Library of Congress Cataloging in Publication Data

HOGAN, ROBERT. (DATE)
  PERSONALITY THEORY : THE PERSONOLOGICAL TRADITION.

  (PRENTICE-HALL SERIES IN PERSONALITY)
  BIBLIOGRAPHY: P. 206
  INCLUDES INDEX.
  1. PERSONALITY. I. TITLE.
BF698.H565   155.2'01   75-16487
ISBN 0-13-658161-7

Printed in the United States of America

10 9 8 7 6 5 4

PRENTICE-HALL INTERNATIONAL, INC., LONDON

PRENTICE-HALL OF AUSTRALIA, PTY. LTD., SYDNEY

PRENTICE-HALL OF CANADA, LTD., TORONTO

PRENTICE-HALL OF INDIA PRIVATE LIMITED, NEW DELHI

PRENTICE-HALL OF JAPAN, INC., TOKYO

PRENTICE-HALL OF SOUTHEAST ASIA (PTE.) LTD., SINGAPORE

**Grateful acknowledgment is made to the following sources
for permission to reprint:**

The collected works of C.G. Jung, ed. by G. Adler, M. Fordham, W. McGuire, and
H. Read, trans. by R.F.C. Hull, Bollingen Series XX, vol. 7, *Two essays on analytical
psychology* (copyright 1953 and © 1966 by Bollingen Foundation), reprinted by permission of Princeton University Press and Routledge & Kegan Paul Ltd.

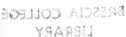

Contents

Contents

Contents

EXPLANATION
SOCIALIZATION
THE UNCONSCIOUS
PSYCHOLOGICAL HEALTH
EVALUATION

chapter eight

George Kelly, *114*

MOTIVATION
SOCIALIZATION AND THE SELF-CONCEPT
EXPLANATION
THE UNCONSCIOUS
PSYCHOLOGICAL HEALTH
EVALUATION

chapter nine

The Sociological Perspective, *128*

EXPLANATION
SOCIALIZATION AND THE SELF-CONCEPT
MOTIVATION AND THE UNCONSCIOUS
PSYCHOLOGICAL HEALTH
EVALUATION

chapter ten

Existentialism, *145*

MOTIVATION
THE SELF-CONCEPT AND THE UNCONSCIOUS
SOCIALIZATION
EXPLANATION
PSYCHOLOGICAL HEALTH
EVALUATION

chapter eleven

Erik Erikson, *164*

SOCIALIZATION AND THE SELF-CONCEPT
MOTIVATION

THE UNCONSCIOUS
EXPLANATION
PSYCHOLOGICAL HEALTH
EVALUATION

chapter twelve

Preface

The goal of this book can be stated simply: it attempts to describe the distinctive contribution that personality theory has made to an understanding of the social nature of human beings. There are certain original and unique conceptions—root ideas—implicit in the literature of personality theory that have profoundly altered our thinking about social behavior. Students of human nature at any level of sophistication should be familiar with these root ideas and the way they developed.

The root ideas—motivation, the unconscious, socialization, the self-concept, psychological health, and explanation—represent the essential contribution of personality theory as a discipline. Consequently, if we can identify those persons who have formulated these concepts in an original manner, then we have a means for deciding whom to include in our discussion. One consequence of using this criterion is that certain otherwise highly esteemed writers will not be treated here. A second consequence is that we will discuss some persons (e.g., Durkheim, Mead, Sartre, Goffman) who are often overlooked in standard textbooks. A third consequence is that the discussion will focus on ideas and their interrelationships rather than on empirical research, emphasizing the importance of personality *theory* as a subject.

The book is organized in the following manner: chapter one presents a brief historical introduction to personality theory, arguing that four traditions (i.e., a literary, medical, empirical, and folk tradition) have combined to form the discipline as it exists today; chapter two introduces and defines the root ideas; chapters three and four are concerned with Sigmund Freud and psychoanalysis (chapter three considers Freud's well-known clinical theory, whereas chapter four is concerned with his equally important but less well-known social theory); chapters five and six discuss Carl Jung and William McDougall. Chapters three through six form a unit, representing the contribution of the medical tradition and dynamic psychiatry to personality theory.

Chapters seven and eight, concerning Gordon Allport and George Kelly, reflect the literary and folk traditions in personality theory. They share a common emphasis on the conscious, rational determinants of social conduct, in contrast with the irrationalist tone of the preceding four chapters.

Chapter nine presents a sociological perspective on the social nature of man. It offers a radical conceptual alternative to the individualistic orientation of psychology, as represented by the writers in chapters three through eight. The sociological perspective is intellectually persuasive and compelling, and future theories of personality must take it into account.

The final three chapters of the book present three possible responses to the sociological perspective. The existentialist contribution, as chapter ten tries to show, is a retreat into a radical form of individualism, a response that attempts flatly to deny the validity of the sociological view. Erik Erikson's more sympathetic reaction is presented in chapter eleven. This response consists of modifying psychoanalysis to accommodate the obvious truths of sociology; the chapter argues that Erikson's modification in fact departs from psychoanalysis to the extent that it represents an alternative conceptual viewpoint. Chapter twelve presents a recent theoretical perspective called psychological role theory.

The reader has probably noted that this book differs from most recent texts in that it discusses Freud's social theory, Carl Jung, William McDougall, George Kelly, the sociological perspective, Erik Erikson, and role theory. The degree to which these topics and writers have been ignored in contemporary psychological literature is inexplicable. One contribution of this book may be to emphasize the continuity and coherence of personality theory as a distinct intellectual enterprise, and to increase modern awareness of the importance of men like Carl Jung and William McDougall to the personological tradition.

I would like to express my sincere gratitude to the following persons who read varying portions of this book in its manuscript form and whose comments notably improved both content and organization: Joseph Adelson, Mary Ainsworth, Diana Baumrind, Robert Brugger, Leonard Cottrell, James Deese, Ellen Dickstein, Doris Entwisle, Louis Galambos, Catherine Garvey, Esther Greif, Harrison Gough, J. C. Hogan, John Holland, Constance Holstein, James Kilkowski, William Kurtines, Maurice Mandelbaum, Harold McCurdy, Peter Rossi, Julian Stanley, C. J. Troll, Forrest Tyler, Mary Viernstein, Roger Webb, and Murray Webster. I extend my special thanks to Richard Lazarus for his extraordinarily helpful editorial assistance.

Personality
Theory

The Personological Tradition

chapter one

Introduction

Much modern personality theory emerged from nineteenth-century psychiatry and the study of mental illness. Today, however, it is less closely tied to psychiatry, resembling what was once called social philosophy: it surveys the results of research from many fields in an attempt to develop a valid description of human nature. Personality theory's contribution to the study of human nature can be summarized in terms of six root ideas that represent the conceptual pillars of the discipline: the unconscious, the self-concept, motivation, socialization, explanation, and psychological health. These six ideas are the central issues with which every substantive personality theory must deal. A consideration of the root ideas serves two functions. It provides a framework in terms of which our discussion can be organized, and it provides criteria by which we can choose whom to include in our discussion. If the essential contribution of personality theory can be defined in terms of these root ideas, then we can limit our discussion to persons who have conceptualized them in a distinctive and original fashion.

Books on personality theory are typically organized in terms of writers who by conventional academic standards are popular and/or important. The content of a book organized around key issues and writers who take original positions with regard to these issues necessarily will be different. Of the nine theoretical perspectives and writers represented here, five (e.g., the sociological perspective, E. Durkheim and G. H. Mead; hormic theory, W. McDougall; personal construct theory, G. A. Kelly; role theory, E. Goffman and others; and E. Erikson's theory of psychosocial development) are virtually unmentioned in standard textbooks. Existentialism and Jungian theory are more frequently discussed, but usually with neither enthusiasm nor understanding.

On the other hand, a number of topics traditionally treated in books of this type are missing here. In most cases these omissions reflect a judgment that the perspectives in question (e.g., factor analytic approaches or Lewinian field theory) have not provided sufficiently original conceptualizations of the root ideas—i.e., the perspectives are either derivative or redundant. There were, however, additional reasons for excluding writers whose approach to personality theory is based on learning theory. In the first place the "principles" of learning theory are primarily based on experimental studies of white rats, and I am skeptical of the relevance of these principles for understanding human behavior. Secondly, the goals of learning theory and personality theory are quite separate. Whereas the former is concerned with analyzing *how* characteristic patterns of behavior are acquired, the latter is concerned with analyzing *which* patterns of behavior are important in social conduct and *why*. Thus it happens that when learning theorists finish setting forth their principles of learning, they must then turn to a substantive personality theory to provide some content for their learning framework (cf. Dollard & Miller, 1950; Rychlak, 1968). Finally, learning theories typically define psychology as the scientific study of behavior (and learning as changes in behavior after new experience). Personality theorists, on the other hand, are rarely interested in behavior *per se*; they see it rather as the matter to be explained, and they use nonbehavioral explanatory concepts that learning theorists often find unintelligible. Thus, there is a historical and philosophical incompatibility between the two disciplines that can be resolved only by a kind of intellectual forced marriage. For these reasons there will be no discussion here of learning theory approaches to the study of personality.

So much for the organization of the book. We now turn to a brief historical survey of personality theory.

HISTORICAL SYNOPSIS

Personality theory is a unique intellectual enterprise for two reasons. First, many concepts drawn from personality theory are explanatory variables for other disciplines within the social sciences. For example, the sociologist Max Weber noted that members of any group are always ranked in terms of their status, and status varies according to a person's power, prestige, or wealth. Weber's observation is a useful generalization about group behavior, a generalization that nonetheless requires explanation. Why do status rankings inevitably emerge from human groups? Here we see the importance of the study of personality: from a reductionist viewpoint (according to which something is explained if it is described using concepts from a more detailed level of analysis), group phenomena must be explained in terms of the psychology of individuals. Thus, history, sociology, anthropology, criminology, political science, and economics must all ultimately appeal to concepts drawn from personality theory in order to explain their empirical generalizations.

The second reason the study of personality is unique is that personality theorists, unlike most other social scientists, have been concerned with developing a scientifically defensible model of man. Gordon Allport once remarked that every theory of personality is also a philosophical statement concerning human nature. If man is primarily rational, then he will act in accordance with his best interests, and his self-defeating actions can be changed by education. If, on the other hand, man is fundamentally irrational, then his actions will be unconsciously determined, and maladaptive behavior can be changed only through massive and intensive retraining procedures. Clearly the psychological assumptions of a discipline will have important consequences for its subsequent conclusions.

In *Consciousness and Society*, the historian H. Stuart Hughes (1958) describes a remarkable change that occurred in the theoretical orientation of the social sciences in the late nineteenth century. It was then, apparently, that scholars such as Freud, Durkheim, Jung, and Weber began to appreciate for the first time the degree to which man's thoughts and behavior are influenced by factors lying outside his aware ness. Modern personality theory began with that conceptual revolution; the origins of the discipline, however, are actually much older. There are four discernible sources of influence on the study of personality: the literary, the medical, the empirical, and the folk traditions.

The Literary Tradition

Personality theory is traditionally associated with literature, and there are several reasons for this. For example, many of these theorists had strong literary interests: Freud received the Goethe Prize for his prose style; G. W. Allport was an accomplished writer; Erik Erikson won a Pulitzer Prize and a National Book Award. Moreover, literary studies of personality are quite old; portraits of universal personality types appear in Plato's dialogues and Aristotle's Ethics. Theophrastus, a student of Aristotle's wrote a series of literary portraits, thirty of which have been preserved. The following description of the "flatterer" is an example of Theophrastus's work:

> Flattery may be considered as a mode of companionship, degrading but profitable to him who flatters. The Flatterer is a person who will say as he walks with another, "Do you observe how people are looking at you? This happens to no man in Athens but you. A compliment was paid to you yesterday in the Porch. More than 30 persons were sitting there; the question was started, Who is our foremost man? Everyone mentioned you first, and ended by coming back to your name" ... Then he will request the company to be silent while the great man is speaking, and will praise him too, in his hearing, and mark his approbation at a pause with "True"; or he will laugh at a frigid joke and stuff his cloak into his mouth as if he could not suppress his amusement ... In short the Flatterer may be observed saying and doing all things by which he conceives that he will gain favour (Jebb, 1909, pp. 39–43).

Character sketches from more recent literature are similar to those found in Theophrastus. Stendhal's Julien Sorel (*The Red and the Black*) is the embodiment of a status-seeking, ambitious young man; James's Daisy Miller (*Daisy Miller: A Study*) is archetypal in her willful self-indulgence; Camus's Meursault (*The Stranger*) is the symbol of contemporary alienation. These elaborate but subtle caricatures are well-known on the college campus. Most sororities have a Daisy Miller; many intense, over-achieving lower class boys resemble Julien Sorel; Meursault's disaffection is mirrored in every dropout.

The appeal of these characterizations is based on the shock of personal recognition. Nonetheless, there are at least four reasons for considering literature as a potentially misleading source of information about human nature. First, literary characters rarely have a historical development; consequently, we seldom know how they came to be the way they are. Second, novelists and playwrights usually seek to entertain rather than enlighten their audiences—the goals of art and science are normally independent, if not actually contradictory. Third, Henry James and Albert Camus notwithstanding, there is no necessary reason to believe that writers as a group are unusually perceptive about people. Although the verbal skill of many writers creates an illusion of perceptiveness, they may be merely projecting their own needs, wishes, and unfulfilled desires into their writing. Fourth, the demands of a literary plot require a consistency in its characters that is rarely found in real life. Thus, although literature may be a useful source of insights into personality, our use of these insights should be properly qualified.

The Medical Tradition

The medical tradition in personality theory began with Hippocrates during the flowering of Greek medicine (c. 400 B.C.). Hippocrates explained the temperamental and emotional differences among people in terms of a crude biochemical theory. Following Empedocles's theory that the world is composed of the four basic elements of air, earth, fire, and water, Hippocrates suggested that people have four corresponding bodily "humors": blood, black bile, yellow bile, and phlegm. Health required that they be mixed in proper proportions; illness resulted from an improper balance of humors. If a particular humor dominated the body, one of four (unhealthy) temperamental types—sanguine, melancholic, choleric, or phlegmatic—would result.

Humors have given way to hormones and instincts over the past 350 years, and two methodological features of the Hippocratic model have had a lasting effect on the medical tradition in personality theory. First, we now see a tendency to understand normal personality in terms of pathological functioning. In fact, the modern attempt to formulate a coherent theory of personality coincides with the renaissance in psychiatry in mid-nineteenth-century France. Charcot and Janet in Paris, and Liébault and Bernheim in Nancy were pioneers in the modern study of neurosis, and their work exerted considerable influence on subsequent generations of personality theorists. In fact, their influence has been so great that psychologists have only recently begun to doubt that the normal personality can be understood in terms of the abnormal.

A second continuing methodological influence of the Hippocratic model is the tendency to specify a set of personality types and then explain their development in terms of physiological or anatomical variables. William Sheldon (1940), for example, suggested that people can be classified in accordance with three body types: endomorphic, mesomorphic, or ectomorphic. Each type is defined by a distinctive pattern of interests and behaviors and is explained in terms of body-build. Freud spoke of oral, anal, and phallic types, defined by certain preferred modes of erotic satisfaction. Similarly, William McDougall postulated a set of twelve biological instincts with which he explained all behavior. To summarize the point, theorists who employ the medical model: (1) try to understand normalcy by studying the abnormal; and (2) postulate certain types of people, and then explain these types in terms of underlying physical variables.

The Empirical Tradition

The empirical tradition is a relatively recent influence on personality theory. It differs from the medical tradition in that it studies cognitive or behavioral *traits* rather than biologically determined personality *types*. The empirical tradition began with the phrenologist Franz Joseph Gall in the late eighteenth century. Gall thought that most differences in human behavior could be explained in terms of mental faculties: "We need faculties, the different distributions of which should determine the different species of animals, and the different proportions of which explain the differences in individuals (1835, Vol. 3, p. 88)."

Gall proposed twenty-seven independent mental faculties or radical powers, whose relative strengths would account for the differences among people. He claimed these faculties were not a product of *a priori* reasoning but were derived from his observations of people.

Today phrenology is something of a joke; the notion that curvatures of the skull reflect structures of the mind seems indeed quite odd. There are, however, other more reasonable implications to phrenology. Specifically, it seems reasonable to assume that the mind has specialized functions, that these functions may be important for social behavior, that they can be assessed independently, and that distinctions can be made among people in terms of the manner in which these mental functions are developed. Concerning Gall's astuteness, MacKinnon (1944, p. 29) observed, "In giving less emphasis to the nomothetic or universal attributes of the mind which had been stressed by other faculty psychologists and in seeking to establish empirically differentiating faculties which could be assumed to be independent of one another, Gall was years ahead of his contemporaries in his treatment of the problem of individual differences and was in more than one sense of the word the forerunner of the modern factor analysts."

As MacKinnon suggested, there is a strong parallel between Gall's work and the research of contemporary factor analysts such as R. B. Cattell, H. J. Eysenck, and J. P. Guilford. Although these men use techniques much advanced over those available to Gall, conceptually they have added little to his original formulations. The two defining characteristics of the empirical tradition are nicely exemplified in the work of Cattell, Guilford, and Eysenck. First, they search for the minimum number of discrete and independent faculties or traits necessary to account for the observed differences among people. Second, whether these traits are identified in an *a priori* or an empirical fashion, they are always atheoretical, the theory follows rather than precedes the discovery of the traits. Because of the strongly atheoretical emphasis of the empirical tradition, it will be discussed only briefly in this book.

The Folk Tradition

Evidence from biology, anthropology, and the study of nonhuman primates suggests that man is by nature a social animal; he is also an intelligent animal. It follows then that man knows a good deal about himself as a result of his natural history. As Scriven (1964, pp. 165, 167) remarks:

> The apparent shortcomings of psychology have nothing to do with its alleged youth. This is partly because it has no youth, the rational study of behavior being the oldest field of human knowledge ... we find, if we view the study of human behavior as an enterprise to produce systematic organized information, that a colossal quantity of this information has ... become a stock part of [what] we all know about human behavior. Psychology as a science must begin beyond that level, and that level was founded upon fifty thousand years of close observation of human beings.

There are three sources of information about social behavior that psychologists sometimes overlook. First, people can often tell us the reasons for their actions. Second, we can study carefully the manner in which certain words in language are used, thereby gaining considerable insight into social behavior. Third, we can directly observe people in everyday social settings. William James's (1890) perceptive and entertaining discussion of the self-concept seems to rest on just such an "ethological" base. In a tradition that extends from James through George Herbert Mead, the influential work of Erving Goffman (1959) is also based on *in situ* observations of social behavior. Barker and Wright (1951) pioneered empirical research in this tradition.

Although personal reports, natural language, and data of everyday life are convenient sources of psychological information, they have definite limitations. People are often mistaken or even self-deceived concerning their own intentions, making their self-reports inaccurate. The limitations of ordinary language are seen in the fact that the goal of science is to pass beyond the conventional wisdom contained in everyday speech. Finally, naturalistic observations based on a single observer are usually unreliable. Perhaps for these reasons the influence of the folk tradition on the study of personality has been substantially less than that of literary, medical, and empirical traditions.

Although these traditions may seem unrelated, they are bound by three common themes. They tell us how or in what ways people are all alike; they tell us how or in what ways all people are different; and they provide a means for explaining particular, enigmatic, and puzzling actions. All personality theories serve the same functions: they account for the nature of human nature and for individual differences among people; and they explain anomalous, idiosyncratic behavior patterns.

chapter two

The
Root
Ideas

This chapter is concerned with definitions. In the following sections we define personality and the root ideas. The word personality, like many other psychological concepts, has been part of ordinary language for some time. The word is used by nonpsychologists in two distinct ways, which are reflected in the German terms *Persönlichkeit* and *Personalität*. Both uses of the word are an inseparable part of its definition.

Personality in the sense of *Persönlichkeit* refers to the distinctive impression that a person makes on others, in the sense that Humphrey Bogart was a unique motion picture personality. The root of the word personality is the Latin term *persona*, the mask worn by an actor to signify his role in a play. Because this form of personality is tied to a contrived public appearance, we are curious about who or what is behind the mask. Personality in this sense is a function of the immediate social situation: it suggests uniqueness in style and superficiality in commitment. Personality as *Persönlichkeit* is most closely associated with the folk tradition; George Kelly, Erving Goffman, and most sociologists use the word in this sense.

Personality in the sense of *Personalität* refers to the fundamental or basic core of man, to the essential person that lives at the center of our being. We have this meaning of personality in mind when we say, for example, that man is a tool-using or pleasure-seeking animal. Personality in this sense refers to the deep, enduring, and often innate structures within a person whose existence, typically, can only be inferred. Because of its innate properties, personality in this second sense is usually seen as autonomous and unchanging: one's overt behavior may vary from situation to situation, but the real causes of one's actions tend to remain constant. Personality as *Personalität* is most closely associated with the medical and literary traditions, i.e., with Sigmund Freud, Carl Jung, William McDougall, Gordon Allport, and the existentialists. Freud and Jung were particularly concerned with the reality that lies behind each person's social mask, defining it in terms of *Personalität*.

The reader should try to keep these two meanings of the word personality in mind in the pages that follow.

MOTIVATION

The first root idea is the concept of motivation, one of the most important in psychology. Stoic philosophers in the fourth century A.D. discussed the nature of human instincts; psychiatrists in the late nineteenth century dramatically reformulated the concept of instinct in ways that changed our thinking about the nature of man. Unfortunately, however, the meaning of the concept has been thoroughly confounded, and today psychologists use the concept of motivation in a bewildering variety of ways. Nonetheless, from a welter of competing definitions it is possible to find two usages that distinguish between *biogenic* and *psychogenic* motives.

Psychogenic motives are cognitive or mentalistic phenomena. They are reasons, intentions, purposes, plans, strategies, or goals. When we ask for example "What was the motive for the crime?", we seek an explanation in terms of psychogenic motives. Such motives are often (but not necessarily) conscious and available to introspection. They are typically the products of experience and can be shaped and modified by further experience. Broadly speaking, each person has a unique set of psychogenic motives. The folk tradition in general, and in particular George Kelly, Gordon Allport, Erving Goffman, the sociologists, and the existentialists use motivational concepts in the psychogenic sense.

Biogenic motives normally refer to biological phenomena such as instinct, drive, biological urge, and need. To ask "Is man by nature aggressive?" is to inquire about biogenic motives. Motives of this type tend to be products of man's biological heritage, not basically changed by experience. Most people share a common set of biogenic motives. The medical tradition—Sigmund Freud, Carl Jung, William McDougall, Erik Erikson—pays considerable attention to these motives. Biogenic motives lie at the conceptual border between psychology and physiology; because of the way these notions straddle the two disciplines, discussions of biogenic motives tend to be rather speculative.

Although every personality theorist uses motivational terms differently, it is usually possible to decide whether they are discussing psychogenic or biogenic motives. The distinctions will recur repeatedly in the rest of the book.

THE UNCONSCIOUS

Of all the root ideas the concept of the unconscious has probably the greatest popular appeal, possibly because of the mysterious connotations of the term. Along with biogenic motives, the unconscious is a distinctive feature of the medical traditions in personality theory, and Freud's use of the term in particular marks a turning point in the history of social thought (Hughes, 1958). As might be expected, it is also difficult to define. In rough terms, the unconscious refers to influences that alter our behavior of whose presence we are unaware. In contrast with Freud, Jung, McDougall, and Erikson, other writers in the personological tradition (e.g., Allport, Kelly, and the existentialists) either deemphasize the importance of the unconscious, or actually deny the term has any meaning.

Schopenhauer's *The World as Will and Representation* (1819), which was quite popular in Germany after 1850, contains perhaps the first version of the modern notion of the unconscious. Schopenhauer thought of the world as governed by will, an evil, blind, impetuous urge that is reflected in various natural forces (e.g., gravity), including human instincts. The will corresponds to the unconscious; man is driven by unknown irrational forces whose primary components are instincts for self-preservation and sexual release. Carl Gustav Carus, a physician and animal psychologist, also provided an influential account of the unconscious in his book *Psyche* (1864). Carus distinguished three levels in the unconscious, described their characteristics, and discussed the manner in which the unconscious was expressed in dreams. Perhaps the most comprehensive and important discussion of the unconscious before Freud, however, was Edward von Hartmann's *Philosophy of the Unconscious* (1869). Hartmann assembled a wide variety of evidence to demonstrate the ubiquitous role of the unconscious in language, religion, history, and all phases of social life. As Brett observed (Peters, 1962, p. 579) "Whatever Hartmann said always came back to the one and only essential conclusion—the Unconscious must be accepted . . . It is true that Aristotle said, 'the understanding moves nothing,' and Hume repeated the idea in the statement that 'the reason doth not move to action,' but it was Hartmann who elevated these phrases to the dignity of a cosmic interpretation, and by sheer force of wide application and manifold repetition, made them subtly penetrate or openly dominate the minds of men."

Not surprisingly, the concept of the unconscious was important in the origins of modern psychiatry. Throughout medical history the symptoms of mental illness seem to have remained constant; explanations of these symptoms, however, have undergone extensive historical development. Early conceptions of mental illness regarded the afflicted person as being under the control of such external agents as demons, spirits, and witches. Gradually these external agents were replaced by forces inside the person. As Ellenberger (1970) points out, exorcism in the Middle Ages gave way to magnetic cures (eighteenth century) and hypnotism (nineteenth century) as treatments for mental afflictions. Magnetic and hypnotic treatments seemed to reveal a new and sometimes more brilliant personality in their subjects. Early investigators were struck by such changes that suggested the new personality had an autonomous life of its own. Ellenberger observes, "The entire nineteenth century was preoccupied with the problem of the coexistence of these two minds [e.g., personalities] and of their relationship to each other (p 145)." This phenomenon led to the concept of *dipsychism*. The occasional discovery of multiple hidden personalities led to the notion of *polypsychism*. Dipsychism and polypsychism provided a ready explanation for mental illness, and psychiatrists in the late nineteenth century referred to these coexisting but unknown states of consciousness as the *unconscious.*

Personality theorists, especially Freud and Jung, are responsible for bringing the unconscious to the attention of psychology and the social sciences. They also provided interesting formulations of this concept that will play a key role in our subsequent discussions.

SOCIALIZATION

The third root idea is socialization, another concept that psychologists have taken from ordinary language. *The Oxford Dictionary of the English Language* tells us that as early as 1828 the verb "to socialize" meant "to render social, to make fit for living in society." The term was adopted by social scientists sometime in the late nineteenth century and refers generally to the social development of the self and personality and to the transmission of culture. Clausen (1968, p. 3) observes that "... the study of socialization focuses upon the development of the individual as a social being and participant in society." Thus, socialization refers to the processes and experiences that help one become sensitive to the expectations of others, to accept the values of one's family and culture. People who are insensitive to social expectations and who reject the norms of their society are "unsocialized." Their behavior is not merely deviant; they lack a basic quality we expect in human nature: responsiveness to the feelings of others.

Although the term socialization is not widely used outside the United States, social scientists everywhere are concerned with the relation of the individual to society. The concept of socialization takes personality theory out of the realm of individual psychology, putting it into that of social concerns; it bridges the gap between individual and group psychology.

Perhaps the best known early discussions of socialization appear in Plato's *Republic* and Rousseau's *Emile* (1762). The success of Plato's ideal state depended on the training of its leaders, the guardians, during their childhood. Plato specified the content of their education in detail, a large portion of which was learning the moral virtues. Rousseau's didactic novel on education, *Emile*, presents a theory of socialization whose influence is still felt today. According to Rousseau, man, who is innately good, becomes wicked through corrupt institutions. The natural inclinations of human nature can therefore be trusted. Children should never be forced to do what they find disagreeable or uninteresting, particularly with regard to their education; rather, they are naturally curious and will at the proper time beg to be taught.

Two themes run through most theories of socialization. The first reflects one's assumptions about the basic nature of man. Some psychologists see culture as an alien institution that must be imposed on people. Culture transforms the naturally brutal inclinations of man and makes social life possible, at the cost of individual freedom. The alternative, more common, notion is that man is by nature a social animal but it is through membership in society that he becomes fully human.

The second theme is a contrast between two views: one, associated with the medical tradition, sees socialization as a biological emergent; the other, associated with folk tradition, regards it as a function of social experience and a sensitivity to the expectations of others.

The writers discussed in this book vary greatly in terms of their concern with the problem of socialization. McDougall (1908) provided the earliest and by far the most explicit analysis of the subject. Freud, Erikson, and the sociologists also thought the problem important. Allport and Kelly gave socialization a cursory treatment, while Jung and the existentialists essentially ignored it, possibly because of their extreme preoccupation with individual development.

THE SELF-CONCEPT

The development of self-awareness in the individual parallels the history of self-concepts in the humanities. Four such parallels reflect forms of the self-concept that can be found in philosophy, literature, and ordinary language, as well as in psychology. The first form of the self-concept—the self as ego, dynamism, as a source of inner direction and will —comes from Hellenistic drama (*circa* 600 B.C.). Bruno Snell (1960, p. 103) argues that the early Greeks discovered or created the self when they realized the possibility of genuine personal decisions. In Homer the gods determined all human action, and man's lot was to suffer and endure; but Greek tragedy (e.g., Sophocles) represented men as ". . . independent agents, acting upon the bidding of their own hearts, instead of merely reacting to external stimuli." Thus, Greek drama in the fifth century B.C. expressed for the first time man's concept of himself as a free agent. Similarly, in the infant the first undifferentiated perception of the self may well be a sense of personal power—e.g., screams can often produce maternal attentions. In this first sense then, the self-concept is similar to a primitive conception of the soul; this is the self as ego, agency, or will, a sense of self-direction and power.

The second concept of the self—the self as an indirect object of knowledge—derives from Plato. With his doctrine of reminiscence Plato concluded that one learns about one's own nature by studying the external world; thus in a sense one's self-concept is determined by one's world concept. The parallel in infant development is obvious: the child learns about himself when, as he begins to crawl, he bumps into things. He discovers noses, fingers, and toes as he jams them against unyielding surfaces; the self is that which acts and the world is that which resists action.

Other people as external entities are unusually powerful determinants of the self-concept. Not only do we learn, for example, what our nose looks like when we see other noses, but with time we may come to see ourselves as other people see us. The self as an indirect object of knowledge is largely a function of regarding ourselves from an outside vantage point and reflecting on ourselves in this manner. Baldwin (1902),

Mead (1934), and Piaget (1964) discuss in detail the manner in which this self-concept (the self as an indirect object of knowledge) develops in children.

The third form of the self-concept—the self as a direct object of knowledge—probably emerged in the fourth century A.D. with Augustine. Plato gives us an image of man seeking self-knowledge by energetically inquiring into the structure of the world; Augustine, however, presents man as a lonely creature living in a small room, listening to the voices of sense experience and God. Descartes modified and expanded this image and provided one of the first clear statements of self-knowledge as simple self-reflection. Although introspection seems to be an immediate source of self-knowledge, it may be that the ability to think in this manner is the result of a long process of cognitive development. As William James observed, "... whether we take it abstractly or concretely, our considering the ... self at all is a reflective process, ... the result of our abandoning the outward-looking point of view, and of our having become able to think subjectively as such, to think ourselves as thinkers (1950, p. 296)." Thus, thinking about one's own thoughts seems to require intellectual attainment at the most abstract level.

Concerning the self as a direct object of knowledge, what do we discover when we look inward? A moment's thought reveals that we do not perceive a fixed image of the self; rather we find a flow of ideas and images. This was precisely the conclusion reached by David Hume, a conclusion subsequently developed by Immanuel Kant. According to Kant, self-knowledge is always an inference based on introspection; thus one's self-concept may not correspond to one's true nature. In Kant the idea of a self-constructed self-concept that is relative to one's experience and that affects the manner in which one thinks about and reacts to the external world appears in its essentially modern form.

The fourth notion of the self-concept is the image that one more or less deliberately presents to those persons he meets each day. This corresponds to the "social self" described by William James in the *Principles of Psychology* (1890). As James observes, a person "... has as many different social selves as there are distinct groups of persons about whose opinion he cares. He generally shows a different side of himself to each of these different groups. Many a youth who is demure enough before his parents and teachers, swears and swaggers like a pirate among his 'tough' young friends (p. 294)." This notion of the self-concept is like a self-constructed role; it is one's conscious attempt to be the person others think he is. To present a consistent and deliberate image to the various people we meet requires considerable social and cognitive skill. Thus the articulation and development of a self in this fourth sense probably does not take place until adolescence.

The four versions of self-concept discussed thus far represent the self as an entity or object. A fifth aspect of the self concerns evaluations of the self-concept, indicated by terms such as self-acceptance, self-confidence, self-worth, and self-esteem. These terms qualify all forms of self as an entity. One may feel good or bad about one's image, as one may be confident or fearful about how others will react to this projected image. These are all aspects of self-evaluation that can be designated by the term self-esteem.

To summarize briefly what has been said in this section, four uses of the word *self* were distinguished: (1) the self as ego and agent—a primitive conception of the self both in terms of individual or collective development; (2) the self as an indirect object of knowledge, discovered through study of the external world and the reactions of other people—a developmentally more advanced conception that depends on the ability to adopt perspectives outside one's self; (3) the self as a direct object of knowledge—a rather sophisticated version of the self-concept requiring a fully developed capacity for abstract thought; (4) the self as the image that one self-consciously projects—a conception of the self that depends on social as well as cognitive development. Finally, it was noted that all four forms of the self-concept are qualified by terms such as self-confidence, self-acceptance, and self-worth, designated most simply by the word self-esteem. The importance of the self-concept in the study of personality is reflected in the fact that earlier writers have occasionally equated the self-concept with personality.

EXPLANATION

In general, psychologists have ignored the problem of explanation, the fifth root idea. As Homans (1967, p. 18) aptly notes, "it is not in its findings . . . that social science gets in trouble, but in its explanations." The subject is complex but deserves serious attention; an investigator's method of explanation limits the kinds of phenomena he studies as well as his conclusions.

As mentioned in chapter one, personality theories are designed to explain three kinds of questions: in what ways are people all alike; in what ways are people all different; and the meanings of specific, enigmatic, anomalous actions—usually neurotic symptoms. Explanations of the first two kinds of questions are normally phrased in terms of the Hempel-Oppenheim or "covering law" model of explanation. This model states four requirements for an explanation (Hempel, 1965):

1. The explanandum (that which is to be explained) must be a logical consequence of the explanans (explanatory statements).

2. The explanans must contain general laws that are actually required for the derivation of the explanandum.
3. The explanans must have empirical content (at least potentially).
4. The sentences constituting the explanans must be true.

In essence this means that two kinds of statements are necessary for an explanation: (1) a statement of the general law or laws governing the class of events under investigation; and (2) a statement of the antecedent conditions that characterize the particular event we are interested in. The event to be explained is then derived from these two sets of statements and the derivation is the explanation.

Suppose, for example, we wanted to explain war. Evidence from anthropology, primatology, and paleontology suggests that members of the hominid line are naturally aggressive and that their evolutionary history has been characterized by intergroup violence. This will serve as a general law. Antecedent conditions are that man is a hominid. Warfare is explained, then, by showing that it is a logical consequence of these propositions.

Individual differences are typically explained by appealing to general laws of human development and the specific developmental history of the person or persons in question. For example, one general law of development holds that human infants need mothering during the first year of life. Children reared in orphanages often receive inadequate mothering. Consequently, such children should behave differently from those who have been adequately mothered (Goldfarb, 1945), and the sometimes disturbed social behavior of orphanage children is explained in this way.

Although the covering law model appears appropriate for explaining general features of human nature and individual differences, it seems inadequate to account for specific, puzzling symptoms and behavior. Specific actions are probably best explained by interpretation, by showing that they are meaningful in terms of everything we know about the person involved. Interpretive explanations are almost never predictive, nor are they subject to experimental verification. Nonetheless, they have functional validity and a good deal of everyday life is conducted in their terms. A doctor, for example, explains a patient's symptoms by interpretation; he evaluates the symptom pattern in the light of all the facts about the patient that he can bring together—family history, previous illnesses, recent emotional pressures, dietary habits—and then interprets the symptoms in terms of a model of physiological processes that will organize all the facts. In most cases lies are detected, insurance risks are appraised, crimes are solved, favors are granted, and the fidelity of lovers assessed in terms of an interpretation based on what we know of the person involved.

The problem with interpretive explanations is that it is difficult to evaluate the merits of competing interpretations. How do we know when we have found the right interpretation? In an essay on the science and the art of interpretation, Hancher (1970) illuminates this problem. To define explanation as interpretation requires two assumptions. First, the meaning of any action must be relatively fixed; it must in principle be possible to assign a finite set of motives to an actor. The second assumption is that any single interpretation will correspond more or less accurately to the true meaning of the act. A scientific interpretation is one that closely corresponds to the actor's (conscious or unconscious) intentions at the time of the action in question. An artistic interpretation is one that is aesthetically attractive, one that places the action in question within a pleasing conceptual framework without regard to the actor's intentions. One obviously ought to choose the interpretation that most closely fits the facts of a case. However, even in the best of circumstances a scientific interpretation is an intellectual creation that ignores at least some relevant facts. Thus, scientific and artistic interpretations often tend to merge, and to choose between them may be difficult if not impossible. Nor is it possible to formulate in advance a clear set of rules for making this choice. Finally, because interpretation depends on the talent of the individual investigator to conceive plausible interpretations, there can be no methodology of interpretive explanation as such.

PSYCHOLOGICAL HEALTH

The sixth root idea—psychological health—refers to the manner in which human effectiveness and proper psychological functioning have been defined by various social scientists. The concept also deals with the causes of neurosis. Conceptions of psychological health and mental illness have changed a good deal over time. Aristotle provided an early but influential analysis in his *Nichomachean Ethics*. He argued that a person is healthy according to the degree to which he has developed his human functions. Since man's intellect is his highest function, the life of the mind is the best life, and psychological health consists of a life fully governed by reason. Aristotle explained mental illness in terms of the Hippocratic theory of humors; neurosis resulted from an imbalance among the four humors.

Aristotle's naturalistic concept of psychological health was repudiated during the Christian middle ages. From the seventh to the sixteenth century A.D., psychological health was defined in terms of piety, and neurosis was seen as demonic possession—a notion that periodically recurs today.

After the sixteenth century, psychological health began to be described once again in naturalistic terms. With the renaissance in psychiatry during the late nineteenth century, theories of neurosis became quite explicit and psychological health was typically seen as an absence of mental illness.

Psychological health is usually defined in one of three general ways. First, it is defined by self-awareness or the absence of self-deception, the resolution of internal conflicts and a stoic acceptance of man's fate. This definition is used by Sigmund Freud, William McDougall, George Kelly, many existentialists, and role theorists. The second definition entails self-realization and self-actualization—the fulfillment of one's innate psychological potentialities, that becomes possible after achieving inner peace, as in a religious conversion. Carl Jung and Gordon Allport adopt this view. The third definition is the degree to which an individual is integrated into a matrix of enduring social relationships, a viewpoint exemplified by Erik Erikson and many sociologists.

These then are the root ideas: motivation, the unconscious, socialization, the self-concept, explanation, and psychological health. They represent the distinctive and unique contributions of personality theory to psychology and the social sciences. In the chapters that follow we will discuss nine persons (or theoretical traditions) who have provided original formulations of these ideas. The discussion should clarify the subject matter of personality theory and the decisive manner in which personality theorists have influenced the modern image of man.

chapter three

Sigmund Freud: The Clinical Theory

There are three good reasons for beginning with Freud. First, many of the persons discussed in this book use Freud as a starting point—in fact they sometimes seem more concerned with criticizing, modifying, or supplementing Freud than with analyzing social conduct in its own right. Second, psychoanalysis is one of two or three major intellectual traditions in the twentieth century, and some familiarity with Freud's thought is an essential part of one's education. Third, Freud is probably the most original figure in the personological tradition; his formulations of some of the root ideas are prototypical.

It is difficult to decide where to begin, because Freud's ideas all interrelate and discussion of a particular concept usually requires knowledge of other portions of the theory. Furthermore, Freud revised his ideas constantly for over forty years, and ideas conceived at different times were never well-integrated. Nor did Freud ever set forth a systematic, well-organized theory of psychoanalysis. Those versions of psychoanalytic theory found in textbooks are patched abstractions from the original prolix source.

Freud belongs to a tradition of German irrationalist thinkers that includes, among others, Schopenhauer, Nietzsche, and Fechner. There are striking parallels in the thinking of these men. Nietzsche and Freud are often erroneously considered to be advocates of the primitive and

Sigmund Freud
Wide World Photos

irrational side of man's nature. They actually represent one of the last modern attempts to reconcile an eighteenth-century faith in reason with the romantic anti-intellectualism of the nineteenth century. Although they argued repeatedly that reason is limited in its scope, they were primarily concerned with extending the limits of reason into the realm of unreason. Freud was the more pessimistic of the two: in his writing he stated repeatedly that one never masters irrationality, that the war against the unconscious cannot, in principle, be won. As Phillip Rieff (1959, p. xxii) notes, "Freud's one small hope, reason, is closely and properly linked to his mixed vision...of the force of death. Reason cannot save us, nothing can; but reason can mitigate the cruelty of living, or give sufficient reasons for not living."

Although we might spend considerable time tracing the influences on Freud's intellectual development, we will mention only five. First were Freud's teachers, most notably Theodore Meynert and Ernst Brücke. These men were his models of professional conduct, and they converted him to a militantly mechanistic and positivistic philosophy of science. Thus Freud adopted a strict version of psychic determinism: there are no psychic accidents, all mental phenomena are meaningful. Although Brücke and Meynert were unusually rigorous in their scientific attitudes, both indulged in what Ellenberger (1970) calls brain mythologies—speculative attempts to describe psychological phenomena in terms of hypothetical brain structures—ideas that Freud later used with dramatic effect.

A second major influence on Freud was the study of sexual pathol-

A 3 7 5 7

ogy, a development that was strongly encouraged by the publication of Richard von Krafft-Ebing's book *Psychopathia Sexualis* (1886). Krafft-Ebing classified sexual abnormalities, coined the terms *sadism* and *masochism*, legitimized the study of sexual pathology in Germany, and generated widespread interest in the subject. Krafft-Ebing knew Freud well enough to nominate him for the position of Extraordinary Professor at the University of Vienna in 1897 and again in 1901.

Pierre Janet also significantly influenced Freud, an impact that is most noticeable in Freud's early work, *Studies in Hysteria*. Although Freud later denied any intellectual debts to Janet, Ellenberger remarks that "... it is difficult to study the initial periods of Janet's psychological analysis and Freud's psychoanalysis without coming to the conclusion that... 'the methods and concepts of Freud were modeled after those of Janet, of whom he seems to have inspired himself constantly'—until the paths of the two diverged (1970, pp. 539–40)."

Freud readily acknowledged a debt to literature—to the Greek tragedians, to Shakespeare, Schiller, and Goethe in particular. Goethe's influence is reflected both in Freud's ideas and in his writing style, and Freud once remarked that he chose his vocation in response to Goethe's poem *On Nature*. In fact, Freud can be seen as a literary figure in his own right: he had good linguistic abilities, a natural feel for language, and a masterful literary style. Even his early technical articles on histology are beautifully written. Freud's present appeal is undoubtedly partly due to his narrative and persuasive skills.

Finally, Freud was heavily influenced by Charles Darwin and evolutionary theory. Darwin proposed a psychology based on instincts (e.g., sex and aggression) and thought of development in genetic terms; i.e., current behavior is determined by past events in human development. Both ideas play an important role in psychoanalytic theory. Darwin accepted the phylogenetic law, the notion that the development of each person is a telescoped version of the history of the species, another prominent theme in psychoanalysis. Freud also adopted Darwin's theory that primitive man lived in brutish hordes under the leadership of a cruel father-despot.

THE UNCONSCIOUS

Freud argued that every man is a stranger to himself, that most people are unaware of the motives and reasons for their actions. He considered self-discovery the most important goal in life, one achieved by making conscious that which was formerly unconscious. Two factors make the task of self-understanding difficult. First, according to Freud, a large portion of the unconscious is essentially inscrutable, and attempts to penetrate its depth are futile. Second, the threatening nature of the unconscious itself produces psychological defenses. Consequently, in most cases we need someone to help us in our search for self-knowledge.

Everything important in the psychoanalytic system is unconscious. To illustrate this idea, Freud compared the mind to an iceberg. Only about ten percent of an iceberg's total mass is ever above the ocean's surface; similarly, we are aware of only a small fraction of our mental life. But what, more precisely, is the unconscious? Freud used the term in essentially three ways. In the first sense, the unconscious refers to mental elements (thoughts, memories) that have been repressed, forced out of consciousness by a direct action of the mind. These elements typically contain material that is threatening in some way. Freud also used the word in a much broader sense to refer to unconscious knowledge —information available to us that we were never taught. Third, Freud felt those experiences that happen to us before we attach verbal labels to them are also unconscious; this is the unconscious as preverbal experience.

Freud regarded the unconscious as an inference that was necessary to account for a range of puzzling physical symptoms present in his first patients. This is obviously insufficient to establish the unconscious as a fact. Is there any scientific evidence available that clearly demonstrates the effects of unconscious motives and impulses on every day life? After years of research on this subject, unequivocal laboratory evidence for the existence of unconscious determinants of behavior has yet to be presented. Perhaps personal experience is ultimately most persuasive. The following is an example of the sort of data that best support the notion of the unconscious. As a graduate student I undertook a course of directed readings with a certain professor. After a time I began to doubt the value of this form of education. One particular afternoon I became increasingly nervous as four o'clock (our appointment time) approached. When I arrived at the professor's office, he seemed surprised to see me, and for good reason. It was actually five o'clock and I had missed my appointment, in spite of the fact that I had been sitting directly in front of a large clock during the previous two hours. This is the kind of experience that leads to the inference of unconscious determinants of behavior. Understandably, not every one will be willing to accept personal experience as reputable evidence. Certainly one ought to be skeptical about the validity of private testimonials; nonetheless, such experience seems to be the best evidence presently available that the unconscious can affect overt behavior.

If the unconscious has manifestations that are observable in daily experience, then it exists in some sense and must be open to investigation. How might we study the unconscious? Freud suggested that we find situations where our critical faculties are relaxed, and where, consequently, more primitive thought forms can appear. These are most often fantasy-related activities or behavior about which one is not normally self-conscious. Eight such situations can be readily identified.

1. Free Association. This is the classic psychoanalytic technique for exploring the unconscious. In order to free-associate, a person must relax mentally and physically, and then say literally whatever comes to his mind. Persons undergoing psychoanalysis typically begin free-associating by revealing a long string of guilty secrets. These are usually irrelevant for the exploration of the unconscious, which only begins after the confession is complete.

2. Resistances. Areas of resistance are hard to distinguish from subjects that a person is simply unwilling to talk about. If, however, in talking with someone a topic arises whose nature and meaning is obvious to everyone but the person concerned, then that topic may be related to the unconscious. For example, once when I was in graduate school, a young lady and her boy friend came to talk to a graduate student with whom I shared an office. The girl, it seemed, had a problem; she was afraid to place objects in compartments—pies in ovens, letters in mailboxes, etc. The problem was quite annoying and she wondered what it was all about. The graduate student asked my opinion. I replied that I didn't know, but that Freud would say she was afraid of becoming pregnant. The girl looked startled and vigorously began to deny the statement. Her boy friend, however, roared with laughter and said it was true.

3. The Pattern of a Person's Dislikes. People often object most strenuously to characteristics in others that they exhibit themselves. A chaplain I knew in the Navy filled his room (which was next to mine) with the pornography he collected in Manila, Hong Kong, and Tokyo. In the evenings at sea, he would pore over this material and periodically pace the passageway denouncing the lasciviousness of Orientals. As Goerg Groddeck (1928, p. 72) wrote, "You will never go wrong in concluding that a man has once loved deeply whatever he hates, and loves it yet, that he once admired and still admires what he scorns, that he once greedily desired what now disgusts him."

4. Life Patterns. Recurring themes in a person's life often reveal the unconscious. Certain people, for example, repeatedly set themselves up for failure by overeating, overdrinking, or oversleeping. When others reject them because they are fat, drunk, or late, the rejection leads to a further round of eating, drinking, or sleeping. Such patterns of behavior suggest a need for punishment or failure, that may be unconscious.

5. *Jokes, Errors, and Mistakes.* In *Jokes and Their Relation to the Unconscious,* Freud argued that humor frequently serves as a means for the unconscious expression of sexual and aggressive thoughts. Similarly, errors and mistakes often seem to result from unconscious influences. Charles Darwin copied examples of evidence that contradicted his theory in a notebook, thereby acknowledging that scientists tend to forget contradictory data. On a more personal level, a young man I once knew was walking in a park with his fiancée, when her engagement ring "accidentally" slipped from her finger and fell in the bordering lake. The meaning of the accident was revealed later when the girl broke off the engagement.

6. *Neurotic Symptoms.* The first psychological problem Freud investigated was the meaning of hysterical symptoms, physical complaints that have no neurological or organic basis. Freud's conclusion—that these symptoms express and are produced by unconscious forces—is fundamental to psychoanalytic theory and therapy. As a common example, sexual promiscuity often arises from deep-seated feelings of personal inadequacy and fear of rejection. The connection is sometimes obscure because such people frequently have lengthy moral and philosophical justifications for their actions.

7. *Works of Art.* According to Freud, artistic creations are neurotic symptoms made public: each work of art reflects more or less directly the artist's unconscious. Freud did feel, however, that the more sophisticated the artist, the more complex were his creations and the more disguised were the unconscious trends.

8. *Dreams.* Freud called dreams the royal road to the unconscious, an idea that seems valid. Once again personal experience illustrates the point most clearly. At a party one evening a bright and aggressive young professor asked me to interpret a dream. He had dreamed he was riding in a car with a man, his father, and the longer they drove the more anxious he became. His fear mounted until he finally awakened, covered with sweat. I said that I could not interpret his dream, but I thought Freud would say he had homosexual impulses about which he felt anxious or guilty. The professor's smile melted, his face turned grey, and he walked away. I learned later that the interpretation was accurate.

To obtain a clearer understanding of unconscious thought, we must inquire more deeply into dream analysis. Freud's major statement concerning thought and its relation to the unconscious occurs in *The Interpretation of Dreams*. Freud considered this book to be his masterpiece; as he remarked, ". . . the theory of dreams . . . occupies a special place in the history of psychoanalysis and marks a turning point; it was with it that analysis took the step from being a psychotherapeutic procedure to being a depth psychology (Freud, 1965, p. 7)." To present the dream theory adequately we must first introduce a distinction between primary and secondary process thinking.

The thought processes of a civilized man, according to Freud, proceed on two separate levels simultaneously, and each level is characterized by its own mental principles. Unconscious thought represents "older, primary processes" that strive only for immediate pleasure or gratification. The unconscious, thus, is characterized by *primary process thinking*, that is guided by the *pleasure principle*, i.e., the pursuit of instantaneous gratification. However, actions that are guided exclusively by the pleasure principle inevitably bring one into conflict with both the human and the natural environment. This is so because the world cannot respond quickly enough to satisfy the pleasure principle.

Unconscious or primary process thought typically has one or more of the following characteristics:

1. The connection between ideas are emotional rather than logical. Consider, for example, the slogan "America—love it or leave it," which expresses the sentiment that a patriot doesn't criticize his country. Clearly the connection between love of country and unquestioning obedience to a particular government is emotional rather than logical.

2. All ideas are expressed affirmatively, without conditions or qualifications. During one of those spasms which gripped our major universities during the late 1960s, I listened to a professor try to rally a group of graduate students to the revolutionary cause. When one student observed that the intended action might harm innocent bystanders, the professor replied, "In times of moral crisis there are no innocent bystanders!"

3. Opposite or mutually exclusive ideas coexist nicely. This form of primary process thought is seen in Rousseau's famous remark that it is sometimes necessary to force people to be free.

4. Synecdoche—a rhetorical or poetic device by which a part represents a whole, or vice versa—is used extensively. President Franklin Roosevelt provided a classic example of this when, in reference to a meeting with Winston Churchill and Joseph Stalin, he said, "England, Russia, and I met yesterday."

5. There is no concern with time. This leads to impulsiveness, as indicated in the following lines by Andrew Marvell:

Now therefore, while the youthful hue
Sits on thy skin like morning dew,
And while thy willing soul transpires
At every pore with instant fires,
Now let us sport us while we may . . .

  This lack of concern for time also leads to a collapse of the temporal
  reference system, so that past events exist vividly in the present.
 6. If blocked in reality, primary process thinking turns to fantasy for
  satisfaction. Thus starving people have fantasies of food, the lonely
  dream of love, and victims plot imaginary revenge.

Summarizing these points briefly, primary process thought can be
described as wish-fulfilling, selfish, and hallucinatory. Although a pre-
dominance of primary process thinking is pathological, it is not necessarily undesirable *per se.* In moderate amounts primary process thought
leads to charm, whimsy, and spontaneity. It is only the exclusive operation of this thought form that is abnormal.

The realization that complete and painless gratification of one's
needs is impossible forces a pause between thought and action that permits the first appearance of the reality principle. Consciousness, Freud
said, is characterized by *secondary process thinking,* guided by the *reality
principle,*—the delay of immediate gratification for the sake of long-term
rewards. In time the reality principle supersedes the pleasure principle;
however, one never replaces or eliminates the other. Rather, the reality
principle safeguards and protects the pleasure principle by providing
dependable sources of gratification. In spite of its greater efficiency, the
reality principle never triumphs because throughout life the unconscious
strives continually to achieve the goals of the pleasure principle.

As a first step in understanding dreams, Freud assumed they were
all wish-fulfilling. While we are asleep the censor or secondary process
thought relaxes, and primary process thinking takes over. Socially unacceptable thoughts, usually dealing with sexual or aggressive themes,
emerge from the unconscious to find fulfillment. Even while one is
asleep, however, pure primary process thought is intolerably threatening.
Thus, these wishes and impulses are scrambled in a chamber called
the *preconscious,* that lies between the unconscious and conscious awareness. They are scrambled, disguised, and then permitted to achieve their
imagined goals in awareness. Thus, every dream has two aspects: a latent
and a manifest content. Latent dream content contains the wishes that
originate in the unconscious and strive for conscious expression, finally
causing the dream. The manifest content is just that—the overt content
of a dream. Analysis of the highly symbolic manifest content will lead us

ultimately to the latent thoughts, from which we may make inferences about the nature of the unconscious.

Although Freud acknowledged that the interpretation of dream symbols was incomplete, he nonetheless described the analysis of symbolism as the most remarkable part of his dream theory. The basis for this evaluation was his conviction that symbolism is a general property of unconscious thought and by no means confined to dreams. Freud assumed that virtually every social act has an unconscious and therefore symbolic component that may be analyzed and interpreted. Thus the real significance of dream analysis lies in the interpretive method rather than the meaning of dreams themselves.

The range and variety of dream images is almost infinite; however the total number of objects represented by these images is quite limited. According to Freud, the number of symbolized objects can be placed in three categories. The first refers to parents and siblings. In our dreams, parents are represented by royalty: kings, queens, emperors, chiefs, presidents, lords, and ladies. In a less elevated vein, children, brothers, and sisters appear as rats, mice, gophers, squirrels, frogs, and foxes.

The second category, by far the largest, contains sexual symbols. The male sexual anatomy is represented by: the mystical number three, sticks, umbrellas, poles, trees, knives, daggers, lances, cannons, pistols, rifles, taps, water cans, pencils, pen-holders, hammers and other tools, airplanes, the dreamer himself flying, reptiles, fish, serpents, hands, and feet. The female sexual anatomy is represented by: pits, caves, jars, bottles, filing cabinets, bureaus, ships, cupboards, stoves, wood and paper, doors and gates, tables, churches, and chapels. Losing teeth symbolizes castration, while blossoms and flowers represent virginity.

The third category contains symbols of a broader and more Jungian variety. Birth is symbolized by going into or coming out of water, a symbol presumably derived from man's evolutionary origins as an aquatic animal and from the liquid environment of the amniotic sac. Otto Rank's book, *The Myth of the Birth of the Hero*, contains detailed evidence that births of many mythical heroes take the same form (emergence from water): e.g., Karma (of the Ramayana), Gilgamesh (from the Babylonian epic); Cyrus, Paris, Hercules, Oedipus, Moses, Siegfried, and Lohengrin. As a final example of symbols found in this category, going away on a journey represents dying.

This list of symbols and their meanings is neither exhaustive nor definitive, but merely illustrative. Freud thought the meaning of dream symbols could be discovered by studying fairy tales, myths, folklore, old sayings, folk songs, poetry, and colloquial uses of language. These sources contain convergences; certain symbols seem to have the same meaning in many different cultures. When such convergences are found, we can usually infer the meaning of the symbol in question. But how can we explain the similarity of symbols across cultures? Freud thought that our knowledge of the meaning of symbols was unconscious, that we have at our disposal a means of symbolic expression that is never taught or learned and is common to people in all cultures.

Freud's observations may seem fanciful. It is useful, however, to distinguish between Freud's analysis of dream symbols on the one hand and his explanation of our knowledge of these symbols on the other. One may accept the meanings Freud assigned to dream symbols without agreeing that our knowledge of these meanings is unconscious.

Dream symbols make up the manifest content of dreams; they are formed by a process called dream work. Dream work transforms latent dream thoughts into manifest dreams; psychoanalysis attempts to find the latent thoughts underlying manifest dream elements. Freud thought four processes were involved in dream work:

1. *Condensation*. The latent content of a dream is always more complex than the manifest content. Although many themes merge to form the manifest dream, the process is never reversed; a manifest dream is never richer in content than its underlying thoughts. Condensation creatively selects and combines latent elements into highly original forms.

2. *Displacement*. Displacement takes two forms. In the first, latent elements are replaced in the manifest dream by substitute thoughts, images, or allusions. Thus a male teacher might stand for one's father, or a girl friend might represent one's mother. In the second form of displacement there is a shift of emphasis; attention is focused on a relatively innocuous aspect of the latent element while the more objectionable elements slide into consciousness in the background. Assume for example, that King Lear was a dream. Although Lear is the dominant figure, analysis might reveal that Lear's fool was in fact the key element in the dream.

3. *Plastic Word-representation*. During this phase of dream work primary process thoughts are transformed into visual images. Ordinarily, words are translations of visual experience; in this case, however, words are reduced back to their original source. Thus the process is regressive.

4. *Secondary Elaboration*. During secondary elaboration the results of the first three stages are combined into a reasonably coherent whole, the finished dream product.

Summarizing briefly, dream formation proceeds through the following steps: an unacceptable, usually sexual, impulse arises from the unconscious and threatens to become conscious; this thought is combined with memories from the preceding day and subjected to dream work; the unacceptable thought, suitably disguised, can now be expressed in consciousness.

Given knowledge of the meaning of dream formation, one can, at least in principle, begin to understand dreams. Bearing in mind that dreams can be properly analyzed only after considering the dreamer's history, how do we know if a dream has been correctly interpreted? There seem to be two tests. The first is frankly intuitive: does the interpretation seem to organize the facts of the dream into an intuitively sensible whole? The second test uses the criterion of consistency: is the interpretation consistent with everything else we know about the dreamer? If the interpretation shows the dream to have a coherent internal structure, and if it agrees with the facts of the dreamer's life, it may be valid.

Freud, however, insisted on a third test. He was quite emphatic about the authority of the analyst in these matters. How do we know if our interpretation of a dream is correct? We must ask an analyst. And how do we know if the analyst's interpretation is correct? Prior to Freud's death he was the final authority. Now it is not clear who is.

A relatively detailed understanding of Freud's dream theory is important for several reasons. In a limited sense, dream interpretation is the primary technique for analyzing the unconscious. As Freud said, "Psychoanalysis aims at and achieves nothing more than the discovery of the unconscious in mental life (1953, p. 397)." More broadly, however, dream analysis formed the basis for all Freud's subsequent work. His model of the psychic apparatus, his ideas about the origins and nature of morality, society, and religion all depend to some degree on findings provided by the dream theory. According to Freud, dream interpretation is the keystone of the entire psychoanalytic structure; the model of analysis presented in *The Interpretation of Dreams* is the psychoanalytic method. Finally, the technique of dream analysis is Freud's interpretive method of explanation; a particular event is explained when it has been interpreted according to the rules of the psychoanalytic method.

Once we recognize how extensively unconscious motives pervade everyday actions, almost anything we do becomes material for interpretation. Freud's analysis of such simple matters as slips of the tongue, lapses of memory, and misperceptions in hearing and reading is revealing. Consider the following examples of misprints (errors on the part of typesetters):

> An error of this sort is said once to have crept into a Social-Democratic newspaper, where, in the account of a festivity, the following words were printed: "Amongst those present was His Highness, the Clown Prince." The next day a correction was attempted. The paper apologized and said: "The sentence should of course have read, the Crow Prince." Again, in a war-correspondent's account of meeting a famous general whose infirmities were pretty well-known, a reference to the general was printed

as "this battle-scared veteran." Next day an apology appeared which read "the words of course should have been, the bottle-scarred veteran"! (Freud, 1953, p. 35).

When such errors occur we normally consider them to be amusing mistakes that express unexpected fragments of truth. The error itself is normally seen as a random event. According to Freud, who believed there was no such thing as a psychic accident, these errors are meaningful mental processes that follow their own purposes: "... they are serious mental acts ... which arise through the concurrence ... of two different intentions (1953, p. 48)." These intentions of course correspond to the latent and manifest content of a dream; one of the intentions is suppressed, and the error represents a "compromise-formation" by which the suppressed intention is expressed. The following personal example should clarify the similarity between the processes underlying such errors and the forces at work in dream formation. As an undergraduate I enrolled in a French course whose instructor was an attractive and worldly young Belgian. I once asked, in reference to a discussion of pronouns used in indirect discourse, "But Mademoiselle, what will we do in the case of indirect intercourse?" Only after several moments of general laughter did I recognize my error. Freud's analysis seems well suited for this example. A normally inadmissible primary process thought was expressed as a result of being combined with an otherwise innocuous question. As Freud would say (pp. 68–69):

> The speaker had determined not to convert the idea into speech and then it happens that he makes a slip of the tongue; that is to say, the tendency which is debarred from expression asserts itself against his will and gains utterance, either by altering the expression of the intention permitted by him, or by mingling with it, or actually by setting itself in place of it ... a suppression of a previous unconscious intention to say something is the indispensible condition for the occurrence of a slip of the tongue.

As in the case with dreams, so it is with slips of the tongue: the "previous unconscious intention" almost always concerns sexual matters.

The same analysis can be applied to most art, except music. The artist, according to Freud, is marginally neurotic. His instinctual needs are unusually powerful; he yearns for "honor, power, riches, fame, and the love of women," but he lacks the means to achieve these goals. Thus he turns to a life of fantasied gratification—a potentially neurotic choice. Through an interesting chain of circumstances, however, the artist (as opposed to the neurotic) may return to reality. Although everyone uses imaginary gratification, most people have strong repressive tendencies, and their fantasies provide only weak gratification. The artist, on the other hand, can modify his daydreams so that their origins are disguised, and nonartists can enjoy these fantasies without repression. The artist "opens out to others the way back to the comfort and consolation of their own unconscious sources of pleasure, and so reaps their gratitude and admiration; then he has won—through his fantasy—what before he could only win in fantasy (1953, p. 385)."

The point to be emphasized here is the similarity between artistic production and dream formation. The artist's unconscious desires demand expression. These unacceptable impulses are condensed, displaced, symbolized, mixed with elements from his experience, elaborated, and set forth in a fashion analogous to dream formation. Thus art is a distortion of reality and a violation of reason; it is also a primary source of information about the unconscious. Art differs from dreams primarily in its public nature. The artist airs his fantasies openly; art contains sharable meanings, dreams do not. The meaning of a work of art, however, must be discovered in the same manner that we interpret dreams: the manifest content must be translated back into its latent content. And, once again, the latent content for the most part expresses sexual themes.

The Symbolic Nature of Neurotic Symptoms. In the early portion of his career Freud was preoccupied with the explanation of neurotic symptoms, in particular with the odd behavior of a class of patients known as hysterics. Hysterics are persons who suffer from physical complaints that have no neurological or physical basis. Hysterics such as Freud treated are no longer common among the educated population of large cities; however, they still appear in rural areas and among the uneducated. The range of hysterical symptoms is enormous. The following are some typical examples: inability to speak; paralyzed limbs; loss of skin sensitivity; sight or hearing defects; tremors, spasms, cramps, and tics; peculiarities of posture; vomiting; diarrhea; loss of appetite, and overeating. When a medical examination shows that these symptoms have no anatomical or physiological basis, it is often assumed that the patient is pretending. According to Freud, however, hysterical symptoms have a symbolic function, they are formed in the same manner as dreams and works of art and may be interpreted in the same fashion.

Powerful, usually sexual, impulses arise from the unconscious and move toward conscious expression. These primary process thoughts are contrary to the reality principle; consequently they are forced out of awareness. As the repressed urges continue to strive toward gratification, they gain symbolic expression in a bodily symptom. Thus hysterical vomiting in women often indicates a desire to become pregnant, because vomiting is associated with "morning sickness" and the early stages of pregnancy.

Freud's analysis of Dora (1963) is the classic example of how, from a psychoanalytic viewpoint, hysterical symptoms are formed. Dora's major symptoms were hysterical coughing and hoarseness. Although these symptoms apparently once had an organic cause, their true meaning was primarily psychological. Dora was caught in a web of intrigue spun by her father, his mistress Frau K., and Frau K.'s husband, Herr K. In the course of a brief and incomplete analysis Freud discovered several meanings for Dora's symptoms. First, the coughing seemed to result from guilt over masturbation, a practice which had once given Dora a slight vaginal infection. By clearing her throat, she was symbolically removing the watery discharge produced by the infection. Second, Dora appeared to be using her illness as a means for diverting her father's attention away from his mistress, whom Dora saw as a rival. Third, the hysterical coughing was a symbolic gesture of revulsion. Herr K. had made a number of sexual advances toward Dora that she unconsciously found arousing. Such pleasurable feelings were consciously inadmissible, and consequently were translated into feelings of disgust, symbolized by coughing. Moreover, the coughing spells occurred when Herr K. was out of town, during which time Dora experienced erotic daydreams apparently prompted by his absence. Fourth, Freud felt Dora had a strong unconscious desire for incestuous relations with her father. Finally, Freud felt the coughing symbolized Dora's homosexual love for Frau K., "the strongest unconscious current in her mental life."

As they are presented here, these interpretations undoubtedly seem forced. To evaluate them properly, one should read the original account whose subtle and persuasive nature is impossible to capture in a brief summary. In Freud's analysis of Dora we see the familiar themes repeated once again. Several unconscious impulses are combined (condensed), displaced (from the genitals to the throat), and mixed with past experience (an earlier cough). Finally, these forbidden impulses, now suitably disguised, are expressed in the form of hysterical coughing.

It was relatively simple for Freud to account for neurotic symptoms in general through his explanation of hysterical symptoms. All such symptoms (e.g., phobias, obsessions, compulsions, anxiety reactions) can be expressed in terms of the Freudian pattern outlined above; the various types of neurosis differ only in their symptoms.

Most if not all forms of mental life may be interpreted in accordance with the psychoanalytic paradigm. Through interpretation, all our hopes, dreams, fantasies, aberrations, and creative achievements are reduced to the same limited number of themes; they are merely the surface wrapping on a relentlessly stereotyped psychological dynamic, four features of which are emphasized by psychoanalysis. First, the themes underlying social behavior are almost always sexual in nature and usually perverse, dealing with incestuous, homosexual, or sado-masochistic forms of sexual desire. Second, such desires are normally unconscious, and therefore the person involved is unaware of them. Third, an analyst is required to bring these unconscious impulses to awareness. If the desires are strong and the person resists acknowledging them for too long, neurotic symptoms will inevitably develop. Finally, there is never a single cause for important psychological phenomena; neurotic symptoms, dreams, errors, and works of art are always "over-determined", the result of several converging lines of influence.

chapter four

Sigmund Freud:
The
Social
Theory

The last chapter discussed Freud's concept of the unconscious mind and described how dream interpretation holds the key to understanding neurotic symptoms. The nature of the relationship between the individual and his unconscious forms the core of Freud's clinical theory, perhaps the best known part of psychoanalysis. This chapter describes Freud's lesser known social theory: his analysis of the relationship between the individual and his society.

MOTIVATION

Freud's ideas about motivation reflect his early training in neurophysiology. His use of the concept of instinct in particular is an attempt to provide links between psychoanalysis and biology.

Freud frequently revised his motivational ideas, giving an ambiguous and even disorganized tone to the theory. Freud himself remarked that "... the science of the instincts is the most incomplete part of psychoanalytic theory." The motivational theory passed through four phases. The first began with *Studies in Hysteria* (1895) and the unpublished manuscript *Project for a Scientific Psychology* (1896). Motivation here was an electromagnetic rather than biological concept; specifically, motivation was defined in terms of "cerebral excitations" and the flow of electric currents. In these early papers Freud developed a concept that he called the "constancy principle," a forerunner of the pleasure principle. The principle of constancy stated, in essence, that people strive to maintain a constant level of cerebral excitation; if this level is exceeded they will be strongly motivated to reduce the surplus excitation. This principle was then used to explain the symptoms of hysteria and the development of anxiety.

The second phase of the motivational theory (extending roughly from 1896 to 1900) developed out of Freud's experience in private practice. He abandoned his physicalistic model, stating frankly that the biochemical nature of instincts was unknown. "The theory of instincts is so to say our mythology. Instincts are mythical entities, magnificent in their indefiniteness. In our work we cannot for a moment disregard them, yet we are never sure that we are seeing them clearly (*New Introductory Lectures*, p. 95)." During this period Freud distinguished two major classes of instincts: libidinal or sexual instincts associated with the pleasure principle and the preservation of the species; and self-preservative instincts associated with the reality principle and the preservation of the individual.

During the third phase, from 1900 to 1923, Freud was primarily concerned with studying sexual instincts, although he continued to recognize the importance of self-preservative impulses. Consequently, the boundary between the second and third phase of the motivational theory is indistinct; it is defined principally in terms of emphasis.

The fourth phase of Freud's motivational theory began about 1920 with the publication of *Beyond the Pleasure Principle*. In this final formulation Freud proposed two classes of instincts, sex and aggression. This last motivational theory has not been well received for reasons discussed below.

Because most accounts of Freud's theory of motivation deal primarily with ideas from his third period, it is worthwhile to examine them in some detail. Instincts exist in a grey region between psychology and physiology, and their precise relationship to the mind is ambiguous. Sexual instincts are the power supply of the mind; they produce psychic energy and periodic states of tension. Much social behavior serves directly or indirectly to relieve this tension. Psychic energy is "invested in" or "cathected to" memories and thoughts of early sources of sexual satisfaction. The greater the cathexis, the stronger the memory.

Underlying most social behavior is a recurring pattern of increasing tension caused by instinctual arousal, followed by goal-directed activity, and then tension release. However, this normal cycle of arousal and release is continually disrupted by four unconscious vicissitudes or perturbations of the instincts:

1. An instinct may develop into its opposite (e.g., love may turn into hate), producing unconscious ambivalence.
2. An instinct may turn around on a person so that, for example, hostility toward one's father may become hostility toward one's self.
3. An instinct may be repressed; repression, however, requires a constant expenditure of psychic energy and is consequently fatiguing in a psychological and emotional sense.
4. The direct expression of an instinct normally provokes anxiety in oneself and others; in some cases, however, it is possible to adapt instincts to the demands of reality (e.g., sexual energy may be channeled into scientific research). Such successful adaptations are called sublimations.

Every expression of the sexual instincts somewhat disrupts the normal work of civilization. Thus, society requires that they be rigorously controlled; but controls are contrary to the pleasure principle and make us unhappy. Moreover, if tension is not periodically released, the psychic system will "explode," resulting in a flood of anxiety, perhaps even in neurosis. If, however, society encouraged every possible form of open sexual expression (a situation unattainable in principle, according to Freud), the vicissitudes of the instincts would make free and uninhibited gratification impossible. Consequently, between the repressive nature of society and the relentless but changeable demands of the instincts, every person is destined to a life of conflict; the sexual instincts are a built-in source of human misery, rather than a source of joy and happiness.

Freud felt that the sexual drive develops through a sequence of stages that is uniform for all persons. These stages of psychosexual development are defined in terms of the region of the body that provides primary erotic gratification at a particular time. Thus, for the first eighteen months of life (known as the oral period) libidinal tension is relieved through stimulation of the mouth, lips, and tongue in the form of nursing. During the second year, the locus of erotic stimulation shifts to the anus. This is called the anal period, and eliminatory behavior is the most important activity at this stage. Around the beginning of the third year of life the child's genitalia become the primary source of sexual excitation; this is the phallic stage. At about five the child enters a latency period wherein sexual activity is minimal. This stage persists until adolescence when the impetus of the sexual drive is greatly increased. At this point the person may move into the final and most mature period of psychosexual development, the genital stage.

At each stage of development one cathects or concentrates on the part of the body that defines that stage. No strong libidinal cathexis is ever completely dissolved, and people retain cathexes that were more appropriate to earlier periods in their lives. These "immature" cathexes are known as fixations. Fixations are primarily unconscious and are a general feature of psychosexual development—everyone has fixations of some kind. The complementary concept is regression—the return to an earlier mode or object of gratification; i.e., one regresses to an earlier fixation. Fixations result from either excessive gratification or undue frustration of a particular mode of satisfaction. In addition to determining the kinds of sexual satisfactions a person will seek, fixations give a distinctive flavor to a person's interpersonal style. For example, excessive deprivation at the oral stage may result in an "oral-dependent" personality, a longing for maternal support that manifests itself as passivity, low self-esteem, and indulgence in such "oral" activities as drinking, smoking, eating, and nail-biting. Excessive oral gratification can produce an "oral-aggressive" personality characterized by a self-confident, quarrelsome, verbal aggressiveness (symbolic biting of the mother's breast).

Children who experience rigid toilet training, according to Freud, may develop severe anxiety about fecal matter. This sometimes results in a fixation at the anal stage and an "anal-retentive" personality. Such people are stingy, pedantic, fussy about rules, compulsively neat and tidy, and overly concerned with the functioning of their bowels. Children who, on the other hand, undergo leisurely toilet training may as adults spend money freely, ignore rules, and appear slovenly in their personal habits; they are not anxious about fecal matter and are known as "anal-expulsives." Fixations at the phallic stage may lead to a "phallic" personality. Such persons are self-preoccupied, intrusive, noisy, inconsiderate, and self-aggrandizing.

Freud meant much more by sexuality than a mere impulse toward sexual union. He used the word sex rather broadly and attributed a sexual component to a variety of emotions. Sympathy, affiliation, loyalty, friendship, filial devotion, parental affection, piety, romantic love, and even aesthetic feelings were all considered to be sublimated forms of sexual attachments.

Most people are aware of Freud's emphasis on sexual instincts as determinants of social behavior, but few realize how profoundly ambivalent he felt toward this subject. Freud urged for the sake of mental health that we acknowledge the realities of sexual motivation, as they tend to preoccupy children and adults alike. Nonetheless, he was no celebrant of the senses. As Rieff (1959, p. 170) observes, "Freud . . . comes to the tacit understanding that sex really is nasty, an ignoble slavery to nature." In the manner of the Stoics, Freud defines sexual pleasure in negative terms, as the absence of sexual tension. The pursuit of pleasure is actually a defense against the buildup of tension. Freud conceives sexual activity in economic terms as a form of bargaining or exchange between persons. However, he regards this exchange as ". . . a bargain of fools each of whom is bound to find out that he has invested far more libido than the 'object' was really worth. Objects disappoint, instincts are stupid, love cheats when it does not delude (Rieff, 1959, p. 172)."

Many people assume that sexual satisfaction is a natural and effortless physical process. For Freud, however, mature sexuality is an achievement made difficult by the fixations of childhood; by the vicissitudes of the instincts; and by a peculiar quality of sexuality itself, that we desire primarily those objects we don't have. Thus, far from advocating sexual license, Freud regarded sexuality as a profoundly troublesome and potentially dangerous force, something to be considered but not praised.

The fourth phase in Freud's motivational thinking began about 1920 with the publication of his monograph *Beyond the Pleasure Principle*. Freud reached this final formulation through studying certain well-known clinical phenomena—sadism, masochism, and repetition compulsions—that seem to contradict the pleasure principle. People who suffer from a repetition compulsion are unable to change behavior that is obviously self-defeating; they seem cursed by an endless chain of bad luck that, on closer examination, appears to be self-inflicted. Because it seemed impossible to explain the self-destructive qualities of masochism and the repetition compulsion, and the aggressive nature of sadism in terms of an erotic drive, Freud hypothesized the existence of ". . . two essentially different classes of instincts: the sexual instincts, understood in the widest sense—Eros, if you prefer that name—and the aggressive instincts, whose aim is destruction (1965, p. 103)." Sexual instincts push one toward change and development, while aggressive instincts urge one toward death.

The life instincts are directed outward in the form of love and sympathy, whereas the death instincts are expressed in the form of aggression. Every cell in one's body is a battlefield in the struggle between the life and death instincts. And every instinctual impulse contains a fusion of these two forces. This means that, for Freud, all human motivation is fundamentally ambivalent; every human action has simultaneously an erotic and an aggressive component that, if not controlled, produce egoistic and antisocial behavior ". . . What we have come to see about the sexual instincts applies equally and perhaps still more to the other ones, the aggressive instincts. It is they above all that make human communal life difficult and threaten its survival. Restriction of the individual's aggressiveness is the first and perhaps the severest sacrifice which society requires of him (1965, p. 110)."

Freud's discussion of aggression and the death instinct has been heavily criticized, even by other psychoanalysts. The death instinct is a puzzling notion on biological grounds; however, the rejection of Freud's ideas about the role of aggression in human affairs is harder to interpret, because an aggressive component in human nature makes biological sense and has empirical support (Mayr, 1963). This criticism may stem in part from the fact that the view of man as naturally aggressive supports a conservative political philosophy, and social scientists tend to be politically liberal. Liberals typically maintain that the human race is ultimately perfectable, that man's inhumanity to man is the result of corrupt social organization. People in general, regardless of their political persuasions, find disagreeable the notion that humans are innately aggressive. Freud on the other hand suggests that man is by nature aggressive and therefore incorrigible, directly contradicting the political assumptions of many social scientists. As Freud (1961, pp. 58, 67) observed:

> ...men are not gentle creatures who want to be loved and who at the most can defend themselves if they are attacked; they are, on the contrary, creatures among whose instinctual endowments is to be reckoned a powerful share of aggressiveness. As a result, their neighbor is for them not only a potential helper or sexual object, but also someone who tempts them to satisfy their aggressiveness on him, to exploit his capacity for work without compensation, to use him sexually without his consent, to seize his possessions, to humiliate him, to cause him pain, to torture and kill him... Who in the face of all his experience of life and of history, will have the courage to dispute this assertion?... I can no longer understand how we can have overlooked the ubiquity of non-erotic aggressivity and destructiveness and can have failed to give it its due place in our interpretation of life... I remember my own defensive attitude when the idea of an instinct of destruction first emerged in psycho-analytic literature, and how long it took before I became receptive to it. That others should have shown, and still show, the same attitude of rejection surprises me less. For "little children do not like it" when there is talk of the inborn human inclination to "badness", to aggressiveness and destructiveness, and so to cruelty as well.

THE SELF-CONCEPT

Freud conceived of personality in terms of both instinctual dynamics and mental structure (his brain mythologies). His ideas about these structures also have a history dating from 1913. His early theory postulated three psychic systems: the conscious, preconscious, and unconscious. In the period from 1913 to 1923 Freud became increasingly critical of this model, and in *The Ego and the Id* (1923) he set forth his structural hypothesis in which mental processes were organized in terms of their functions. Here Freud described the origins and development of the id, the ego, and the superego, and analyzed their inter-relationships.

The id is the "dark, unaccessible part of our personality." It is the "core of our being," the primitive, relentlessly demanding, and wholly unconscious portion of the psychic apparatus that was discovered through the study of dream work. The id is the reservoir of psychic energy that, as we have seen, comes from two sources (sexual and aggressive instincts), and it strives constantly after instinctual gratification in accordance with the pleasure principle and the "laws" of primary process thought. It is the source of the impulses that become converted into manifest dreams and neurotic symptoms. The id is virtually equivalent to the unconscious.

Initially the mind is all id and primary process; but slowly, some time within the first six or eight months of life, the ego begins to be differentiated from the id. The ego is not a single mental structure; it is a shorthand expression for a set of structures that are concerned with the person's interaction with the external world. The early tasks of the ego include gaining control of one's muscles, coordinating sensory perception with motor movement (i.e., developing hand-eye coordination), and building up a fund of memories useful for dealing with the environment. The energy required to carry out these activities is taken from the id—it is denatured or desexualized psychic energy—and all the ego's activities, directly or indirectly, serve the pleasure principle. Freud's ego structures, therefore, correspond to the first notion of the self-concept discussed in chapter two, the self as dynamism, agency, or ego.

As a result of repeated frustrating encounters with the world, the ego learns to discriminate between signals from the id and signals from the external world. This process, called reality testing, is never completed even in adulthood. Failures of reality testing have serious social consequences. Don Quixote tilting windmills is an example of what happens when a person acts in accordance with his hallucinations (signals from the id). Oceanic religious experiences that produce feelings of oneness with the universe also suggest a collapse of ego boundaries and a failure of reality testing.

Perhaps the most important function of the ego, and one that the id neglects, is self-preservation. Although the ego structures cannot be destroyed, they can be disorganized and portions turned back into id. The ego can be overwhelmed by excessively strong libidinal impulses (such as tend to occur at the outset of adolescence) or by unusually powerful stimuli from the external world. When the ego feels itself in danger it sends out bolts of anxiety as warning signals. The ego then develops defenses such as repression or even neurotic symptoms to protect a person from anxiety. This conception of anxiety as a warning signal is quite different from Freud's earlier notion that excess libidinal energy is discharged directly as anxiety. Freud's later formulation, called the concept of signal anxiety, implies that the ego can anticipate unpleasant social occurrences and in some sense takes charge of the pleasure principle.

Ego Psychology

The bulk of Freud's writing is devoted to analyzing the relationship between the individual and his unconscious. For various reasons Freud gave relatively little attention to the origins and development of the ego and one's relations with social reality. The major development in psychoanalysis since the death of Freud is a movement called ego psychology, a movement that has been primarily concerned with this neglected aspect of psychoanalysis emphasizing the nature of ego structures and their development. Hartman (1939), who is perhaps the principle figure in this movement, suggested that the ego and the id emerge together from an earlier, undifferentiated stage of psychic development. He toyed with the notion that the ego has its own energy supply but concluded that its power comes from a continuous supply of neutralized libidinal energy. Both the id and the ego are assumed to have inherited features so that each infant is born "preadapted to the average expectable environment." The ego is considered to be autonomous; unlike Freud, Hartman suggested that the ego develops independently from the id. Consequently, it develops in a "conflict-free sphere," being spared some of the conflict between instinct and reality that Freud thought was inevitable. Not only is the ego innately autonomous vis à vis the id, but also some of its functions develop what Hartman called secondary autonomy. That is, exercising some of the ego's processes (e.g., playing ball, solving problems, climbing trees) may be intrinsically rewarding; the pleasure derived from their use does not come from the id. Hartman placed particular emphasis on this ego-derived "pleasure in activities themselves, in overcoming difficulties," a form of enjoyment that he called *Funktionlust* or pleasure in functioning. The ego psychologists emphasize genetic or developmental studies of children that they feel will furnish information about the ego that the study of adult neurotics is unable to provide. As a consequence, many of the ego psychologists are specialists in child development.

Ego psychology represents the mainstream of current psychoanalytic thought. It ties in well with academic psychology, and the ideas and research it has stimulated are an invaluable contribution to contemporary social science. However, the actual relationship of this movement to Freud is problematical. For example, the notion of the ego developing in a "conflict free sphere" is quite anti-Freudian, given that Freud thought conflict and unhappiness were a necessary and unavoidable part of the human condition. Ego psychology seems an attempt to add a little brightness to Freud's dark vision of man's fate; by attempting to remove some of the bitterness from Freud's original ideas, the ego psychologists seem to attentuate the force and power of his analysis (Marcuse, 1955). An analogous effect would be achieved in literature if Hamlet, Macbeth, and King Lear were rewritten so that each had a happy ending. Such revisions might make some theatergoers happy, but Shakespeare would surely suffer as a result.

SOCIALIZATION

Thus far we have discussed the biological or psychosexual development of the individual. We now turn to social development, a process explained in terms of the evolution of the superego. The origins of socialization are found both in the history of each person's development and in the history of the species. Thus Freud offers an ontogenetic and a phylogenetic explanation of socialization. We shall consider the ontogenetic process first.

The Ontogenesis of Socialization

Freud analyzed the ontogenesis of socialization in two closely related ways; both analyses involve the concepts of identification and the Oedipus complex. Freud distinguished between two different and unrelated forms of love. The first is respect and affection based on identification; the second is sexuality narrowly defined. Identification is basic to the process of socialization, and the earliest form of an emotional bond with another person. Through identification a little boy takes "a special interest in his father; he would like to grow like him and be like him and take his place everywhere." That is, through identification a little boy takes his father as an ideal. "This behavior has nothing to do with a passive or feminine attitude toward his father (and toward males in general); it is on the contrary typically masculine. It fits in very well with the Oedipus complex for which it helps to prepare the way (Freud, 1960, p. 46)." At the same time that a boy begins to identify with his father, or perhaps a little later, he begins to develop a desire for incestuous relations with his mother. "He then exhibits, therefore, two psychologically distinct ties: a straightforward sexual object-cathexis toward his mother and an identification with his father which takes him as his model. The two subsist side by side for a time without any mutual influence or interference. In consequence of the irresistible advance toward unification of mental life, they come together at last (Freud, 1960, p. 46);" and the Oedipal crisis begins.

Briefly, the Oedipal crisis results from the conflict between a boy's incestuous longings for his mother and his desire to please his father. This conflict mounts as a boy's love for his mother becomes increasingly passionate. It reaches a peak when a boy is about five years old and he receives (or thinks he has received) a threat of castration from his presumably jealous father. To avoid castration and retain his father's love, a boy resorts to a defensive strategy known as "identification with the aggressor." He takes the image of his father inside himself, renounces (at least consciously) his sexual desires for his mother, and seems symbolically to say, "See, I'm just like you; there is no point in your hating me, you'll just be hating yourself." The boy actually takes the image of both parents inside himself, and this internalized image is the superego, the final set of psychic structures conceived by Freud. The superego prevents the subsequent appearance of any desires or actions that one's parents would not approve of.

Superego formation for little girls is different and less complete. Here the problem centers on the Electra complex; it begins when a small girl discovers that she lacks a penis. This causes her to turn away from her mother whom she feels has betrayed her and to invest her love in her father. This love quickly turns into incestuous desires, but then the Electra complex begins to disappear, partly because of the girl's fear of losing her mother's love. The resolution of the Electra complex is ambiguous according to Freud, and women lack well-defined and objective superegos as a result.

The events we have just described are only half the story of socialization. The child has repressed his sexual impulses, but his aggressive desires remain largely untouched. And, as we saw earlier, aggression is an even greater threat than eros to a stable social order.

Freud's discussion of the socialization of aggression arises from his analysis of the origins of guilt. In the early stages of development a child conforms to his parents' wishes out of fear of punishment or losing their love. When parental authority is internalized through the establishment of a superego, however, prohibited thoughts and actions are followed by feelings of guilt that persist until the person undergoes some form of punishment.

During weaning, toilet-training, and other instruction, parents inevitably frustrate their children. Children consequently develop considerable resentment toward their parents, but there is little they can do about it. They must give up both their libidinal pleasures (free access to the breast, leisurely excreting, free sex-play) and the satisfaction of revenge—hostility toward their parents would produce punishment and rejection. Children are thus caught in a powerful, instinctually-based dilemma: their aggressive impulses demand expression, yet there are no safe outlets for them. They again resort to the defensive strategy of identification with the aggressor, and by so doing, place the unattackable authorities inside themselves. This internalized authority becomes a child's superego, and it has all the aggression at its disposal that the child originally felt toward its parents. When aggression is turned inward and taken over by the superego, the superego can direct it against the ego. "The tension between the harsh superego and the ego that is subjected to it, is called . . . the sense of guilt; it expresses itself as a need for punishment (Freud, 1961, p. 70)."

Conscience begins with the repression of one's aggressive impulses. Once a conscience is established, further repression of aggression is guaranteed, because the superego will not allow its expression. Moreover, each subsequent repression turns that much more aggressive energy over to the superego to be used against the ego. This produces a snowballing effect that leads to an interesting moral paradox: every denial of one's aggressive instincts increases the severity and intolerance of one's superego. The more virtuous a man is, the more severe and distrustful is his superego; those who are most saintly reproach themselves constantly with the worst sinfulness: they experience constant moral indigestion.

Thus, for Freud socialization consists of placing one's sexual and aggressive impulses under the control of a superego, that will then punish one for socially incorrect expressions of either instinct. Socialization thus consists of turning libido outward and aggression inward.

The superego has two major functions: the first is called conscience and the second is called the ego ideal. Conscience results from defensive identification (identification with the aggressor); its actions are primitive, unconscious, and unrealistic. Conscience always acts contrary to the pleasure principle. According to Freud, if conscience had its way the human species would perish (because people would cease to procreate). Conscience punishes us for our real and imagined misdeeds by making us feel guilty. One of Freud's most interesting insights is that this superego function rather than the id is the ultimate source of irrationality in our lives: conscience not instinct is the final foe of reason.

The ego ideal, on the other hand, is the product of anaclitic identification (identification based on respect and affection). It is an idealized parental image or standard against which we evaluate our conduct. The superego will punish us if we fail to live up to our ego ideal. The purpose of the ego ideal is to regulate social conduct by telling us what we ought to do, in contrast with conscience, which tells us what we ought not to do.

One major consequence of superego development is that it preserves the continuity of culture across generations. The superego is made up of social norms; therefore, it is the primary vehicle of cultural transmission between parents and children.

Secondly, a person who lacks a superego will be hostile, disrespectful of authority, and probably delinquent. One with a well-defined superego, however, will be over-repressed, unduly respectful of authority, and sexually maladjusted. According to Freud, the major problem in life is not sexual adjustment *per se* but establishing a proper relationship to authority in the form of one's superego. The Oedipal crisis is the most important event in human development.

A final consequence of superego development is that the sense of guilt caused by the superego is identical with any other form of anxiety, including that associated with neurosis. Thus, civilized living places extraordinary demands on people. It requires first that we give up certain important sources of instinctual satisfaction thereby reducing our general level of happiness. More importantly, however, for Freud civilized behavior is a neurotic defense against superego anxiety; we comply with the norms of society to avoid being punished by the superego. Although morality may be the hallmark of civilized culture, it is also a sick compromise one makes for the benefits of living in society. The goal of psychoanalytic therapy is thus to make the patient less moral by relaxing the excessive demands of the superego, because the problem of neurosis is typically the problem of over-socialization.

The Phylogenesis of Socialization

A complete account of Freud's structural hypothesis requires that we say something about the phylogenetic origins of the superego. The phylogenetic theory first appeared in *Totem and Taboo* (1912). This wide-ranging book traces a number of parallels in the thinking of neurotics and primitive peoples (primarily Australian aborigines). Freud observed, for example, that neurotics and primitives share an unusually strong abhorrence of incest, that neurotic phobias and primitive taboos are quite similar, and that both neurotic fantasies and primitive magic are characterized by a childish faith in the omnipotence of thought. In the latter part of the book Freud attempts to explain these parallels.

Freud adopted Darwin's suggestion that primitive man lived in small hordes dominated by powerful and despotic males. He also adopted the notion first proposed by the Scottish anthropologist Robertson Smith, that sacrifice at an altar was a universal characteristic of primitive religions. Such sacrifices usually entailed killing and eating the tribe's totem animal; this was normally forbidden because the totem animal was regarded as a kin and a god. Freud assumed that totem animals symbolized father figures. He further believed that adult neurotics always have an unconscious desire to kill their fathers, impulses that are also reflected in dreams and in children's play. On the asumption that in the beginning man actually did what he only dreams of doing today, Freud concluded that prehistoric man actually murdered his father.

As Freud described it, life in the original primal horde was hard for the sons of the despotic ruling male. The father, who symbolizes the reality principle, controlled the women and the supplies, and sons who offended him were killed, castrated, or driven out of the horde; older sons were driven away as a matter of course. The banished sons lived in a community united by homosexual bonds. At some point the sons sensing their combined strength, returned and murdered their father, ate him, and engaged in an orgy of incest. Each son then wanted to take his father's place as leader and monopolize the women. The group was consequently faced with the possibility of total anarchy. Moreover, rebellion against the father had also meant the overthrow of biologically justified authority (the father was the group's most competent male), which threatened the life of the group as a whole. Finally, the sons in a sense loved as well as hated their father (they needed to be dominated by him), and therefore felt guilty after his murder. Thus, as soon as the sons gained their freedom they missed their domination; they felt a craving for authority. To ease their guilt, to forestall a chaos of murder, and to satisfy their need to be dominated, the brothers mutually agreed to restrict their sexual behavior and to obey a father substitute. They also established their murdered father as a god whose forgiveness they asked for their primal crimes of patricide and incest. Thus, Freud observed, the ultimate reinstatement of the primal father was as inevitable as his murder.

No other portion of Freud's writing has been as strongly attacked and universally rejected as *Totem and Taboo*. There are probably two reasons for this. First, the book unquestionably has problems with regard to its logical consistency and its presentation of man's evolutionary past. According to anthropologists, a tribe whose adult males were not joined together as a cohesive social unit would have been at a serious competitive disadvantage in the struggle for survival. Moreover, leadership in primate groups seems not to depend on the physical strength of the leader, but on his ability to persuade other males to assist him in physical confrontations with his adversaries. Thus the primal horde was almost surely not structured as Freud describes it.

Totem and Taboo is most properly seen as a Freudian allegory concerning man's ambivalent relationship to authority. If one assumes with Freud that memories of the primal crime and sense of guilt are somehow part of the unconscious and that similar events have reoccurred throughout man's history, then, as Freud suggests, a number of consequences follow. First, conflict between fathers and sons is inevitable. Second, cultural history should consist of one revolution after another, however each revolution will be followed by renewed repression. Third, as Thomas Hobbes suggested, man is anarchic and needs society to save him from chaos; consequently, he conforms to the rules of society out of fear of anarchy. Freud agreed, but added that man also conforms out of an unconscious desire to be dominated. Fourth, although society is repressive, rebellion is unjustified because the leaders of the revolution are always motivated by envy, revenge, and the desire to become masters themselves. Finally, all political and religious history subsequent to those bloody events in the primal horde can be seen as a record of man's repeated, irrational attempts to reinstate the primal father in the form of Caesars, Stalins, Hitlers, and Perons.

Totem and Taboo contains some markedly antipolitical themes that are repeated in *Group Psychology and the Analysis of the Ego* (1922). This later book is ostensibly concerned with an explanation of mass or crowd behavior, a topic that fascinated political and social philosophers in the nineteenth century. A close reading suggests, however, that Freud actually used the book to extend the analysis presented in *Totem and Taboo*, to clarify further the relationship between the individual and the group.

Freud remarked at the beginning of *Group Psychology and the Analysis of the Ego* that "... individual psychology ... is at the same time social psychology as well (1960, p. 3)"; and the primary questions of social psychology concern the changes that occur when we enter a group. In groups people's thinking comes to resemble that of children and primitives. They seem impulsive, changeable, and irritable; they lose their critical faculties and become extraordinarily credulous and suggestible. People in groups develop an exaggerated respect for authority and tradition; their desire to be dominated makes them conservative and unwilling to deviate from group norms. Thus, when one enters a group, the power of the superego declines and primary process thinking takes over much as if one were asleep. How, asked Freud, can we account for these remarkable changes?

Group members seem to be bound by strong emotional ties in two directions: the first is to the leader, the second is to the other members of the group. These ties that form rather easily, distinguish a group from a mere collection of people. For example, whenever a group of persons work together toward a common goal, emotional bonds develop between them based on identification. These bonds account in part for the power of a group over the individual. However, the strongest factor in group formation is the leader. Freud equated the relationship between a group member and his leader with that of a hypnotic subject to his hypnotist. Indeed, he suggested that a hypnotic relationship is a group—a group, however, with only two members. The hypnotist establishes a powerful emotional (libidinal) tie with his subject; the tie is so powerful that the hypnotist takes the place of the subject's superego. A group functions because "...a number of individuals...have put one and the same ...person (the leader) in the place of their ego ideal and have consequently identified themselves with one another in their ego (p. 61)." This description of a group closely parallels Freud's discussion of man in the primal horde. As Freud states, "...the group appears to us as a revival of the primal horde. Just as primitive man survives potentially in every individual, so the primal horde may arise once more out of any random collection of people; in so far as men are habitually under the sway of group formation we recognize in it the survival of the primal horde. We must conclude that the psychology of groups is the oldest human psychology...(pp. 69–70)." This oldest human psychology is activated the moment we leave the privacy of our rooms to join our colleagues at the office, in the laboratory, or on the playing field. In the voices of the drill sergeant, the president, the family patriarch, and the scoutmaster we hear echoes of the primal father, and at some level we respond accordingly.

Since the beginning of man there have been two kinds of psychologies, that of the individual group members, and that of the father, chief, or leader. Although members must comply with the norms and conventions of their group, the leader like the primal father is free. He is strong and independent, he loves no one but himself, and he is interested in other people only in so far as they serve his needs. "He, at the very beginning of the history of mankind, was the 'superman' whom Nietzsche only expected from the future. Even today the members of a group stand in need of the illusion that they are equally and justly loved by their leader; but the leader himself need love no one else, he may be of a masterful nature, absolutely narcissistic, self-confident and independent (p. 71)." This leads Freud to an interesting analysis of the meaning of social justice: it is the situation wherein everyone is persecuted equally. Since society is always repressive and political leadership psychopathic, this is the only definition Freud considered possible.

Freud's discussion of the psychology of leaders has been criticized in contemporary research. However, such leaders as politicians, generals, business executives, and football coaches tend to ignore this modern view, and, by their actions, they often seem to support Freud's analysis.

EXPLANATION

We can now summarize Freud's rather complex model of explanation. He accounts for the universal features of human nature in three ways: first, in terms of his motivational theory—all men are unconsciously driven by sex and aggression; second, in terms of his ontogenetic models of psychosexual development and socialization—everyone passes through the oral, anal, and phallic stages of development and the major event in childhood is the Oedipal crisis; third, in terms of the phylogenetic theory of socialization—at a deep or unconscious level we all have incestuous tendencies, we all resent authority, and yet we all need to be dominated. Thus, Freud describes human nature in terms of general laws of motivation, sexual and social development, and the evolutionary history of the species.

Freud explains individual differences primarily in terms of social experience. People differ from one another as a result of fixations at different stages of development that create character types (e.g., oral, anal, and phallic) defined in terms of a particular style of social behavior. People also differ as a result of the way they have dealt with their Oedipal conflicts. Finally, the parental image that a child internalizes at the end of the Oedipal period produces additional differences among people.

The third set of phenomena that personality theories attempt to explain are specific puzzling symptoms, anomalous actions, and curious errors and mistakes. Freud explained these by interpretation, and the best account of this explanatory procedure is found in his dream theory. The process of interpretation is independent of the phenomena to be explained and takes the same form in every case. The explanandum (the matter to be explained) is seen as a "compromise formation," a symbolic expression of an otherwise unacceptable, usually sexual impulse. This impulse is condensed, displaced, mixed with what remains of the person's earlier experiences, shaped by secondary elaboration, and then made public. The process of interpretation reverses this sequence by tracing the manifest content or symptom back to its latent and unconscious source. Such interpretive explanations place considerable demands on the intuitive and imaginative powers of the investigator; he must invent hypotheses that will plausibly organize a wide range of facts concerning the phenomena under question. Freudian interpretations are sometimes compelling *tours de force*; on other occasions, however, they are less than convincing.

PSYCHOLOGICAL HEALTH

In the Freudian model unhappiness is inescapable; the most we can hope for is to master *some* of the sources of our misery. Our problems lie both in the past and the present. From the past, fixations and immature cathexes cause us to seek inappropriate modes of libidinal gratification (e.g., thumb sucking, fingernail biting, excessive drinking, etc.), that only lead to further frustration, anxiety, and rigidity, and prevent us from trying more appropriate means of obtaining satisfaction. Early trauma caused by premature weaning, punitive toilet training, or difficulties during the Oedipal period, prevent us from managing our instincts in a mature and reasonable manner. An unusually strict superego will inhibit any expression of the instincts and will force one to expend large amounts of psychic energy to keep these inhibitions in place. Such persons have little energy left to deal with reality.

Problems arise in the present because human instincts are constantly demanding, but civilization is implacably repressive; one must give up free instinctual gratification in order to live in society. If, however, one manages to devise socially-approved means for libidinal gratification, the nature of the instincts themselves is such that they will disrupt organized patterns of tension release. One is trapped between the demands of the id, the superego, and society as a whole. For these reasons most people, according to Freud, are to some degree neurotic; psychological health is an ideal, not a statistical norm. Moreover, although we are unhappy because of the conflicts between instinct, conscience, and reality, there are other sources of misery in our lives. From *Group Psychology and the Analysis of the Ego* we also know that all group or collective actions will tend .to be irrational, guided by the most primitive and immature impulses.

Certain characteristics then, are necessary for psychological health. The first is self-awareness: everything that might cause problems in the unconscious must be made conscious. Unnecessary unconscious repressions must be lifted, and the energy that was required to keep them in place must be turned over to the ego. Unconscious childhood experiences must be relived and "worked through," thereby permitting one to give up infantile sources of gratification. Ultimately, however, true self-awareness is not possible until the unrealistic and superfluous controls of the superego have been broken down. Because the unconscious portions of the superego reflect the prohibitions and ideals of one's parents (and produce in us an irrational respect for authority), psychological health requires that a flexible and rational ego replace our rigid and moralistic conscience. This does not mean that, as unconscious superego controls are weakened and repressed desires are made conscious, we can begin a life devoted to pleasure. Self-awareness, not hedonism, is the main ingredient for psychological health; and in the mature person repression of instinctual desires is replaced by condemnation. Under the guidance of a rational and conscious ego we may exchange our neurotic unhappiness for the common misery of mankind.

But self-awareness is not enough for a healthy psyche. As we have seen, social living itself is a potential source of unreason. Freud held a nearly tautological belief in the irrationality of group actions. He considered all political movements, democratic or totalitarian, revolutionary or reactionary, to be corrupt. Consequently, Freud proposed rational alienation from public enthusiasms as a final criterion of psychological health. Skepticism about social ideologies and political leadership and a carefully cultivated individuality are the final defining features of the mature man.

EVALUATION

Before closing this discussion of Freud, it is appropriate to offer a brief evaluation of his contribution. In making this evaluation I will concentrate on the theory itself and ignore the question of how well psychoanalysis has been supported by empirical test. This same procedure will be followed at the end of subsequent chapters as well.

There are five aspects of psychoanalysis that now seem questionable. First, psychoanalysis presents a profoundly condescending and distorted image of women. Like Nietzsche and Schopenhauer, Freud was a misogynist. Women are described as weak, immature, emotional creatures, innately inferior to men in terms of both moral and intellectual development. Many writers in the nineteenth century took a patronizing attitude toward women, and Freud seems to have reflected the spirit of his times. Nonetheless, the antifeminist trends in psychoanalysis should be recognized for what they are and the model judged accordingly.

Second, history suggests that certain forms of social injustice can occasionally be eliminated. However, social reform always depends on people acting together in a political fashion. Although Freud's observations concerning the narcissistic and psychopathic character of politicians and the irrational nature of group actions are well taken, the net effect of psychoanalysis is to support the status quo. From Freud's perspective social freedom is both illusory and a contradiction in terms. Yet any observer of human affairs knows that at least some citizens of every society are victims of the system. Thus, the reactionary trends in psychoanalysis should also be recognized for what they are.

Third, there is an annoying tendency in Freud not to acknowledge his intellectual antecedents. His ideas about the socialization of aggression and the concept of repression, for example, are clearly influenced by if not taken directly from Nietzsche. On occasion Freud actually denied ever having read Nietzsche, yet to anyone familiar with the writings of both men, the assertion is obviously false.

Finally, the concept of resistance effectively guarantees that psychoanalysis will be immune to those self-correcting tendencies that characterize most scientific activities. According to Freud, the subject matter of psychoanalysis is so personally threatening that objections to the theory can only be motivated by resistance. The disquieting nature of the subject matter guarantees that one cannot have an honest intellectual disagreement with Freud; it is in principle impossible to criticize psychoanalysis in the same way one might, for example, criticize Keynesian economics. This tendency in psychoanalysis is unacceptable and somewhat dishonest.

In spite of some very serious problems in the systematic theory of psychoanalysis, Freud remains for several reasons a towering figure within the personological tradition and the social sciences generally. First, Freud's ideas about motivation, explanation, the unconscious, socialization, and psychological health are original, complex, and quite distinctive. Whether he was right or wrong, Freud's originality must be acknowledged.

Second, in discussing the origins of society and morality in an evolutionary and biological framework, Freud suggested important linkages between the biological and social sciences. More time will be necessary to determine the truth of these insights, but recent research in such areas as ethology, and behavior genetics indicates some validity in Freud's biological emphasis.

Third, by emphasizing childhood sexuality and connecting early experience to the formation of adult personality, Freud prepared the way for the subsequent study of child development in its own right—a movement that is beginning to make important contributions to psychology and the other social sciences.

Finally, Freud gave form and substance to the nineteenth-century existentialist protest against the rationalism of the eighteenth century. The movement was sparked by the writings of Dostoevsky, Kierkegaard, and Nietzsche. Freud strengthened their attack on narrow scientific rationalism first by pointing out that our actions are controlled by forces outside our awareness, and second, by using reason to understand these forces. If we take Freud's analysis seriously, we will no longer be able to accept at face value people's reasons for their actions. Nor can we assume that social progress is inevitable, that our associates and leaders are guided by benevolent motives, that man's inhumanity to man results exclusively from ignorance or poverty. Rather, the unconscious strives constantly for expression, and our task is to learn to recognize and then condemn its manifestations when they appear.

Certain logical inconsistencies in psychoanalysis have deliberately been de-emphasized here in order to present the model as forcefully as possible. It should be mentioned, however, that over seventy years of research have provided only equivocal support for the systematic theory of psychoanalysis. In view of the inconsistencies of the model and its arguable empirical status, psychoanalysis seems to exert a negative influence over theory and research in personality today. Even such prominent contemporary spokesmen for psychoanalysis as Bowlby and Erikson hold positions that are incompatible with a strict Freudian view. In light of all this I would like to offer two final comments. First, the most important part of psychoanalysis may be the insights it provides rather than the systematic theory it develops. The suggestions that people inevitably deceive themselves about their social motives, that there are fixed limits to human nature that are impervious to social change, and that man is naturally aggressive as well as loving seem far more important than the question of where the ego gets its energy or how the meaning of dream symbolism is acquired. In short, Freud's insights may outlast the theory he developed to explain them. It seems to me that the most important task of the future is to develop an intellectually defensible alternative to psychoanalysis that at the same time preserves the best of the Freudian insights.

chapter five

Jung

Opinion differs greatly today concerning the importance of Carl Jung in the personological tradition. Many persons regard Jung as a romantic and a mystic whose only contribution has been to trivialize some important Freudian insights. Others such as H. Ellenberger and H. S. Hughes, consider him to be a boldly imaginative thinker, one of the eight or ten most influential men in modern social science. It is easy to understand this ambivalence toward Jung. For one thing, he was a dreadful writer. Although his historical and philosophical perspective was much broader than Freud's, Jung's wisdom "was of no profit to him: he was unable to express what he had learned in any unambiguous form ... and his writings are a trial to anyone who attempts to discover in them a logical sequence of ideas (Hughes, 1958, p. 160)." Moreover, Jung's writings have not attracted the number of interpreters who were drawn to Freud, and it is these persons who give a semblance of order to Freud's otherwise disconnected writings. Another source of hostility toward Jung is in the Freudians themselves. Psychoanalysis remains the dominant theoretical viewpoint in psychiatry and clinical psychology, and many clinicians keep alive the animosity between Freud and Jung that developed prior to their break in 1913. Perhaps most importantly,

Carl Jung
Wide World Photos

however, many of Jung's ideas have a mystical flavor that offends academic sensibilities, more so than the equally extravagant Freudian sexual theories.

The intellectual backgrounds of Freud and Jung were similar in many ways. Both were influenced by Carl Gustav Carus, Arthur Schopenhauer, and Edward von Hartmann, the great philosophers of the unconscious. The broad influence of Goethe and Nietzsche is apparent in both men, as is that of Pierre Janet, Freud's brilliant contemporary and one-time mentor. However, two aspects of Jung's life made a distinct impression on his later thinking. First, as a child Jung was preoccupied with the history of his family and community. He greatly admired his paternal grandfather, a legendary figure in the history of Basel who was both scientist and playwright, as well as a supposed illegitimate son of Goethe. In his childhood Jung saw the philosopher-historian Jacob Burckhardt on the streets of Basel and heard people speak of their former neighbor, Friedrich Nietzsche. Thus, as a boy Jung developed a strong sense of history that led naturally to an interest in myths and religion. Jung's concern with the psychology of religion was reinforced by the death of his father, a Presbyterian minister who lost his faith and subsequently committed suicide. A religious crisis in Jung's boyhood that culminated in his fabulous dreams of the underground Jesus and the destruction of the church at Basel (Jung, 1961, pp. 11–13, 39) stimulated even further his curiosity concerning the psychology of religious belief.

The importance of these experiences will become more apparent in our later discussion.

Jung's association with Freud and the Vienna psychoanalytic circle during the early 1900s also strongly influenced his intellectual development. Jung was greatly impressed with Freud and, to a lesser degree, with Alfred Adler. A major stimulus to his early psychiatric thinking was his desire to resolve some of the theoretical contradictions between Freud and Adler. Although Jung respected Freud's contribution to psychology, he was critical of Freud's ideas concerning the sexual origins of dream symbols and neuroses, and the importance of the Oedipus complex.

THE UNCONSCIOUS

Jung thought Freud had demonstrated once and for all that conscious thoughts and attitudes are mere rationalizations of powerful, unconscious desires. According to Jung, however, Freud's analysis of the unconscious was incomplete in several ways. For one thing, the repressed thoughts in the unconscious are not exclusively sexual. For example, some people find strong emotions unpleasant and tend to repress them, as they do with unpleasant experiences that embarrass, frighten, or threatened them in some way. Because one's parents and family are often a source of unhappy early experience, childhood memories are frequently repressed. Such memories and emotions cluster in the unconscious to form "complexes", constellations of mental elements that absorb psychic energy. The repressed portions of the unconscious are thus composed of complexes that are always troublesome but not necessarily sexual in nature.

Painful experiences that have been repressed form what Jung called the personal unconscious. The personal unconscious is a major source of neurosis, especially in young people, and Jung spent the early years of his career studying it. Gradually, however, he came to believe that certain psychic phenomena could not be explained in terms of repressed childhood experience. Some images that reoccur in our dreams and fantasies suggest the presence of unconscious materials that were never experienced and therefore were never repressed. Materials of this second type belong to the collective unconscious. "We have to distinguish between a personal unconscious and an impersonal or transpersonal unconscious. We speak of the latter also as the collective unconscious, because it is detached from anything personal and is entirely universal... (1956, p. 76)." Because Freud dealt almost exclusively with the personal unconscious, Jung thought his analysis was relatively superficial and incomplete.

What, more precisely, is the collective unconscious? "There are present in every individual, besides his personal memories, the great 'primordial' images, as Jacob Burckhardt once aptly called them, the inherited powers of human imagination as it was from time immemorial ...I have called these images or motifs 'archetypes', also 'dominants' of the unconscious... The primordial images are the most ancient and the most universal 'thought-forms' of humanity. They are as much feelings as thoughts; indeed, they lead their own independent life rather in the manner of part-souls..." The archetypes are the basic units of the collective unconscious; they provide "a kind of readiness to produce over and over again the same or similar mythical ideas." They can be regarded as inherited predispositions to respond to situations and stimuli in an organized but unconscious manner. And what is their source? "It seems to me that their origins can only be explained by assuming them to be deposits of the constantly repeated experiences of humanity (Jung, 1956, pp. 75–76)."

There are a great number of archetypes. The following, presented in the order in which they appear during analysis, are the most important and widely discussed: the persona, the shadow, the anima or animus, the hero, the self.

The persona, one's social mask or public personality, is composed of attitudes taken from one's social class, occupation, ethnic heritage, religious affiliations, and nationality. On the surface each persona seems unique. Yet, according to Jung, "the persona... is only a mask for the collective psyche, a mask that *feigns* individuality and tries to make others and oneself believe that one is individual, whereas, one is simply playing a part in which the collective psyche speaks (Jung, 1956, pp. 166–67)."

The second archetype is the shadow, the repulsive personal characteristics that we try to hide from ourselves and others. They are often projected as devils, sorcerors, or other dark, satanic figures. The following is a clinical example. Jung asked a patient in the early stages of analysis, "...'how do I seem to you when you are not with me?'... she said, 'Sometimes you seem rather dangerous, sinister, like an evil magician or a demon. I don't know how I ever got such ideas—you are not a bit like that.'" Jung then suggested that the woman was projecting her shadow. She replied, "'What, so I am a man, and a sinister, fascinating man at that, a wicked magician or a demon?... I cannot accept that, it's all nonsense. I'd sooner believe this of you!'... Her eyes flash, an evil expression creeps into her face, the gleam of an unknown resistance never seen before . . . In her glance there lurks something of the beast of prey, something really demonical . . . What have I touched? What new chord is vibrating? Yet it is only a passing moment. The expression on the patient's face clears, and she says, as though relieved, 'It is queer, but just now I had a horrible feeling you had touched the point I could never get over . . . It's a horrible feeling, something inhuman, evil, cruel. I simply cannot describe how queer this feeling is.' " Jung remarked that the patient's repression broke at this point and she entered a new phase of analysis (Jung, 1956, pp. 101–3).

The third archetype is the anima or animus. It is one's idealized vision of the opposite sex and a potential source of creative inspiration and insight. The anima is seen in a man's distorted perception of the women in his life (his mother, sister, lover, spouse); the animus is the female version of the same archetype. According to Jung, the anima evolves through four stages whose images are projected on the women in question. In the first stage woman is equated with mother, symbolized by Eve or "Mother Earth," and her nurturant and reproductive capacities are emphasized. In the second stage she is placed on an aesthetic and romantic level; Helen of Troy symbolizes this level of the anima. In the third, spiritual, stage woman becomes the personification of the Heavenly as in Mary, Queen of Angels. In the fourth stage the anima becomes fully intellectualized as Sophia or wisdom. Societies with rigidly pre-scribed sex roles force people to ignore the opposite sides of their sexual nature, with serious consequences. Men who are under the anima's influence appear nervous, irritable, and weepy; women dominated by the animus are stubborn, argumentative, and aggressive. In either case the person appears to be out of touch with an important aspect of the collective unconscious.

The next archetype is the hero, as exemplified in the universal hero myth. Hero myths vary enormously in detail; however, they tend to be quite similar in basic structure, even when developed by groups that have had no cultural contact. Heroes always have miraculous but humble births (Moses, Christ); and they provide early proof of their superhuman powers (young Arthur drew a heavy sword from a stone, the infant Hercules slew serpents, and the three-year-old Davy Crockett killed a bear). The hero typically rises rapidly to power, has a triumphant struggle with the forces of evil, falls victim to the sin of pride, and meets his end either through betrayal or heroic sacrifice (Oedipus, El Cid, Abraham Lincoln). There are aspects of the hero archetype appropriate to the various periods in the life cycle. The image of the hero evolves in such a manner that it reflects or parallels the evolution of personality. If one is aware of this archetype, it can serve as a guide, model, or aid during difficult periods in one's development. Once past these tests and embarked on a new phase of the life cycle, the hero myth will lose its relevance (Henderson, 1964).

The final and most central archetype is the self. The power of this primordial image is reflected in man's longings for wholeness and unification, and in symbols of oneness and transcendence. The self archetype is discussed in detail in a later section of this chapter.

A variety of sources support the notion of the collective unconscious. One experience that first suggested the idea of archetypes to Jung happened while he was a resident at the Burgholzli Psychiatric Hospital in Zurich. An old, constantly hallucinating schizophrenic patient remarked that the sun had a phallus whose movements produced the wind. While puzzling over the meaning of this delusion, Jung discovered that in the liturgy of the once powerful Mithraic religion of the Middle East the wind is produced by a tube hanging from the sun. Numerous coincidences of this sort convinced Jung that there are universal symbols that occur in religious myths as well as psychotic delusions (Ellenberger, 1970, p. 705). Certain recurring themes in art, myths, and legends also suggest the presence of such universal images. As always, however, the most persuasive evidence comes from personal experience; the following is a simple example of how quickly primitive thought forms can take hold of otherwise civilized persons. While in graduate school a friend and I took a brief vacation in the mountains. We hiked a considerable distance into a remote section of Sequoia National Forest in northern California. Some time after the sun went down on the first day, we both experienced powerful but inexplicable feelings of uneasiness and dread. In retrospect it was clear that we were afraid of the dark, a fear that would normally seem strange in grown men. Yet up in those mountains where, according to the Indians, Sasquatch (or Big-Foot) prowls—Sasquatch, the legendary and fearsome man-monster whose mere howl drives camp dogs mad—surrounded by a forest full of strange rustlings and sudden movements, considerable effort was required to remain calm and unconcerned. According to Jung, such fears are predictable, for they are natural responses to the dark woods arising from the collective unconscious.

The collective unconscious is Jung's most provocative and controversial concept. Oddly enough, many persons who criticize this aspect of Jung's thinking nonetheless accept Freud's ideas about the Oedipus complex and dream interpretation. Yet the universal nature of the Oedipal conflict and the meaning of dream symbols can be explained only by assuming that they are also part of the collective unconscious.

As noted in the last chapter, Freud assumed that hostility toward one's father (and authority in general) and sexual longings for one's mother are universal. On the basis of his own clinical experience, however, Jung found no evidence for such universal tendencies. Although neurotics may have repressed incestuous desires, these are the symptoms rather than the cause of their neuroses. Jung considered it absurd to suppose that every little boy was in love with his mother and jealous of his father. Rather, normal children tend unconsciously to admire, respect, and identify with the parent of the same sex. In little boys, unconscious identification typically extends beyond the father to the paternal ancestors.

We can summarize the discussion thus far by reviewing Jung's criticisms of Freud's analysis of the unconscious. First, people repress a variety of unacceptable emotions and impulses in addition to sexual desires, and repressed sexuality is by no means the only cause of neurotic behavior. Second, the largest part of the unconscious, according to Jung, is never repressed; it is simply given as a portion of man's biological heritage. Third, for Freud the contents of the unconscious are implacably antisocial; for Jung, on the other hand, they are potentially helpful (as in the discussion of the hero archetype presented earlier). Finally, the Oedipus complex is not a universal part of the unconscious as described by Jung.

According to Jung, the unconscious is the most powerful and determinative force in our lives; it is the source of both madness and creative inspiration, and one must come to terms with it. The primary key to the unconscious, for neurotics and normals alike, is dream analysis. The manner in which dream symbols are interpreted is therefore critical for understanding the unconscious. Jung contrasts causal-reductive or *objective* interpretation with synthetic or *subjective* interpretation. The former, as developed by Freud, assumes that dream images always correspond to objects in the real world (e.g., royalty signifies parents, money is equated with fecal matter), and the analyst translates somewhat mechanically these dream images into their real-world counterparts. Moreover, the correctness of an analyst's interpretation does not depend on a dreamer's agreement. According to Jung, however, dreams are most accurately interpreted when every part of the dream—images, actors, settings—is referred back to the dreamer himself. Thus, the meaning of a dream image usually lies within the dreamer rather than in the external world, and the analyst must constantly check with the dreamer concerning the accuracy of his interpretations.

Freud's causal-reductive or objective method also assumes that the manifest dream content is a screen that disguises the true nature of the latent content. Jung observes, "I have long maintained that we have no right to accuse the dream of, so to speak, a deliberate maneuver calculated to deceive . . . Nature is often obscure or impenetrable, but she is not, like man, deceitful. We must therefore take it that the dream is just what it pretends to be, neither more nor less (1956, pp. 110–11)." Jungian dream interpretations are, consequently, often more common-sensical than Freudian interpretations of the same material.

How, more specifically, does one interpret dream images? Jung offered some basic suggestions. First, most dreams are compensatory and indicate that some portion of the psyche is being ignored. Second, a dream's meaning is usually not hidden. Third, if the dreamer finds an interpretation unacceptable, then it is probably wrong. Fourth, free association is a useful technique for discovering obscure meanings. Finally, dreams often contain hints concerning the advisability of intended actions. However, these rules are misleadingly simple. For Jung, dream analysis is not a parlor game but requires unusual erudition. Because dreams are often fragments of old (but universal) myths and legends, one must have considerable knowledge of anthropology, art history, linguistics, literature, and religion before one can understand these images. And how do we know when we have correctly interpreted a symbol? The next dream may tell, or perhaps the interpretation will be followed by an upsurge of repressed emotion and energy. Incorrect interpretations are always a possibility, as Jung notes: ". . . the reward of a correct interpretation is an uprush of life . . . [however] an incorrect one dooms itself to deadlock, resistance, doubt, and natural desiccation (1956, p. 122)."

Perhaps a personal example will clarify the differences between Freudian and Jungian dream analysis. In a particularly vivid dream I found myself driving across the country, accompanied by my wife and my father. We stopped for gas at a small town in Wyoming. Two children were walking behind the gas station along a small dirt road bounded by a barbed wire fence. Suddenly, from the direction in which the children had come, a small herd of frightened cattle appeared; behind the cattle was a group of Indians. The cattle quickly overtook, trampled, and killed the children. The gas station attendant ran down the highway toward a cluster of buildings crying, "The Indians are coming." A great deal of noise and confusion followed; it soon became clear that after a long series of mutual atrocities war had erupted between the cowboys and the Indians. The remainder of the dream involved dodging arrows, while trying to convince the cowboys to stop shooting. From a Freudian perspective the dream concerned the classic Oedipal triangle (myself, my father, and my mother—symbolized by my wife). From a Jungian viewpoint, however, the dream dealt with the futility of trying to mediate between quarreling parties. Perhaps coincidentally, for several weeks before the dream I had been trying without success to reconcile the differences between two groups of my associates. In this case a Jungian interpretation not only made sense of the dream, but it felt better as well.

MOTIVATION

Jung's contribution to motivational theory, although original and important, is not well known and the fault is his own. He presents his ideas in such a disorganized manner and gives motivational status to so many unrelated concepts that the theory is nearly incoherent.

Four sets of factors make up Jung's motivational theory. First, repressed desires, memories, and emotions tend to cluster in the personal unconscious and form complexes; these complexes often attain motivation power. Complexes are typically dissolved in the early stages of Jungian analysis through exploration of the personal unconscious.

Psychic energy or libido, the second component in the theory, is Jung's best-known motivational concept. Opposition between the conscious and unconscious portions of the psyche, between extroversion and introversion, between sensation and intuition, thinking and feeling (1956, pp. 101–8) produces tension, and this tension is the source of psychic energy. Psychic energy, whose effects can be described as "generalized intentionality", is responsible for most everyday social behavior. Although psychic energy cannot be measured directly, relative differences can be assessed with techniques such as "The Word Association Test." The number of associations and the amount of emotion elicited by the test words will indicate the presence of complexes, repressed memories, and emotions that have attracted large amounts of psychic energy.

Symbols are external representations of psychic tendencies that can transform or release psychic energy. When a symbol is internalized or identified within the unconscious, a certain amount of psychic energy is liberated and can be used at a conscious level. For example, the religious and magic rites of primitive people before a hunt or battle (or those of contemporary Americans before a football game) are means of using symbols to release energy for specific purposes. Nonetheless, this psychic energy can be consciously directed only for short periods of time. The unpredictable nature of psychic energy allows Jung to make a characteristic plea for greater tolerance of unreason: "Much indeed can be attained by the will, but . . . it is a fundamental error to try to subject our own fate at all costs to our will . . . reason and the will . . . are valid only up to a point. The further we go in the direction selected by reason, the surer we may be that we are excluding the irrational possibilities of life which have just as much right to be lived (1956, pp. 59–60)."

Archetypes are the third element in Jung's motivational theory; however, the precise nature of their role is ambiguous. On the one hand, archetypes are patterns that give form to the expression of instincts: "There are . . . no amorphous instincts, as every instinct bears in itself the pattern of its situation. Always it fulfills an image (archetype), and the image has fixed qualities . . . the instinct cannot exist . . . without its image (Jung, 1956, p. 71)." On the other hand, archetypes have a motivational status of their own: ". . . when an archetype appears in a dream, in a fantasy, or in life, it always brings with it a certain influence or power by virtue of which it either exercises a numinous or fascinating effect, or impels to action (1956, p. 80)."

By giving motivational status to archetypes, Jung blurred the distinction between them and the instincts, the final portion of his motivational theory. A great number of instincts affect human behavior. Three are particularly important: eros, power, and the need for meaning. Freud considered the influence of the instincts to be constant throughout life; Jung thought the importance of a particular instinct was relative to a person's age. There are four periods in the life cycle: childhood, youth, middle age, and old age. The first, childhood, extends from birth to adolescence; for Jung this is not a necessarily critical stage in life, because ". . . when normal, the child has no real problems of its own. It is only when a human being has grown up that he can have doubts about himself and be at variance with himself" (1933, p. 100). Nor is old age important, because like childhood, old age "vanishes into the unconscious." The second phase of the life cycle, youth, begins when one is confronted with the two great tasks of this period—choosing a mate and a vocation. Youth extends from adolescence to middle age (sixteen to forty). During this period the instincts of eros and power are primarily important. If, upon entering youth, a person cannot deal with sexuality in a straightforward and natural manner, he will be unhappy and potentially neurotic. Thus Freud's theory of neurosis was true as far as it went. However, Jung thought Adler had shown that ambition and the drive for worldly achievement, the need for power, is also a potential source of neurosis. This "mighty demon" can be satisfied by fame, prestige, wealth, or even infamy. The need for power cannot be reduced to sublimated sexuality; it is a separate and autonomous instinct that must be dealt with on its own terms. Youthful neurosis may result from both repressed sexuality and feelings of inferiority resulting from frustrated ambition.

However, "it is a great mistake to suppose," as Freud and Adler did, "that the meaning of life is exhausted with the period of youth and expansion... The afternoon of life is just as full of meaning as the morning; only, its meaning and purpose are different (1956, p. 84)." When a person enters middle age, the third great instinct is activated, and the course of one's life may change abruptly. "We are here outside the range of Freudian and Adlerian reductions; we are no longer concerned with how to remove the obstacles to a man's profession, or to his marriage, or to do anything that means a widening of his life, but are confronted with the task of finding a meaning that will enable him to continue living at all (1956, pp. 83–84)." Moreover, the manner in which one has adjusted to the demands of eros and the need for power are irrelevant during the third stage of the life cycle, because the problem here is entirely different.

There is ample evidence that the problem of meaning can decisively influence the course of one's life. The first three lines of Dante's *Divine Comedy* provide an archetypal statement of the dilemma:

Midway this way of life we're bound upon
I woke to find myself in a dark wood
Where the right road was wholly lost and gone.

Tolstoy admirably expressed the problem in *My Confession* (James, 1958, pp. 130–32):

I felt that something had broken within me on which my life had always rested, that I had nothing left to hold on to, and that morally my life had stopped. An invincible force impelled me to get rid of my existence, in one way or another. It cannot be said exactly that I *wished* to kill myself, for the force which drew me away from life was fuller, more powerful, more general than any mere desire. It was a force like my old aspiration to live, only it impelled me in the opposite direction. It was an aspiration of my whole being to get out of life.

All this took place at a time when so far as my outer circumstances went, I ought to have been completely happy. I had a good wife who loved me and whom I loved; good children and a large property which was increasing with no pains taken on my part. I was more respected by my kinsfolk and acquaintances than I had ever been; I was loaded with praise by strangers; and without exaggeration I could believe my name already famous. Moreover I was neither insane nor ill. On the contrary, I possessed a physical and mental strength which I have rarely met in persons of my age. I could mow as well as the peasants, I could work with my brain eight hours uninterruptedly and feel no bad effects... And yet I could give no reasonable meaning to any actions of my life.

This is no fable, but the literal incontestable truth which every one may understand. What will be the outcome of what I do today? Of what I shall do tomorrow? What will be the outcome of all my life? Why should I live? Why should I do anything? Is there in life any purpose which the inevitable death which awaits me does not undo and destroy? These questions are the simplest in the world. From the stupid child to the wisest old man, they are in the soul of every human being. Without an answer to them, it is impossible, as I experienced, for life to go on. "But perhaps," I often said to myself, "there may be something I have failed to notice or comprehend. It is not possible that this condition of despair should be natural to mankind." And I sought for an explanation in all the branches of knowledge acquired by man ... and I found nothing. I became convinced, moreover, that all those who before me had sought for an answer in the sciences have also found nothing. And not only this, but that they have recognized that the very thing which was leading me to despair—the meaningless absurdity of life—is the only uncontestable knowledge accessible to man.

The biographies of Tolstoy, William James, Freud, and Jung himself suggest that the problem of meaning can assume crisis proportions in the lives of sensitive and reflective persons. And here we come to the most important and original aspect of Jung's motivational theory. On the basis of evidence such as that contained in Tolstoy's biography, Jung concluded that an irrational commitment to an ideology such as might be found in political theory, history, or religion is essential for normal development. We all need to believe in something. Yet modern man is crippled in this regard because all the traditional ideologies have been discredited. In particular, Jung thought the major problem of twentieth century Western man was the failure of the Christian myth, a failure that left many people without a coherent world view. Furthermore, in conjunction with Christianity's demise has come a corresponding decline in man's myth-making powers. Although the problem of finding a meaning in life remains basic to man, modern man has become estranged from his traditional solution. The sources of estrangement are complex but may be the result of what Jung described as the "insanely narrow rationalism of the twentieth century," encouraged by the triumphs of science and technology. Jung further maintained that until a new solution to the problem of meaning is found, mankind will be continually swept by conflicts between such competing ideologies as communism and capitalism, Judaism and Islam, and Protestantism and Catholicism.

Jung treated the need for meaning as equivalent to a psychological predisposition to religious belief, an aspect of his thinking that has annoyed many psychologists. Freud considered persons who are bothered by the problem of meaning to be neurotic by definition. Two points might be mentioned concerning this aspect of Jung's theory. First, it is an empirical question as to whether nonneurotic persons can be troubled by a lack of meaning in their lives. If the answer is yes, then conventional psychology has been wrong to ignore such an important source of human motivation. Second, Jung calls attention to the problem of meaning but suggests no answers. Rather, he notes that the "... serious problems in life are never fully solved. If it should . . . appear that they are, this is the sign that something has been lost. The meaning and design of a problem seem not to lie in its solution, but in our working at it incessantly (1933, p. 103)."

EXPLANATION

As noted above, most dreams are compensatory and indicate that portions of the psyche are out of balance. There is constant tension between the conscious and unconscious parts of the psyche, and there are sources of tension arising from the structure of the mind itself. Jung's ideas about this are presented most fully in *The Psychological Types* (1921), a book that he wrote to explain why Freud and Adler disagreed so strongly concerning the dynamics of hysterical neuroses. Freud thought hysterical symptoms were symbolic expressions of repressed sexual desires; Adler thought they were tools that neurotics used to control others as a means of satisfying their need for power. Jung found both arguments persuasive and concluded that the theories of neurosis proposed by Freud and Adler were in fact projections of their own personalities, Adler being an introvert and Freud an extrovert. "The first attitude is normally characterized by a hesitant, reflective, retiring nature that keeps itself to itself, shrinks from objects, is always slightly on the defensive and prefers to hide behind mistrustful scrutiny. The second is normally characterized by an outgoing, candid, and accommodating nature that adapts easily to a given situation, quickly forms attachments, and . . . will often venture forth with careless confidence into unknown situations. (Jung, 1956, pp. 54–56)."

Introversion and extroversion are attitudes or cognitive styles—basic habits of mind present in everyone in varying degrees. Introverts attend primarily to internal subjective events, and extroverts pay most attention to the external world. It is difficult to classify people precisely using this typology, since most people are a combination of both attitudes. The balance between introversion and extroversion leads to one of the most important principles in Jungian psychology: when one attitude is highly developed in consciousness, the other develops proportionally as a compensation in the unconscious.

Introversion and extroversion are the two superior categories of the mind; in conjunction with the four fundamental "functions" of the conscious psyche they form the basis for Jung's most interesting contribution to the problem of explanation. The four functions are divided into two categories: the rational and the irrational functions. The irrational functions are modes of perception that govern the way we take in information about the world. They are called irrational because Jung thought rational and logical processes played no part in perception. There are two perceptual modes—sensation and intuition—and every person has a preferred mode. Persons who prefer sensation are hard-nosed empiricists who rely primarily on the five senses for information about the world. Persons who prefer intuition tend to be creative and original; they take in information by filtering it through the unconscious, which permits them to detect the hidden possibilities implicit in sensory data.

The rational functions are thinking and feeling; they govern the manner in which a person comes to conclusions or judgments about information previously taken in. Persons who prefer the thinking mode operate in a logical and rigorous fashion, primarily trying to decide whether the information they have received is right or wrong. Persons who have developed the feeling mode evaluate data in terms of personal considerations through a process of appreciation. They react to data not on the basis of whether it is true or false but if it is sympathetic, antagonistic, agreeable, or disagreeable.

Everyone has all the attitudes and functions, and certain combinations of them eventually gain control of the psyche, producing one of eight psychological types. Four of these are introverted and four are extroverted.

The *thinking-extrovert* directs his life in accordance with fixed rules, and his thinking is positive and dogmatic (Freud may have been Jung's model for this type). The *feeling-extrovert* is conservative, respectful of authority and conventions and very emotional. The *sensation-extrovert* is pleasure-seeking, affiliative, easygoing, and socially adaptive. The *intuition-extrovert* is socially acute and may be a talented entrepreneur or politician.

Friedrich Nietzsche was Jung's model for the *thinking-introvert*; these are persons with poor practical judgment—socially inhibited, isolated individuals with bold ideas and an obsessive desire for knowledge. The *feeling-introvert* is unassuming, quiet, enigmatic, and hypersensitive (possibly a musician); feeling-introverted women are presumed to exert a mysterious power over extroverted men. The *sensation-introvert* is also quiet, but is esthetically sensitive, and has a bemused and detached view of human affairs (perhaps an art collector). The *intuitive-introvert* is an odd, eccentric daydreamer, completely absorbed with his inner thoughts; Jung may have been thinking of himself here.

Although certain attitude-function combinations inevitably dominate consciousness, their dominance leads to psychic imbalance. If this imbalance remains unconscious, it will produce pathological consequences.

We can now outline Jung's model of explanation. All people are alike, according to Jung, in the way their lives are influenced by unconscious forces. These influences are independent of individual experience; they arise from the collective unconscious, a storehouse of psychic dispositions that is innate in each of us. Mankind also shares a common set of instincts, the most important of which include sexuality, power, and the need for meaning. Finally, according to Jung, human development takes the same form everywhere. Sexual and power needs are universal problems in youth and early adulthood; a need for meaning is the major problem of adulthood. Thus, Jung explains the similarities among people in terms of the collective unconscious, common instincts, and universal patterns of human development.

From a Jungian perspective individual differences arise from three sources. First, differences among people result in part from the persona, the roles people develop in order to participate in society. Second, as we have seen, differences result from the way people use their minds. That is, the manner in which a person typically obtains and then uses information about the world produces a distinctive social style; a great deal of the variety in interpersonal behavior can be attributed to differences in cognitive styles. Although Jung does not emphasize this point, it seems to be one of his more original and important insights. A final source of differences among people arises from the degree to which they have become aware of the unconscious. Awareness leads to maturity, creativity, and personal balance; lack of awareness produces one-sided rigidity, personal stagnation, and even mental illness.

Jung explained particular anomalous actions by interpreting them within the context of his theory. His interpretive method differs from Freud's in several ways. First, the validity of an interpretation depends in part on the agreement of the person whose actions are in question. Second, proper interpretation of thoughts, dreams, symptoms, and behavior requires information about the balance between a person's conscious and unconscious attitudes and psychic functions. It is also necessary to know what memories and emotions have been repressed and are seeking conscious expression. Finally, an interpretation depends on the person's awareness of the collective unconscious; it is important to know the extent to which primitive thought forms are being denied conscious expression. Most inner action can be explained in terms of these aspects of the unconscious: repressed emotions and experience, undeveloped attitudes and psychic functions, and manifestations of the collective unconscious.

SOCIALIZATION

In contrast with Freud, who discussed socialization in great detail, Jung seemed relatively unconcerned with the topic. This may reflect his general lack of interest in overt social behavior and his preoccupation with man's inner life. He regarded socialization as neither traumatic for the child nor problematical for the social scientist. "It should never be forgotten—and of this the Freudian school must be reminded—that morality was not brought down on tables of stone from Sinai and imposed on the people but is a function of the human soul, as old as humanity itself. Morality is not imposed from the outside; we have it in ourselves from the start—not the law, but our moral nature without which the collective life of human society would be impossible (1956, p. 36)."

Loosely speaking, Jung explained socialization in two ways. The first involves the persona. Those whose personas are undeveloped are socially inept; they seem blundering, tactless, and socially maladroit. Developing a persona causes one to act in accordance with the social expectations of others, that is part of what it means to be socialized. The second explanation, found in an essay entitled "The meaning of the father for the destiny of the individual," suggests that all children unconsciously conform to family attitudes as if infected by psychic contagion. These attitudes, once fixed, persist through life. Jung's account actually raises more questions than it answers and consequently tends to mystify the socialization process.

Jung was almost exclusively concerned with individual development. He maintained, however, that individual development depends on a person's being firmly rooted in the collective; those who are alienated from society can never experience self-development. Socialization is therefore a necessary antecedent of psychological health.

THE SELF-CONCEPT
AND PSYCHOLOGICAL HEALTH

According to Jung, modern man has become neurotic because of his estrangement from the irrational and unconscious side of his nature. Generally speaking, Jung's view of neurosis is more complex than either Freud's or Adler's, whose theories Jung regarded as "destructive and reductive." Freud and Adler thought neurosis is without exception undesirable. Jung thought that neurotic symptoms not only reflect attempts to cope with infantile trauma but also represent attempts to deal with present and future reality. Neurosis can lead to worldly success as well as social incompetence, as it did with Nietzsche who "more than once acknowledged how much he owed to his malady (1956, p. 57)." Moreover, Freud and Adler were exclusively concerned with the neuroses of the young; however, Jung felt such neuroses are unrelated to the problems of maturity. Thus neurotic symptoms can be understood only when placed in the context of the life cycle.

In most cases, the cause of neurosis is one-sidedness. This can occur in many ways, two of which are particularly important. In the first case the person remains preoccupied with goals that were appropriate to an earlier stage in the life cycle. A young person who is obsessed with the problems of his childhood will be unable to deal effectively with the demands of eros and social competition. A middle-aged person who is still concerned with sexuality and social status is equally misdirected, because these should no longer be the salient issues in his or her life. In the second form of one-sidedness, a basic attitude or function may become overdeveloped, or the person may begin to take his persona too seriously; the person becomes inflexible and is unable to adapt to the changing conditions of his life. But if neurotic tendencies are sometimes associated with high level achievement, why is one-sidedness undesirable? There are two reasons. First, neurotics are social liabilities; they are, in Nietzsche's terms, "pale felons" who evade their social obligations and place extra burdens on others. Second and more importantly, one-sidedness blocks the individuation process. The ultimate goal of Freudian and Adlerian psychology is to reconcile the individual to the demands of society. Jung regarded this as merely the first, necessary, step toward individuation: "There is a destination, a possible goal, beyond reconciliation ... that is the way of individuation. Individuation means becoming a single, homogenous being, and, in so far as 'individuality' embraces our innermost, last, and incomparable uniqueness, it also implies becoming one's own self. We could therefore translate individuation as 'coming to selfhood' or 'self-realization' (1956, pp. 182–83)."

The requirements for individuation and the cure for one-sidedness are almost always the same—self-awareness achieved through an exploration of the unconscious. Individuation "... is a natural process, a manifestation of the energy that springs from the tension of the opposite, and it consists in a sequence of fantasy-occurrences that appear spontaneously in dreams and visions (1956, p. 90)."

The individuation process is unique to each person; its meaning and purpose, however, "... is the realization, in all its aspects, of the personality originally hidden away in the embryonic germ plasm; the production and unfolding of the original, potential wholeness (1956, p. 121)." Because individuation requires that one be "capable of attaining wholeness," Jung thought that a certain number of people in any society are doomed to incompleteness.

What is involved in individuation? In simplest terms it consists of a progressive differentiation of the ego, or consciousness, from the unconscious, so that the person becomes steadily more aware of the degree to which his thoughts and motives arise from the collective unconscious. However, differentiation of consciousness is only half the story. Simultaneously with this differentiation, the conscious and unconscious portions of the psyche must be reintegrated—but at a higher level of awareness. This reintegration is crucial because the tendency to ignore the unconscious is the source of modern man's discontents. "We should never identify ourselves with reason, for man is not and never will be a creature of reason alone ... The irrational cannot and must not be extirpated (1956, p. 82)." Here we see another difference between Freud and Jung. Freud could not conceive of an excess of consciousness. Jung, on the other hand, felt that too much as well as too little consciousness was pathological, and in this respect he may have had the more balanced position.

Jungian therapy is a telescoped version of the individuation process; as such it clarifies the steps involved. The first stage concerns the dissolution of the persona. This happens when one realizes that society's goals are artificial. Although one must fulfill the demands of his social roles, one must also see them in perspective. The second stage requires becoming fully aware of the shadow; one must understand that basically he is not only decent and unselfish but also capable of almost any crime imaginable—treachery, sodomy, murder, and cannibalism. An encounter with the shadow may lead to depression and social withdrawal. Sometimes, however, it leads to an attempt to return to one's earlier life-style by throwing oneself into a whirl of social activities (what Jung called "a regressive restoration of the persona"). Self-awareness, however, is a one-way street, and it is not possible to return to more primitive levels of consciousness. The third step in individuation involves coming to terms with the anima or the animus. For men this requires recognizing the feminine aspects of their nature; for women, the masculine aspects. Successfully integrating the anima (or animus) into consciousness has two effects: it releases previously unsuspected sources of creative inspiration, and it frees a person from the still-active influences of his childhood. Men finally become emancipated from their mothers, as women do from their fathers.

Persons who have completed the first three stages of individuation may experience what Jung called "the mana personality." They feel an unnatural sense of power and (falsely) think they are completely self-aware; consequently, they set themselves up as prophets. Jung felt this had happened to Freud, whose hostility to religion and obsessive concern with sex betrayed an essential one-sidedness.

After encountering the persona, the shadow, and the anima, one final barrier to selfhood remains—the problem of meaning. Jung's child-hood dreams of the destruction of the Basel cathedral and the revelation of the underground Jesus suggested to him an answer to this problem: one must recognize the dark and irrational side of man's nature. The "demonic" has to be acknowledged in order to gain access to its therapeutic potential. It is necessary to recover not the action of the irrational but its symbolism, and that will save us from our "insanely narrow rationalism." A personal commitment to a primordial fantasy will resolve the problem of meaning; such a commitment will simultaneously free one from the unconscious power of the archetypes and release their creative energy because psychic energy is released when symbols are internalized. Primitive man intuitively understood this principle—American Plains Indians had vision quests and Australian aborigines went on "walk-abouts" in search of precisely such images or symbols. Thus the task for the psychologist, according to Jung, is to determine when and how it is possible to make a commitment to an illusion. The final stage of therapy, therefore, involves the discovery and encouragement of the religious impulse. Only through an irrational commitment to art or religion, to a symbol of some sort, is the final attainment of selfhood possible.

There are many barriers to self-actualization, but the urge toward individuation is so insistent that Jung called it an instinct. The unconscious contains a "driving force" that, "so far as it is possible for us to grasp it, seems to be an essence—an urge toward self-realization (1956, pp. 193–94)." Ultimately then, the archetype of the self is the dominant force in psychic growth; consequently, the self-concept is the most important element in Jung's theory. What more precisely is the self? In an individuated person the conscious and unconscious portions of the psyche complement one another and form a totality that is the self, "...a quantity that is superordinate to the conscious ego...There is little hope of our ever being able to reach even approximate consciousness of the self, since however much we make conscious there will always exist an indeterminate and indeterminable amount of unconscious material which belongs to the totality of the self. Hence the self will always remain a superordinate quantity (pp. 186–87)."

When achieved, the self becomes the center of the psyche. "I have called this centre the self...It might equally well be called the 'God within us.' The beginnings of our whole psychic life seem to be inextricably rooted in this point, and all our highest and ultimate purposes seem to be striving towards it (p. 250)." "So ... the self is our life's goal, for it is the completest expression of that fateful combination we call individuality ... (However) we can say nothing about the contents of the self. The ego is the only content of the self that we do know. The individuated ego senses itself as the object of an unknown and super-ordinate subject. It seems to me that our psychological inquiry must come to a stop here, for the idea of a self is itself a transcendental postulate which, although justifiable psychologically, does not allow of scientific proof (p. 252)."

For Jung, then, psychological health and the achievement of self-hood amount to the same thing. Three criteria define selfhood. First, repressions must be released, tensions between the conscious and the unconscious attitudes and functions must be relaxed, and through self-knowledge one will achieve internal peace. Second, one must give symbolic expression to the unconscious. Third, through a personal faith-fulness to a private symbol or myth, a person can approach selfhood. According to Jung, selfhood is an elusive state of being: "In order to discover what is authentically individual in ourselves, profound reflection is needed; and suddenly we realize how uncommonly difficult the discovery of individuality in fact is (1956, p. 165)." Buddha and Christ are presented as examples of persons who finally achieved individuation.

EVALUATION

Before closing this discussion of Jung, we should assess briefly his contribution to the personological tradition. Several features of Jungian theory are troublesome. First, if bad writing reflects bad thinking, then a number of Jung's concepts seem confused. Selfhood is described as a state of being, yet Jung repeatedly refers to the self as an entity, a "part-soul", and an archetype. His motivational concepts are, if possible, even more confused. Libido is postulated as the "prime mover" of the psychic apparatus, then primary motivational status is given to the need for meaning. Still later the self-archetype is described as the most important source of human motivation. Finally, it is hard to know the meaning of the Jungian dictum that everything developed in conscious-ness has its counterpart in the unconscious.

Second, Jung's concept of psychological health presents a barrier to social change. Each person, according to Jung, should become actualized while remaining in his prescribed socio-economic niche. Thus a cobbler should be content with cobbling and find the real meaning of his life in the individuation process. Consequently, Jung's notion of psychological health directly supports the status quo. Related to this aspect of Jung's thinking is a well-defined strain of elitism. It becomes clear that only bright, well-educated, articulate persons who have considerable leisure time are eligible for individuation. Jung was quite clear about this point: self-actualization is reserved for a particular, self-chosen elite, and the vast majority of mankind is necessarily excluded.

Third, it may be true that people need to believe in something that transcends them and gives meaning to their lives; it does not follow, however, that they *ought* to organize their lives around an enduring irrational commitment of some sort. In *Varieties of Religious Experience* William James deals seriously with this problem, and his analysis is remarkably parallel to Jung's. However James quite properly avoids suggesting that one ought to act on one's religious impulses. Although reason is limited and the modern world does seem to be afflicted by the narrow, positivistic metaphysics of scientific thought, reason nevertheless remains the only guide we have. We seem to need more rather than less reason—reason in the sense of balanced judgment as opposed to the impoverished rationalism of technology. To argue otherwise seems to be a form of intellectual treason.

Certain inconsistencies in the ideas of Jung represent shortcomings in his theory. His notion of socialization, for example, is too poorly developed to be useful. Nevertheless, he did provide original conceptualizations of five of the six root ideas. This along with other aspects of his thinking more than compensate for the shortcomings of his theory. These other contributions should also be noted.

First, Jung's emphasis on the phylogenetic origins of the unconscious implies a psychic unity of mankind, a feeling that human development is in a real sense universal. In contrast with the environmental explanations so popular in much academic psychology today, Jung suggested that, at a deep level, the nature of the mind and the origins of personality are remarkably similar, both across cultures and historical periods.

Second, an adequate conceptualization of any important phenomena must begin with a set of assumptions that are sufficiently complex to do justice to the problem under consideration. The image of man that Jung develops is more complex, more balanced, and in some ways more intellectually satisfying than the Freudian model. Although Jung stressed that conflicts are an inevitable part of psychic development, these conflicts never achieve the tragic proportions they do for Freud. If Jung's view of man is less tragic than Freud's, his optimism and faith in man's potential for growth are a pleasant contrast to Freud's relentless pessimism.

Third, Jung is one of a surprisingly small number of psychologists to propose that normal people need to believe that their lives have meaning and purpose. Although one might argue that the problem is primarily important for middle-class intellectuals and one might disagree with Jung's solution, Jung nonetheless deserves great credit for emphasizing this source of human motivation. Furthermore, unlike repressed sexuality, the problem of meaning seems as insistent today as it was in the late nineteenth century—it may be an enduring aspect of the human condition.

Finally, Jung's concept of selfhood contains an important idea that is often overlooked. Self-realization—the fullest possible development of one's innate potentialities—may be the most important goal in life. Yet, according to Jung, this fact should never be used as a justification for self-centered or thoughtless behavior. Those who ignore social conventions and the feelings of others are immature, and antisocial conduct inevitably destroys the social bonds on which further individuation depends.

chapter six

William McDougall

William McDougall is the forgotten man of the personological tradition. His books are out of print and he is rarely mentioned in modern textbooks. He apparently expected this: "Most of my early papers seemed to be stillborn; but at that time I was not troubled by the fact ... I still had the naive belief that sound and original work is sure of recognition in the long run.... However the publication of my *Social Psychology* was like dropping a stone into a bottomless pit ... About this time [1911] I began to find it difficult to believe in the value of my work, a difficulty which has grown steadily greater (1930, pp. 206, 209)."

Because McDougall was probably the best trained scientist in the personological tradition and the most philosophically sophisticated psychologist since William James, the lack of interest in his ideas today is puzzling and unfortunate. Two factors may explain this. First, compared with Freud and Jung his writing seems bland and unexciting. In place of Freud's view of man living at the mercy of dark forces beyond his control, McDougall describes in an orderly and unpoetic way how thought evolves out of and then comes to control man's instincts. Compared with Freud, McDougall's writing is systematic, factual, and tame. Second, McDougall seems to have been a victim of a change in intel-

William McDougall
Wide World Photos

lectual fashion; his interest in the instinctual basis of human behavior ran contrary to the American enthusiasm for behaviorism. Consequently, starting in 1919 and continuing for ten years thereafter, McDougall's ideas were the target of a ceaseless barrage of behaviorist criticism. The result, as Murphy and Kovach (1972, p. 445) note, was not only to suppress his writings, but also "to leave social psychology, toward the end of the twenties, without any generally accepted theoretical basis and without any common agreement as to the kinds of entities or principles to which the complexities of social life should be reduced."

McDougall is the only man in the personological tradition whose ideas, at least initially, were not influenced by psychoanalysis. His background was that of a British physician-scholar of the Victorian period, and his writings reflect the influence of his two distinguished British predecessors, James Ward and G.F. Stout. Both considered the individual to be an active organizing agent (rather than the passive victim of unconscious forces) whose organizing tendencies are important for understanding mental life. Stout argued in particular that consciousness has three defining properties: thinking (cognition), feeling (emotion), and willing (conation). He emphasized will as the most obvious fact of consciousness in striving toward selected goals. These themes occur repeatedly in McDougall's writing.

McDougall took his concept of the unconscious from the German philosopher of education, Johann Friedrich Herbart. According to Herbart, consciousness is composed of a mass of mutually supportive ideas. Those that are incongruent with this dominant mass are forced below a "limen of consciousness"; ideas below the limen of consciousness, though unconscious, continue to strive toward consciousness. Thus, for Herbart and McDougall thoughts become unconscious through their interaction with other ideas; this contrasts with the Freudian notion that unconscious thoughts have been forced out of awareness by the ego, a mental agency.

The most important influence on McDougall's thinking, however, was biology and evolutionary theory. A brilliant student, McDougall finished his secondary education at fourteen, studied biology at the University of Manchester, and then completed a second undergraduate degree at Cambridge, again specializing in biology and physiology. He did further work in physiology in medical school, where he studied under the illustrious Sherrington. (This extensive education was apparently effective—McDougall was active in laboratory research throughout his career and was elected a fellow of the Royal Society in 1912 for research on the psychophysics of vision.) Perhaps more than any other writer in the personological tradition McDougall took Darwin seriously and believed that psychology was ultimately a biological science.

MOTIVATION

McDougall considered the nature of human motivation to be the primary problem in psychology. He was influenced in this belief by Darwin, who thought instincts were the source of man's social conduct; McDougall elaborated on this theme in detail.

He defined an instinct as ". . . an inherited or innate psycho-physical disposition which determines its possessor to perceive and to pay attention to objects of a certain class, to experience an emotional excitement of a particular quality upon perceiving such an object, and to act in regard to it in a particular manner, or, at least, to experience an impulse to such action (1908, p. 25)." That is, instincts do three things: (1) they sensitize an organism to perceive certain stimuli (e.g., newborn goslings have an innate tendency to detect moving objects); (2) they promote a specific emotional response to such perceptions (e.g., goslings, upon perceiving a moving object, may experience "joy"); (3) they produce characteristic patterns of behavior (e.g., goslings follow moving objects; since these are usually mother geese, survival is thereby facilitated).

Intelligence, habit, imitation, and experience modify instinctive behavior in the higher animals. Many people think of instinctive behavior in terms of fixed behavior patterns. McDougall, however, defined instinctive behavior in terms of fixed goals. He considered instinctive activity as a complex, organized sequence of actions that is sustained until some natural goal is reached. Ultimately then, McDougall defined instincts functionally, in terms of invariant goals, rather than behaviorally, in terms of invariant action patterns.

Instincts are initially nonspecific; for example, a newborn gosling will follow virtually anything that moves. Over time, however, the stimuli necessary to elicit an instinct become progressively more specific, as the older gosling will follow only its mother. Although instincts become closely associated with particular stimuli, significant objects, according to McDougall, always produce more than one instinctual response, thus a child may both love and fear his father.

As people gain experience and maturity, habits develop. Habits may acquire a motivational power of their own; however, they fade when they cease to serve instincts. Nor are pleasure and pain, in themselves, ever motivational variables. Rather, they modify habits and other behavior patterns; pleasure prolongs any mode of action and pain cuts it short.

McDougall suggested that twelve instincts along with five "nonspecific innate tendencies" are "all that we can recognize with certainty." He modified this list only slightly during the remainder of his career. As he observed, "Lightly to postulate an indefinite number and variety of human instincts is a cheap and easy way to solve psychological problems (1908, p. 75)." The instincts are subdivided into minor and major categories. Although the minor instincts lack a strong emotional component, they are important in social life and include the following:

1. The instinct of *reproduction* that underlies all male-female relations. (Thus, in McDougall's hands Freud's Eros has dwindled to the status of a minor instinct.)
2. The instinct of *food-seeking* that is elicited primarily when we are hungry.
3. The instinct of *acquisition* that leads to such hobbies as stamp and book collecting and obtains a pathological form in miserliness and kleptomania.
4. The instinct of *construction* that requires doing things with one's hands, from building mud pies to bookcases.
5. The instinct of *gregariousness* that prompts us to seek and enjoy the company of others and was important in the development of society.

The seven major instincts listed below are characterized by the presence of a strong emotional response.

1. The instinct of *survival* produces the emotion of fear and a tendency to flee or hide; it is brought on by a variety of (usually unfamiliar) stimuli. The survival instinct tends to promote the welfare of an individual at the expense of his social group.

2. The instinct of *aversion* is stimulated by bad smells, tastes, or tactile sensations (e.g., sliminess) and prompts feelings of disgust and avoidance reactions.

3. The instinct of *curiosity* is the stimulus for science and religion and gives rise to feelings of wonder.

4. The instinct of *aggression* is matched only by survival in terms of its strength and the intensity of the emotion—anger—that it generates. This instinct is prompted by "... any obstruction to the activity to which the creature is impelled by any one of the other instincts. And its impulse is ... to destroy whatever offers this opposition (1908, p. 51)." Thus, aggression leads us to overcome obstacles.

5. The instinct of *self-display*, accompanied by positive self-feeling, is found in most social animals at mating time, in children, in the boasting of men and the vanity of women. One practices self-display when feeling superior to another.

6. The instinct of *self-abasement* and negative self-feelings, as reflected in a submissive posture and an attempt to avoid attention results in shame and bashfulness.

7. The *parental* instinct prompts humans to care for their young. It is elicited by the sight or thought of a distressed child, and consequently serves to preserve the species.

Five nonspecific tendencies, together with the twelve instincts described above, round out McDougall's motivational theory. These are:

1. *Sympathy*, "... a suffering with, the experiencing of any feeling or emotion when and because we observe in other persons or creatures the expression of that feeling or emotion (1908, p. 79)." Primitive sympathy is a reflex; it implies none of the "higher moral qualities." Too much sympathy may render one incapable of effective action, and consequently it can be maladaptive.

2. *Suggestibility*, accepting "... with conviction ... a communicated proposition in the absence of logically adequate grounds for its acceptance (1908, p. 83)." Children are particularly suggestible; this is the reason "... that they so rapidly absorb the knowledge, beliefs, and especially the sentiments, of their social environment (1908, p. 86)." Thus, suggestibility facilitates socialization.

3. *Imitation*, the tendency to mimic the emotions or actions of another.

4. *Play*, a natural tendency present in the young of higher animals. Play serves two purposes: (a) it allows the young to practice those specialized activities on which their adult survival will depend; and (b) it teaches the young cooperation, leadership, and the ability to substitute group goals for individual ends. Thus play is an important vehicle for socialization.

5. *Habit*, a tendency "... for every process to be repeated more readily in virtue of its previous occurrence and in proportion to the frequency of its previous repetition (1908, p. 99)."

These twelve instincts and five nonspecific tendencies form the basis of personality and social behavior. McDougall, like Freud and Jung, thought most human action was instinctive in origin; unlike Freud and Jung, however, he did not regard instinctive behavior as necessarily irrational. On the contrary, he thought that instincts lead to behavior that is rational in both its methods and results.

McDougall gave priority to the problem of motivation; however, he was equally preoccupied with the problem of explaining the organization of behavior. Instincts provide the first level of organization of behavior, and without them our actions would be completely random. Clearly, however, the action of the instincts must itself be organized; according to McDougall, this is produced by the sentiments.

A sentiment, McDougall suggested, develops when the mental image of an object becomes "... linked with one or more [instincts] in such a way that ... when the corresponding object is perceived ... the [instinct] is also brought into action and engenders its peculiar [response] directed upon the object (1932, p. 223)." Anything that consistently triggers an instinct will become the object of a sentiment. McDougall used the term "sentiment" much as contemporary writers use the word "value": sentiments like values become attached to objects or ideas and serve to organize our conduct. If an object becomes the stimulus for several instincts, a whole system of sentiments will develop around it. Thus one's mother, for example, might have regularly elicited one's instincts of gregariousness, survival, self-display, and self-abasement, and produced a complex maternal sentiment. Such sentiment systems correspond to Jung's notion of a complex, or to a nonpathological Freudian fixation. Each sentiment is a unique system of ideas and response dispositions; taken together, sentiments are the major structural and functional units of the mind.

McDougall is often wrongly criticized for explaining all social behavior in terms of instincts. He thought "... the activities of the adult man ... derive their energy [from] ... the sentiments within which the [instincts] are organized (1932, p. 227)." There are three types of sentiments: the first concerns such concrete objects as one's favorite coat, shoes, pen, or tennis racket. The second type of sentiment is directed toward collective objects: "... our church, our school, our gang, our party, our nation ... of all group sentiments ... devotion to the family is perhaps the most nearly universal (1932, pp. 229–30)." Finally, we can develop sentiments for abstract objects. "The abstract objects which

most commonly become objects of sentiments are the qualities of...
honesty, courage, strength of character, generosity, fair play, cruelty,
meanness, ruthlessness, fickleness ... such objects are ... the essence of
morality ... (1932, p. 231)." For McDougall, the more abstract sentiments
organize the less abstract ones in a hierarchical fashion. The first level
of organization in behavior is in terms of instincts; the second level is
in terms of sentiments; and at the third level sentiments themselves
become organized under abstract moral qualities into a system called
character.

THE SELF-CONCEPT AND SOCIALIZATION

McDougall thought socialization was crucial for the development
of the individual and the stability of society. "If we would understand
the life of societies, we must first ... understand the way in which individuals become moulded by the society into which they are born ...
how ... they become fitted to play their part in it as social beings—how,
in short, they become capable of moral conduct (1908, p. 150)."

Like Freud, McDougall conceptualized socialization in both ontogenetic and phylogenetic terms (his discussion, however, predates Freud's
by about five years).

McDougall explained the development of socialization within the
individual in terms of the growth of the self-concept and self-consciousness. One's self-concept develops through interactions with others, reflecting how we see ourselves in relation to others—this is the self as an
indirect object of knowledge.

The "genesis of moral conduct and character" (socialization) passes
through four stages, each defined by one's self-concept at that stage. In
the first the child is primarily aware of the difference between his body
and the external environment; his instinctive behavior is controlled
only by pleasure and pain.

In the second stage the child can distinguish between inanimate
objects and other persons. He is increasingly aware of people and begins
to imitate them. His behavior in this second stage is controlled by the
physical rewards and punishments administered by adults.

In the third stage behavior is controlled by social praise and blame.
According to McDougall, concern about the opinion of others coincides
with the development of the self-regarding sentiment—self-esteem, self-
respect, or pride. When properly formed, self-regard contains a blend
of gregariousness, self-display, self-abasement, and sympathy that produces
a balance between positive and negative self-feelings. Gregariousness

and self-display are satisfied when the person is paid attention. The positive self-feelings that result from being noticed cause one indiscriminately to seek social attention. Consequently, the negative self-feelings associated with self-abasement must be stimulated to produce "an attitude of receptivity, of imitativeness and suggestibility." These negative self-feelings, evoked in children by "inflexible authority," cause them to understand that the attitudes of their parents represent "the attitudes of... organized society." The final step in the development of the self-regarding sentiment is the emergence of active sympathy. "Active sympathy impels [one]... not only to seek to bring the feelings and emotions of his fellows into harmony with his own, but also, since that is often impossible, to bring his own into harmony with theirs (1908, p. 173)."

With maturity one tends to extend the self-regarding sentiment to one's children and family: one becomes concerned with what others think about one's family. This leads to a concern for their welfare, but this concern is ultimately self-serving. For McDougall, then, altruism results from recognizing that social judgments of one's family reflect equally on oneself.

Behavior governed by the self-regarding sentiment is still relatively immature. It is egoistic, tied to social approval, and dependent on the values of one's culture. But, as McDougall remarked, occasionally "... a man may stand apart from his group and from the whole of organized society, defying the general opinion and... saying 'You are mistaken; this is right and I will do it, though I go to prison and disgrace, or to hell' (1923, p. 441)." This represents moral autonomy and is the final stage in the development of socialization.

Autonomous behavior seems to depend on a highly developed self-regarding sentiment and on a concern with how one's actions will appear when judged from the viewpoint of eternity (sub specie aeternitas). "The man who stands up against the prevailing public opinion... has found some higher court of appeal, the verdict of which he esteems more highly... and whose approval he desires more strongly, than that of the mass of mankind... In short, he has learned to judge his conduct as it would appear to a purely ideal spectator... In this way... a man may become, as it is said, a 'law unto himself' (1923, pp. 441–42)."

The emergence of moral character in the fullest sense also requires that a person incorporate within his self-regarding sentiment such moral ideals as honesty, self-control, and justice, so that his sense of self-worth depends on the maintenance of these ideals.

As the preceding discussion indicates, McDougall's ideas about the self-concept and the socialization process are complex and closely interrelated. Socialization passes through four stages, each defined in terms of a different conception of the self. In the first stage a child only distinguishes between "me" and "not-me," and his actions are guided by pleasure and pain. In the second stage, a child divides the world of "not-me" into people and things, begins to attend closely to people, and regulates his behaviors in terms of their rewards and punishments. In the third stage the egoistic self-regarding sentiment emerges, and conduct is controlled by social approval and disapproval. In the final stage, reached only by some people, behavior is controlled by the opinions of an "ideal spectator"; to others such behavior appears autonomous and self-directed.

McDougall's phylogenetic theory of socialization resembles Freud's and is framed in terms of the natural history of aggression. According to Darwin and others, primitive man lived in families consisting of a patriarch, his wives and children. As young males matured sexually, the jealous father drove them away from the family. The young males formed bands and lived on the perimeter of the family circle. These sons would periodically challenge the patriarch to mortal combat. If successful, one would assume control of the family; if unsuccessful, he would be killed. Consequently, the primal father ". . . constantly weeded out the more reckless of his male progeny, those least capable of restraining their sexual impulse under the threat of his anger . . . Hence this ruthless selection among the young males must have led to the development of prudence (1908, p. 245)." Prudence implies "self-consciousness" and "a capacity for deliberation." Thus, this selection process produced ". . . a succession of patriarchs, each of whom was superior to his rivals, not merely in power of combat, but also . . . in power of far-sighted control of his impulse (1908, p. 246)." Over time then, according to McDougall, natural selection produced in primitive man the capacities for self-consciousness and self-control.

Individual families eventually joined together to form villages or tribes. The survival of these social groups depended ". . . not only on the vigor and ferocity of individual fighters, but also . . . upon the capacity . . . for united action, upon good comradeship, upon personal trustworthiness, and upon the capacity of individuals to subordinate their impulsive tendencies and egoistic promptings to the ends of the group and to the commands of the accepted leader (1908, p. 246)." Those groups that had more efficient social organization were at an immediate adaptive advantage: they could exterminate the less organized groups (a view held by such contemporary writers as Ardrey, 1970). For McDougall, then, socialization results from selection pressures operating on aggression at both the individual and group level.

McDougall based these speculations on observations he made while living in Borneo for a year. The tribes of Borneo in the late nineteenth century were arranged in a particular fashion. Those along the coast were peaceful; they were inadequate warriors who fought only in self-defense. The tribes in the central regions were extremely warlike and a "constant source of terror" to those living below. Between the central and the coastal tribes

> ...were others that served as a buffer between them, being decidedly more bellicose than the latter but less so than the former. It might be supposed that the peaceful coastwise people would be...superior in moral qualities.to their more warlike neighbours; but the contrary was the case. In almost all respects the advantage lay with the warlike tribes. Their houses were better built, larger, and cleaner; their domestic morality was superior; they were physically stronger, were braver, and...in general are more trustworthy. But, above all, their social organization was firmer and more efficient.... And the moderately warlike tribes occupying the middle regions stood midway between them and the people of the coast as regards these moral qualities (1908, p. 248).

McDougall's analysis suggests that through evolution aggression has fostered self-consciousness, prudence, self-control, and tendencies toward group loyalty. Aggression has subsequently become ritualized and turned into competitive play, a socializing force in itself. Furthermore, when persons share experiences active sympathy develops between them. Active sympathy is equivalent to the Freudian concept of identification, and it is an additional cohesive force in society. When the evolutionary consequences of aggression and man's innate playfulness are combined with the powerful socializing effects of suggestibility and sympathy, we see that man is strongly predisposed by his phylogenesis (or biological makeup) toward social living.

McDougall's account of the socialization process, though complex, skillfully blends biological predispositions and social experience. It is the most sophisticated treatment of socialization in the personological tradition, and represents a distinct theoretical advance over Freud's and Jung's analyses of the same subject.

EXPLANATION

McDougall was keenly aware of the problem of explanation, to which he devoted a chapter of his *Social Psychology*. An explanation of human conduct, he noted, requires an "adequate conception of behavior in general." Behavior at any level of complexity has four defining features: (1) the person moves persistently towards an end; (2) he varies his means as necessary to achieve the end; (3) the energy of the whole person seems concentrated upon the task; and (4) over time the person becomes more efficient at obtaining his goal. Actions that lack these four characteristics are not, properly speaking, behavior; they are random events and consequently do not require explanation. Instincts are the original or initial cause of behavior; an account of the origins of instincts themselves, however, is beyond the realm of psychology. For McDougall, then, instincts provide the major explanation of behavior. "When, and not until, we can exhibit any particular instance of conduct or of behavior as the expression of . . . [instincts] which are ultimate constituents of the organism, we can claim to have explained it (1908, p. 312)."

McDougall explained the universal or common characteristics of human behavior (personality as *Personalität*) in terms of instincts. The human race, as a species, shares a common set of innate action tendencies, derivatives of man's evolutionary history, that set him apart from the other animals.

Differences among people (personality as *Persönlichkeit*) are explained in two ways. First, according to McDougall, one must take into account individual differences in the strength of the instincts and in temperament or bodily constitution. As we know from genetics, people differ widely in terms of these biological characteristics. Second, individuality depends on the nature and organization of a person's sentiments, especially the sentiment of self-regard. Because each person's life experiences are unique, the sentiments will also be organized in a manner that is specific and particular to the individual. Thus, with his concepts of instinct and sentiment McDougall specified in what ways we are alike and different.

Finally, to explain particular, puzzling patterns of behavior, McDougall constructed an interpretation based on the way the action developed, taking account of the person's life history, the innate tendencies that might have impelled it, and the sentiments that seemed to guide it. Consequently, although the concepts differ (i.e., instincts, sentiments), McDougall, like Freud and Jung, explained specific actions in terms of an interpretive model of explanation.

THE UNCONSCIOUS

McDougall had a mixed regard for Freud. As he observed, "I believe that Professor Freud has done more for the advancement of psychology than any student since Aristotle. At the same time . . . I regard much of the current psychoanalytic doctrines as ill-founded and somewhat fantastic (1926, p. viii)." McDougall worked for five years during World

War I as an army psychiatrist, treating combat-related neuroses and psychoses. During this time he came to doubt that the unconscious was composed of mental elements that have been either inherited or forced out of consciousness by an unconscious action of the ego. In his *Outline of Abnormal Psychology* McDougall remarked, "I shall not make use of 'the Unconscious' as an explanatory principle. The use of that term tends ... to a vague and mystical way of thinking; authors too readily fall into the way of solving all obscure problems by invoking 'the Unconscious' ... and leaving them illuminated only by that dim and uncertain radiance (1923, p. 26)." He also doubted that the mind was composed of two or more structures (e.g., the ego and superego) set apart from and often in conflict with one another. According to McDougall, one can speak of two such structures only in the case of a dual personality. He thought that the mind is in most cases a unified whole. He agreed with Freud, however, that only a portion of all mental activity is at any time available to introspection; the other portions of psychic life can be perceived only with great difficulty. McDougall labelled these more obscure activities "subconscious."

The next question concerns how thought becomes subconscious; the answer shows the difference between Freud's and McDougall's treatment of the unconscious. There are two ways that a thought may become subconscious: through the interaction of mental elements as described by Herbart, and through a form of repression that can be called suppression.

According to Herbart, the relationship between any pair of ideas can be positive, negative, or neutral. Positively related ideas attract, and negatively related ideas repel one another. The mind is composed of these ideas arranged in dynamic equilibrium. A dominant mass of related thoughts makes up consciousness; a subordinate mass of related thoughts is forced below the limen of consciousness because each thought is incompatible with those in the dominant mass. Thus, each subconscious thought becomes so by virtue of its relationship to the ideas within the dominant mass of consciousness. Yet each thought is instinct-based and, consequently, continually strives for expression in awareness. Thoughts from below the limen of consciousness typically appear in awareness as distortions of conscious thought and behavior.

Thoughts also become subconscious through repression. In contrast with Freud, however, McDougall did not consider repression to be an unconscious process. Rather, the self-regarding sentiment is the cause of repression. One ignores or represses those ideas that are too discrepant from one's ideal self-image or that reflect badly on the self. For Freud, repression is a function of an unconscious censor, and we tend to repress socially unacceptable impulses; for McDougall, repression is based on conscious choice, and we tend to repress (or ignore) personally embarrassing ideas regardless of their social acceptability.

According to McDougall, everyday experience provides "abundant illustrations" of subconscious mental activity. For example, the biographies of highly creative men such as Coleridge and Pascal suggest that ". . . all creative production, especially of the higher kind, issues from a vastly complex train of activity which in large part is subconscious (1932, p. 246);" moveover, the thinker may be unaware of these processes, but can recover them with concentration. Like Freud and Jung, McDougall believed that subconscious thinking is seen most clearly in dreams. Most dreams "have some significance not immediately clear to the dreamer." They reveal upon analysis "some tendency at work subconsciously;" this mental tendency is subconscious because it is "repugnant in some way to the dominant tendencies of the dreamer (1932, p. 247)." McDougall (1932, pp. 246–47) offered as an example the following dream of a neurasthenic army officer:

> An English officer, who, during the Great War, had served several years at the front without receiving promotion or other recognition of his services, dreamed that he went to a tea-party at Buckingham Palace to meet the King and Queen. To his chagrin the other guests were regaled with various delicacies, but nothing was offered to him. The dream seemed to him utterly silly and without significance. It was only when I . . . prompted the dreamer to undertake a candid self-examination, that his inner state of brooding discontent and resentment (hitherto strongly repressed from both the world and himself) was revealed and acknowledged; a state of long-continued conflict that had engendered the symptoms of neurasthenia.

Two points about this interpretation are important. First, like Freud and Jung, McDougall recognized that dreams provide information about the subconscious conflicts that produce neurotic symptoms. Second, McDougall thought that dreamers, when pressed, could recover the meanings of their dreams themselves.

PSYCHOLOGICAL HEALTH

On the basis of his own clinical experience McDougall was highly critical of Freud's explanation of neurosis. He thought that Freud's theory of motivation was entirely too narrow, and that there are instinctually-based sources of conflict beyond those produced by sex and aggression. We need to understand normal functioning before we can explain neurotic behavior; according to McDougall, Freud's explanation of neurosis was limited by his inadequate conception of normalcy. Finally, Freud thought the cause of hysteria was repression and the major symptom was physical impairment with no organic basis; McDougall thought the cause was dissociation and the major symptom was multiple personalities (in Ellenberger's terms, di- and polypsychism—see page 12 above). Freud not only ignored the problem of multiple personalities, he actually denied their existence, arguing that such cases "... might better be denoted as shifting of consciousness—that function—or whatever it be—oscillating between two different psychical complexes which become conscious and unconscious in alternation (McDougall, 1926, p. 523)." But, McDougall added, Freud offered no reasons for dismissing a phenomenon that so intrigued such distinguished contemporaries as William James, Morton Prince, and especially Pierre Janet, under whom Freud began his study of neuroses. Like McDougall, Janet argued that dissociation, not repression, was the cause of neurosis. Janet, McDougall, and others pointed out that the Freudian unconscious could not be directly experienced; it was an inference used to explain other mental phenomena. They maintained, on the other hand, that their notion of a dissociated subconscious refers to phenomena that we can experience for ourselves—e.g., hypnotic suggestion, sleepwalking, unconscious problem solving, and talking to one person while listening to another (for an interesting modern discussion of dissociation, see Hilgard, 1973). Moreover, as McDougall noted, the study of subconscious activities does not suggest that the mind is divided into a conscious and unconscious portion; it suggests, rather, "... a hierarchy of minor integrations which, under favorable circumstances, becomes the integrated system we call the normal personality (1926, p. 523)."

If the mind is normally "a hierarchy of minor integrations," why does the integration break down? Conflict produces dissociation when incompatible motives impel one to incompatible goals. Conflict prepares the way for the general class of disorders that Freud was concerned with: hysterical symptoms, amnesias, phobias, obsessions and compulsions. According to McDougall, these neuroses are always purposive: they are the means by which a neurotic achieves some important goal. By taking flight into a disease, the neurotic is able to control others, avoid responsibility, and compel consideration. McDougall acknowledged that there are neuroses that confer no benefits to the neurotic. "But in the ordinary neuroses one always finds on close inspection an advantage from the disease (1926, p. 53)." Neurotic symptoms, however, are inefficient means for solving problems, and they are even unpleasant to the neurotic, since he must first actually experience the disease to achieve his goal. McDougall (1926, pp. 242-43) provided the following example of the perverse but serious nature of an hysterical paralysis:

A young gipsy labourer, working on a hayrick, was caught by the left hand in some of the mechanism ... He was violently dragged high in the air and left suspended for some time by the left arm. When he was released from his predicament, it was found that the whole of his left fore limb was in a condition of complete flaccid paralysis and total anesthesia. He remained in this condition for more than a year before he was sent to me. He had been examined and treated by several medical men. One had applied electrical stimulation with such vigour that the skin of the arm bore several deep scars burned by the strong current. Another, a surgeon, had offered to cut away the useless limb, that dangled like a flail ... With the failure of every such attempt at treatment, the patient's conviction that the arm was permanently useless had become more firmly established; and thus the case was a difficult one. He seemed to be much depressed by his paralysis and the prospect of diminished economic efficiency through life. Hypnotic suggestion produced no immediate effect. It was only through a course of education, persuasion and suggestion and encouragement continued over some weeks that the cure was effected. The essential step was to shake and undermine his fixed belief in the permanent nature of the paralysis.

Although McDougall does not specify the dynamics of this case, the young man's paralysis presumably served a purpose of some sort. Through it the patient may have forced his family and friends to take care of him, he may have avoided military service, or perhaps extracted additional concessions from his former employer.

Neurotic symptoms can be classified along a continuum of increasing dissociation. Simple hysterical symptoms, as seen for example in the gipsy labourer, are caused by superficial dissociations. Amnesias represent a more serious lack of integration; and finally, cases of multiple personality indicate extreme dissociation.

According to McDougall there are four causes of neurotic dissociation. The first is hereditary; some people are born with "an unfortunate temperament" that predisposes them to dissociation. The second is a poor home environment, where a child receives "unwise training" and possibly imitates a neurotic parent. Third, because no one is completely integrated, almost anyone will break down under prolonged periods of stress. Finally, dissociation results when a conflict works "... obscurely, unrecognized ... and especially ... when one of the unrecognized motives is of a nature such that we will not, dare not, recognize it, but rather repress it (1926, p. 217)." Thus, it is not conflict but the self-deception or repression that a conflict of motives will engender, that leads to dissociation and neurotic symptoms.

As the preceding discussion indicates, the key to McDougall's conception of psychological health is integration, the development of a "unitary personality." A healthy person's sentiments are organized into a system that both reduces conflict and coordinates the expression of the instincts. The sentiments are integrated by coming under the control of more abstract sentiments. The highest form of integration is achieved by the development of a master sentiment that dominates the whole system of sentiments, subordinating their impulses to its own. The master sentiment may be (and often is) love of wealth, power, or worldly success; however, master sentiments such as these indicate flawed character development. Occasionally two incompatible master sentiments may develop (e.g., love of learning and of wealth); this also leads to internal conflict and a divided personality. According to McDougall, only a self-regarding sentiment that takes "the form of a self-conscious devotion to an ideal of character" can effectively organize the personality. Psychological health is possible only when one has personally identified with a moral ideal (e.g., justice, freedom), when one's self-respect depends on maintaining that ideal, and when a violation of that standard is experienced as a personal outrage.

Despite this elaborate discussion, McDougall believed that a harmoniously integrated character is an ideal that few people actually achieve. Furthermore, he thought personal integration would become increasingly difficult in an industrialized age characterized by the collapse of traditional religious and moral values, by conflict among the ideologies of competing life styles, by the decline of ethnic and national loyalties, by mounting crime and divorce rates, and by an emerging technocracy and occupational structure in which work is basically dull and alienating.

Three points concerning McDougall's analysis of psychological health should be emphasized. First, there is close agreement between McDougall and Jung concerning the importance of integration for personal maturity. Second, and in contrast with Freud, McDougall defined maturity in terms of greater integration rather than increased consciousness. The total amount of subconscious psychic activity in a normal and a neurotic is the same; the difference is that a normal person has substantially fewer subconscious conflicts. McDougall also opposed the concept of dissociation to the Freudian notion of repression as an explanation for neurotic symptoms. Third, and in sharp disagreement with Freud, McDougall equated psychological health and character development. For Freud the superego was unconscious, irrational, and the source of neurosis; for McDougall a well-developed conscience was the hallmark of maturity.

EVALUATION

As a brief summary of this chapter it would be useful to mention the positive and negative aspects of McDougall's contribution. We will begin with the shortcomings. First, reflecting the influence of his predecessors, Stout and Ward, McDougall was often too scholastic in his analysis of an issue. He frequently tried to solve empirical questions by force of logic alone, and he sometimes saw social behavior as more orderly than everyday experience suggests it is. Second, he repeatedly interrupted himself to pursue metaphysical problems that had little relevance to the psychological issues at stake. His speculative flights obscure the fact that he could be (and often was) a very pragmatic, issue-oriented writer with great respect for evidence. Third, although Mc-Dougall regarded intrapsychic conflicts as inevitable, the model of man he developed was in fact quite rational. He felt that man is fundamentally reasonable, the cause of neurosis is ignorance, and the cure is education. Yet available historical evidence seems to support Freud's skepticism concerning human rationality. Finally, McDougall regarded man as naturally social and benevolent. Conflicts between the individual and society are infrequent and pathological by definition. There is no morality beyond that given by one's society, even though few people ever actually embody these principles at their finest. Freud and Jung also endorsed an ethic of conformity; however, they were highly skeptical of social morality and political leadership, and both considered civilization as a necessary evil. McDougall lacked this skepticism; consequently, even more than Freud and Jung he seemed wedded to the status quo.

On the positive side, McDougall was an important and original thinker who formulated unique concepts of several root ideas: motivation, the self, socialization, the unconscious, and psychological health. In so doing, he raised an interesting criticism of the tendency, latent in the ideas of Freud and Jung, to regard neurotics as victims of forces beyond their control, a tendency that permits the neurotic to avoid responsibility for his own life. By explaining repression and neurotic symptoms without postulating an unconscious censor, McDougall placed the burden of responsibility in neurosis back on the patient. Another unique characteristic of McDougall's writing is that, perhaps more than any other major psychologist, he made a conscientious attempt to explore systematically the implications of biology and evolutionary theory for a science of human nature. Not surprisingly, among contemporary social thinkers it is the ethologists (Konrad Lorenz, Niko Tinbergen) who are most closely related to McDougall. From the perspective of the 1970s, the ethological and comparative study of social behavior seems to be one of the most interesting and promising analytical models available. As psychoanalysis and behaviorism lose popular appeal, McDougall's biological perspective may enjoy a revival after fifty years of obscurity.

McDougall's ideas about the structure and dynamics of human personality, judged in terms of their scope, internal consistency, and congruence with external facts, may represent the most formally adequate theory in the personological tradition. His first book, *Social Psychology* (1908) was an attempt to provide a complete account of individual social behavior. The account is systematic, well-organized, comprehensive, and philosophically sophisticated; in my judgment McDougall's ideas represent the best theory of personality that we have.

Perhaps McDougall's most important contribution, however, is his careful and sophisticated analysis of socialization. McDougall placed the acquisition of values at the center of social development, and three aspects of his analysis of "moralisation" are distinctive. First, he was one of the first psychologists to recognize the importance of play, games, imitation, and peer interaction for moral development. Second, he was one of the first persons to relate the self-concept to socialization. Third, and most importantly, McDougall contradicted Freud by equating moral development and psychological health. Self-actualization theorists as different as Aristotle and Nietzsche have traditionally argued that personal maturity and character development are interrelated, but psychologists, perhaps as a result of Freud's influence, have ignored their insight.

In view of McDougall's striking originality, it seems safe to conclude that his importance to the personological tradition is equalled only by Freud and Jung and that his ideas merit close attention from anyone seriously concerned with the study of human nature.

chapter seven

Gordon Allport

Gordon Allport's position in the personological tradition is unique in several ways. Freud, Jung, and McDougall exemplify the medical tradition, whereas Allport represents the literary and folk traditions. He paid great attention to language as a source of information about human nature, he was one of the finest writers in his discipline, and his ideas are an engaging blend of literary insight and common sense. Allport is also distinctive in terms of his relationship to academic psychology. Freud and Jung showed an ostentatious disregard for academic opinion. Mc-Dougall cared a great deal about it, but was pilloried by his academic colleagues, particularly in America. Allport was as critical as McDougall of the philosophical and methodological dogmatism of American psychology, yet he had by all conventional standards an enormously success-ful career. He introduced the study of personality to America with his 1937 textbook, *Personality: A psychological interpretation*, and at the end of his life was regarded as the grand old man of his discipline. All-port is also unique in that, compared with Freud, Jung, and especially McDougall, he "had no talent for science (Allport, 1968, p. 384)." Rather

Gordon Allport
Wide World Photos

he was primarily an essayist and described his own point of view as "empirical humanism."

In view of Allport's literary and humanistic orientation, it is not surprising that as a young man he found the climate of ideas in American psychology (i.e., radical behaviorism) uncongenial and that he described his graduate training at Harvard as intellectually unproductive. Allport formed his most important ideas while traveling in Germany after graduate school. His thinking seems to have been shaped almost exclusively by European influences: *Gestalt* psychology, William Stern, and William McDougall.

The primary principle of *Gestalt* psychology is that the whole cannot be explained in terms of its constituent parts; it is a protest against elementarism or atomism, exemplified in American psychology by behaviorism. According to *Gestalt* psychology, we will never understand structured wholes by studying their ingredient elements. Rather, if we can achieve some insight into the structure of the phenomenon in question, we may then understand its components. Allport remarked that he knew nothing of *Gestalt* before leaving Cambridge for Germany. Once there, however, he found ". . . the kind of psychology I had been longing for but did not know existed (1968, p. 387)."

Allport described himself as a student of William Stern, a prominent member (and friendly critic) of the *Gestalt* movement. Stern is best known in the United States for his books on child development and differential psychology. An original thinker, he invented the concept of the I.Q.; he subsequently denounced it as "pernicious" because of the manner in which it had been used to classify schoolchildren. Three aspects of Stern's psychology of personalism are reflected in Allport's writings. The first is Stern's eclecticism. The term *eclectic* contrasts with *systematic*; it refers to theories that are composed of whatever ideas the theorist finds compatible, regardless of the original context. Although this often results in confusion, ideas taken from different theories may sometimes be assembled to form a more integrated perspective. Allport was self-consciously eclectic, in contrast with Freud, Jung, and particularly McDougall, who were all systematic. Stern's second influence on Allport concerned his ideographic (as opposed to normative or nomothetic) perspective. According to Stern, the individual person, rather than generalized notions of human behavior as found in psychoanalysis, is the subject matter of psychology. An ideographic method studies each person with regard to him or herself and not in comparison with others. Allport was the champion of the ideographic approach in American psychology, the reason he is often regarded as a "humanistic psychologist." Stern's third influence on Allport concerned his motivational theory. Stern was deliberately unsystematic in his discussion of motivation; as a result, he lumped an array of unrelated ideas together under the concept of motivation. Allport followed Stern's example here as well.

Allport also seems to have been very much influenced by William McDougall. He adopted McDougall's concept of sentiment or value, especially the notion of a master-sentiment, as an explanatory concept. He was also impressed with McDougall's analysis of the self-concept. But McDougall's influence is most pronounced in Allport's concern with the problem of organization and integration of personality.

MOTIVATION

Freud, Jung, and McDougall thought of motivation in biogenic terms as instincts. In so doing Allport believed they reflected the major tradition in motivational theory. This tradition began with Schopenhauer and later Darwin, and was a reaction against the naive tendency to ignore man's ability to give self-justifying rationalizations for even the most obviously selfish and immoral conduct. Schopenhauer, Darwin, Freud, Jung, and McDougall were, for Allport, irrationalists who thought the source of man's behavior was unconscious and beyond his control. Their ideas have dominated Western psychology for over a century and, according to Allport, have produced "... a kind of contempt for the 'psychic surface' of life. The individual's conscious report is rejected as untrustworthy, and the contemporary thrust of his motives is disregarded in favor of a backward tracing of his conduct to earlier formative stages. The individual loses his right to be believed. And while he is busy leading his life in the present with a forward thrust into the future, most psychologists have become busy tracing it backward into the past (1960, p. 96)."

Allport raised four criticisms of the biogenic or "irrationalist" tradition in motivational theory. First, although neurotics may be unwilling (or unable) to discuss their motivations with a psychiatrist, normal people often freely discuss theirs. Indeed, the degree to which a person is willing to admit unpleasant facts about himself may be an index of adjustment (Jourard, 1971). As Allport observed, "The story is told of a patient who remarked that a Rorschach card made him think of sexual relations. The clinician, thinking to tap a buried complex, asked him why. 'Oh, because,' said the patient, 'I think of sexual relations all the time anyway' (1960, p. 97)." Second, biogenic theories of motivation are an attempt to imitate the natural sciences whose prestige psychologists envy. Allport maintained that psychology differs from the natural sciences precisely because it must take psychogenic as well as biogenic motives into account. That is, people are self-motivating; they make plans and organize their actions accordingly. Consequently, biogenic theories of motivation are inadequate to the facts of everyday experience.

Allport's third criticism is that irrationalist theories of motivation are essentially reactive; they present man as reacting to internal and external stimuli in a purely passive way. This is contrary to common sense. Man is active as well as reactive, he lives in the future as well as the past; indeed, healthy people may have their motivation primarily in the future.

Allport's final criticism is that the medical tradition cannot explain the fact that adult motives are infinitely varied, self-sustaining, contemporary systems, rather than derivations from one's past. Appealing to common experience, Allport argued that although one may initially have gone fishing or worked in the garden in order to please one's father, fishing or gardening in adulthood is motivating in itself. Thus, he concluded, there is no way to derive a mature interest in poetry, an adult love of hard work, or a sailor's longing for the sea from a small list of instincts or biological urges.

According to Allport, there are four characteristics of an adequate theory of motivation. First, motives are contemporaneous: for a motive to be a motive, it must be one now; thus, the past is important only if it can be shown to be dynamically active in the present. Second, a proper motivational theory will allow for motives of many types. Instincts tend to be deficit motives and are important in childhood. Growth motives, however, are much more important in adulthood. These include curiosity, ambition, and the needs for competence and meaning; and all foster personal growth and expansion. The third characteristic of an adequate motivational theory is that it will ascribe causal status to cognitive concepts such as plans, intentions, and values (psychogenic motives). The final requirement of an adequate theory of motivation is that it will "allow for the concrete uniqueness of motives"—it will take account of the fact that each person has a unique and specific set of motives.

As the foregoing suggests, Allport gave equivalent motivational status to both biological abstractions (instincts) and cognitive concepts (plans, values, intentions). Thus, he ignored the distinction between biogenic and psychogenic motives. This curious lapse in one ordinarily so careful with language reflects the influence of William Stern.

Beyond his general critique of biogenic theories of motivation, Allport's own contribution was twofold: the first concerns how motives develop, the second involves the nature of motivational units themselves. Allport described the development of motives with one general law that he called the functional autonomy of adult motives. Functional autonomy—Allport's best known and most controversial concept—refers to the phenomenon that adult interests usually begin as responses to some external demand but later seem to become motivational in themselves. "Functional autonomy, then, refers to any acquired system of motivation in which the tensions involved are not of the same kind as the antecedent tensions from which the acquired system developed (1961, p. 229)."

Allport demonstrated that motives become functionally autonomous through examples and appeals to introspective evidence. "For example, a student who first undertakes a field of study in college because it is required, because it pleases his parents, or because it comes at a convenient hour may end by finding himself absorbed in the topic, perhaps for life. The original motives may be entirely lost. What was a means to an end becomes an end in itself (1967, p. 235)."

Allport readily granted that not all motives become functionally autonomous, raising the question of how to tell which are and which are not. Unfortunately, Allport's answer to this was somewhat circular. Functional autonomy can never be determined in advance; rather, functionally autonomous motives are those that become so. Moreover, in calling a motive functionally autonomous Allport avoided the problem of why that particular motive developed in the first place. To this difficulty Allport replied somewhat enigmatically that "... historical explanation is *not* functional explanation. In a very real sense a functionally autonomous motive *is* the personality. We cannot ask for any further reduction. Life itself is the energy and the 'explanation.' We need not, and cannot, look 'deeper'—not if the motive is functionally autonomous (1961, p. 244)."

Allport's second contribution to motivational theory concerns the analytical or structural units most appropriate to the study of personality.

As he observed, "Man's nature . . . seems to be composed of relatively stable structures." The success of psychology depends on its ability to identify them. The most important structural units according to Allport are motives. "What is the relation between units of motivation and units of personality? I would suggest that all units of motivation are at the same time units of personality (1960, p. 118)."

Each person's behavior contains certain consistencies that characterize him or her. This is reflected in everyday speech by such trait words as dominant, hostile, sexy, and sociable. Allport thought these terms mirrored in a rough, general way, psychological reality; that is, traits underlie the observed consistencies in each person's behavior. He therefore proposed the concept of a trait as his major motivational concept and as the most important structural unit in personality. A trait is ". . . a neuropsychic structure having the capacity to render many stimuli functionally equivalent, and to initiate and guide equivalent (meaningfully consistent) forms of adaptive and expressive behavior (1961, p. 347)." The psychologist and the man on the street think about other people in terms of traits and use the same means to define them; ". . . the *frequency* with which a person adopts a certain type of adjustment is one criterion of a trait. A second criterion is the *range of situations* in which he adopts this same mode of acting. A third criterion is the *intensity* of his reactions in keeping with this 'preferred pattern' of behavior (1961, p. 340)."

Allport believed that traits literally exist somewhere in the nervous system and that neurophysiologists will ultimately uncover the mechanisms by which they are formed. Trait terms found in ordinary language are only crude approximations to the real thing; they are labels that we as observers more or less arbitrarily pin on other people. According to Allport, some traits can be more correctly assigned to a person than others. He made a distinction between common traits and personal traits. Common traits are those that are shared by all members of a society, culture, family, or other social unit; they are the variables assessed by most personality tests and inventories. Common traits are categories into which people are forced by an external observer. When we see a person's profile on the Minnesota Multiphasic Personality Inventory, for example, we can locate that person with regard to the test author's frame of reference and describe him using a set of common traits. This is called the normative or nomothetic approach to the description of personality.

On the other hand, personal traits, which Allport called personal dispositions, are unique to only one individual. Common traits are categories into which an individual is forced; personal traits reflect the individual's personality structure. When we accurately classify someone in terms of personal dispositions, we locate him with regard to his own (as opposed to an observer's) frame of reference. This is called an ideographic approach to the description of personality.

Allport acknowledged that there are two problems associated with describing personality in terms of personal dispositions. First, no single act is ever the product of a single personal trait; personal dispositions can be detected only by observing a person over a wide variety of situations. Second, it is impossible to specify in advance the amount of consistency necessary to define a personal disposition. Nonetheless, Allport thought personal dispositions were the analytical units of choice in the analysis of personality.

Within each individual personal dispositions vary in significance. Allport called the most pervasive and important of these cardinal dispositions; almost everything a person does can be traced to their influence. Such a disposition—often called an eminent trait, a ruling passion, a master sentiment, or a radix of life—is so overt and obvious that a person may even become famous for it; an example would be Tolstoi's passion for simplicity. At a lesser level are central personal dispositions; these are the sorts of things we mention when we write a careful letter of recommendation for another person. At the third level are secondary personal dispositions, that are regarded by others as idiosyncracies. Although it is nearly impossible to determine the number of personal dispositions a person has, we can estimate the number of cardinal dispositions necessary to describe someone. Drawing on Ralph Barton Perry's biography of William James, Allport pointed out that Perry nicely described James with only eight cardinal dispositions. Thus, Allport concluded, "When psychology develops adequate diagnostic methods for discovering the major lines along which a particular personality is organized (personal dispositions), it may turn out that the number of such foci will normally vary between five and ten (1961, p. 367)."

Summarizing this discussion, Allport criticized "conventional" motivational theory (as represented by Freud and McDougall) for focusing exclusively on unchanging, unconscious, universal, biogenic motives. He proposed a general law describing the development of adult motives; i.e., they become functionally autonomous of their infantile and/or biological origins. He then suggested that the most appropriate motivational unit for the study of personality is the personal disposition. The term personal disposition refers to nonbiological traits and interests such as ". . . ambitions, compulsions, phobias, general attitudes, inclinations, hobbies, values, tastes, predilections—all are personal dispositions and all are at the same time motives (1961, p. 373)." According to Allport, personal dispositions are more "truly motivational" than biological drives or instincts; unlike instincts, however, personal dispositions are perfectly unique to each person. Thus, in direct contrast with Freud, Jung, and McDougall, Allport argued that each person must be characterized ideographically in terms of his particular set of motives.

THE SELF-CONCEPT

Allport remarked that the image of man developed by contemporary psychology is that of the ideal subject of a totalitarian state—colorless, stereotyped, passive, and conforming. This image largely resulted from psychology's obsession with general laws to the exclusion of the question of uniqueness. According to Allport the basic problem of psychology is to understand the patterned uniqueness of each individual.

The first step toward this goal is to determine what is more or less important for each person. One's personality is organized around those matters that are most personal and most personally important to him. Allport used the term *propriate* to describe such things. Taken altogether, these propriate factors comprise the self or proprium; the self is a shorthand expression for the set of personally relevant matters that give organization to personality and account for uniqueness.

Allport distinguished eight functions and properties of the self or proprium. The first he called *the sense of the bodily me*, composed of sensations that arise from within the body. These experiences are usually sensed only dimly; nonetheless they are a necessary part of an infant's initial sense of self. Moreover, the sense of the bodily me is "a lifelong anchor for our selfawareness (1961, p. 114)."

The second propriate function is *self-identity*, the feeling of self-continuity over time—e.g., the person I see in the mirror this morning is the same one I saw yesterday. This sense of self is closely tied to the development of language, most importantly in a child's own name. "By hearing his name repeatedly the child gradually sees himself as a distinct and recurrent point of reference. The name acquires significance for him in the second year of life. With it comes awareness of independent status in the social group (1961, p. 115)."

The third aspect of the self is *egoism* or *self-seeking* (McDougall's self-regarding sentiment), that usually results in pride and self-esteem. Self-esteem depends on success and failure in one's ability to deal with the world. In the two-year-old self-esteem is related to the need for autonomy, as seen in the child's negativism during this period. By age six or seven self-esteem becomes tied to successful peer group competition and peer approval.

The fourth aspect of the proprium, *ego-extension* (McDougall's quasi-altruistic extension of the self-regarding sentiment), begins to develop sometime after age four. During this period the child learns the meaning of the word *mine*. He develops love for his parents, pets, dolls, and other possessions; this love brings with it the capacity to extend his sense of self to these external objects. In a passage reminiscent of McDougall, Allport observed, "As we grow older we identify with groups, neighborhood, and nation . . . Later in life the process of extension may go to great lengths, through the development of loyalties . . . focused on abstractions and on moral and religious values. Indeed, a mark of maturity seems to be the range and extent of one's feelings of self-involvement in abstract ideas (1955, p. 45)."

Sometime between ages four and six the next form of the proprium —the *self-image*—starts to emerge. The self-image has three components. The first is the child's perception of his abilities and status relative to other people. The second is a composite of other persons' expectations of him. Through social interaction a child comes to know what his parents, relatives, teachers, and others expect him to be. Finally, during this period the child may begin to formulate goals for himself that also become part of his self-image.

The sixth form of the proprium starts to appear after a child enters school. Allport calls this the *self as rational coper*. He thought that the self as a coper closely corresponds to Freud's definition of the ego: it is the conscious portion of the personality concerned with resolving the problems caused by one's biological impulses, the demands of the environment, and the prohibitions of one's conscience.

The seventh aspect of the proprium—*propriate striving*—begins to appear sometime after adolescence. Propriate striving is a motivational concept; it has to do with formulating a long-range goal or purpose for one's life. According to Allport many psychologists assume that motivation consists entirely of a need to reduce instinctual tensions. The characteristic feature of propriate striving, however, is that it increases or maintains tension. Allport used the biography of Roald Amundsen as an example. From the age of fifteen Amundsen dreamed of being a polar explorer. He persisted in this dream despite seemingly insurmountable obstacles; his tenacity, in fact, finally led to his death in the Arctic. Nor was Amundsen unique; according to Allport most of us have insatiable desires that can be explained only very superficially in terms of tension reduction. Propriate striving not only maintains tension and causes conflict but also promotes unification of personality. Mental patients have conflicts, but these are not produced by problems arising from long-range goals. As Allport observed, "The possession of long-range goals, regarded as central to one's personal existence, distinguishes the human being from the animal, the adult from the child, and in many cases the healthy personality from the sick (1955, p. 51)."

In addition to the seven aspects of the proprium just outlined, Allport felt there is a cognizing self, or *self as knower*, that transcends and oversees all the other propriate functions. In so doing, he raised an issue typically ignored by psychologists and confounded by philosophers. Cutting through mountains of obscure rhetoric with a good-natured appeal to common sense, Allport observed that something must be aware of the various aspects of the proprium just outlined. That something that promotes self-recognition and self-consciousness is the self as knower. This final aspect of the self or proprium is never experienced directly; however, it is a necessary inference based on everyday experience (this was Kant's position—see chapter two).

Allport's conception of the self, like his viewpoint concerning motivation, is complex and sometimes confusing. He felt, however, that this complexity was necessary in order to present an accurate image of human nature: "While it is surely the task of science to bring order among facts without needless proliferation of concepts, yet oversimplification brings discredit upon science, and psychology may succeed only in caricaturing human nature (1955, p. vii)."

EXPLANATION

Allport defined personality as ". . . the dynamic organization within the individual of those psychophysical systems that determine his characteristic behavior and thought (1961, p. 28)." As this definition suggests, Allport was not very interested in general laws of human nature. He explained the similarities among men (personality as *Personalität*) in terms of three sets of innate factors. The first are the instincts, that promote survival. The second are gene-linked characteristics normally associated with "family, stock, and race." Genes, for example, explain why we have two eyes, hair, and similar internal organs. The third set of innate factors are less obviously biological. According to Allport, every human infant has the capacity to learn, to develop a conscience, a sense of self, and a hierarchical organization of personal dispositions; each person is born with a propensity to become an organized, self-maintaining, and self-regulating being.

Allport believed that the major task of personality theory is to explain the organization and growth of the individual person. Uniqueness and organization can be explained in terms of the self-concept, the characteristic patterns of propriate striving. In particular, uniqueness can be described as the manner in which values, interests, and intentions are organized within each person. As Allport observed, values and intentions integrate biological impulses with social meanings to produce the distinctive marks of an individual personality. Intentions are an individual's primary means of orienting him or herself to the future, and "values are the termini of our intentions (1955, p. 90)." Values "... are unique for each person, and tend to attract, guide, inhibit the more elementary units to accord with the major intentions themselves (1955, p. 92)." Thus, intentions organize values, values organize interests, and each person's uniqueness is explained in terms of his particular hierarchy of intentions and values. If the word sentiment is substituted for value, Allport closely resembles McDougall in this aspect of explanation.

Allport was an academic rather than an applied or clinical psychologist, and perhaps for this reason he was not interested in the explanation of specific actions. In his discussion of values and intentions, however, there is a hint as to how he might have handled the problem. Because such men as Roald Amundsen live their lives primarily in the future in pursuit of certain overreaching goals, their present actions are means for achieving these goals. This must be a general rule. As Allport observed, "... recent empirical investigations have abundantly proved that personal values do in fact steer and select perceptions, judgments, and adjustments, although there is still inadequate recognition of the theoretical significance of this discovery (1955, p. 89)." Thus, specific actions can be explained in terms of the person's values or purposes, that always serve certain larger scale intentions. For Freud, Jung, and McDougall, values and intentions are discovered by interpretation. Allport, however, would simply ask the person what he intended on any particular occasion, and the answer would serve as an explanation of his actions.

SOCIALIZATION

Allport, like Freud and McDougall before him, understood the importance of socialization for personality development. As he stated, "... the primary problem in the psychology of becoming is to account for the transformation by which the unsocialized infant becomes an adult with structured loves, hates, loyalties, and interests, capable of taking his place in a complexly ordered society (1955, p. 29)."

Each infant is both socially dependent and utterly anarchistic. Even at age two when he is walking and trying to talk, the child is "an unsocialized horror" from whose depredations we are saved only by his size and incompetence. Unless the child's natural tendencies are radically altered, it will become a potentially evil adult; as Hobbes observed, the wicked man is but a child grown strong.

Drawing on the work of the ego-psychologists (see chapters four and eleven), Allport observed that serious disturbances in the early mother-child relationship through death, social dislocation, or maternal rejection are associated with various forms of anti-social conduct in later life. Thus, the process of socialization depends on an initial rapport between the child's needs for love and security and his social environment. If these needs are not met, a child will become hostile and aggressive. If, on the other hand, these early needs are adequately met, socialization will proceed naturally because conscience development is an innately regulated process.

Children need both affiliation (love and security) and autonomy. A child's early affiliative needs promote conformity to family and group norms. On the other hand, a child's needs for autonomy produce antagonism toward group pressures. Throughout later life a person must deal with tension produced by the contradictory needs for affiliation and autonomy. But the need for autonomy also provides a means by which one can resist the occasionally immoral demands of conventional society.

Conscience development undergoes a profound qualitative change over time. "Broadly speaking, we may consider the evolving conscience in childhood a *must* conscience, and the mature, adult form an *ought* conscience (1961, p. 134)." The child's *must* conscience evolves out of a combination of his affiliative needs and the expectations of his parents. This form of conscience corresponds to a Freudian superego. Gradually, as the self-image develops and the individual acquires personal ideals, the negative *must* conscience gives way to an autonomously directed conscience; the emphasis shifts from parental and social control to individual control, and as McDougall observed, the person may become a law unto himself. Thus, although theories of socialization derived from Freud tend to define it in terms of conformity, Allport, like McDougall, recognized the need for an element of autonomy in moral behavior.

THE UNCONSCIOUS

Throughout his career Allport felt ambivalent toward Freud and the concept of the unconscious. The term unconscious is not even mentioned in *Becoming* (1955), perhaps the most systematic single statement of Allport's overall point of view. The difference between Freud and Allport on this point is exemplified in an anecdote that the latter told about himself. In the summer of 1920, a year after finishing his undergraduate degree at Harvard, Allport was in Vienna visiting his brother. "With a callow forwardness," he wrote to Freud asking for an interview, that Freud graciously granted. Later, after Allport was seated in Freud's inner office, Freud merely gazed at him, silently but expectantly. Allport was apparently unprepared for this and somewhat desperately invented a conversational gambit. "I told him of an episode on the tram car on the way to his office. A small boy about four years of age had displayed a conspicuous dirt phobia. He kept saying to his mother, 'I don't want to sit there . . don't let that dirty man sit beside me.' " Because the boy's mother was a fastidious and domineering German mother, Allport thought the point of the story was obvious. Freud, however, observing the prim and compulsive young man sitting across from him, remarked, "And was that little boy you?" The experience made a great impression on Allport and ". . . taught me that depth psychology, for all its merits, may plunge too deep, and that psychologists would do well to give full recognition to manifest motives before probing the unconscious (1968, p. 384)." Even a critic of psychoanalysis might think that Allport missed the point and that Freud's comment was insightful and appropriate.

Allport's reluctant final position concerning the unconscious was that ". . . most of what goes on in our personalities belongs in some way to an unconscious stratum (1961, p. 140)." This raises a simple but crucial question: does the conscious mind *always* serve the needs of the unconscious, as Freud argued, or can consciousness serve needs of its own?

To answer this question, Allport adopted Freud's early topographic model in which the mind is depicted as having a conscious, a preconscious, and an unconscious level. Allport then argued that a normal person's thought is characterized by conscious dominance, with the preconscious providing the memories that are used in creative problem solving; the unconscious, according to Allport, plays only a small role in the lives of normal persons. Creative artists are characterized by preconscious dominance, while the conscious and unconscious layers of the mind play lesser roles. Among neurotics the unconscious is dominant and the preconscious and conscious portions are seriously reduced in their effectiveness. Thus, Allport concluded, Freud was correct in his analysis of the importance of unconscious processes in the mental lives of neurotics but wrong about unconscious dominance in normals. For Allport, then, there is no "psychopathology of everyday life."

PSYCHOLOGICAL HEALTH

Neurosis, according to Allport, is primarily the result of "poor mental hygiene." Neurotics may have been severely traumatized in the early portion of their lives by disturbed mother-child relations, or they may have strong escapist tendencies that lead them to protect their needs, impulses, and ideas from reality.

Although Allport was rather vague concerning the dynamics of neurosis, he was quite specific about the definition of a neurotic. A neurotic cannot engage in the sort of "balanced give-and-take" necessary for friendship, pleasant relations at work, and domestic happiness. He "... is demanding and possessive, jealous and self-pitying, hysteric and accusatory; he (she) may develop physical ('conversion') symptoms: ulcers, eczema, functional deafness, lameness, even paralysis. Although disorders of love life are often, perhaps always, involved, there are also other fierce but unguided motives in the neurotic pattern: hate, fear, resentment. The truest and most general statement about the neuroses seems to be that they are a reflection of uncontrolled self-centeredness. Someone has said that the neurotic will do anything to be loved except to make himself (herself) lovable (1961, p. 151)."

According to Freud, we are all somewhat neurotic. According to Allport, however, there is a "great gulf," a qualitative difference, between the neurotic and the normal personality. Neurotic behavior is dominated by the unconscious; it has a compulsive, driven, and self-defeating character about it, and the source of neurotic motivation is typically in the past. In contrast, the behavior of normal persons remains consciously directed, self-insightful, autonomous (as opposed to compulsive), and normal motivation lies primarily in the future.

Since the end of World War II there have been a number of empirical investigations of the nature of personal soundness. This research has yielded fairly consistent results, summarized by Allport in terms of six criteria of maturity.

The first criterion is called the capacity for self-extension. Children are naturally egocentric; but with maturity people acquire interests outside themselves, including concern for the welfare of others. In order to develop self-extension, one must authentically participate "in some significant sphere of human endeavor." One must be in Sartre's terms *engagé*, committed to some activity in the world. Those persons who display a high degree of personal soundness are involved in life. Thus, Allport concluded, "Everyone has self-love, but only self-extension is the earmark of maturity (1961, p. 285)."

The second criterion of personal maturity concerns the manner in which one relates to or interacts with other people. A mature person is capable of deep and intimate involvement with others, in particular with his family and friends. Although mature persons are involved with others, they are never intrusive or possessive. Rather they have a certain detachment and they appreciate the basic mortal condition of all men.

Allport called the capacity to form these kinds of relationships *compassion*, a quality that is achieved ". . . through an imaginative extension of one's own rougher experiences in life (1961, p. 285)." One becomes compassionate through personal suffering and the realization that ultimately the same fate awaits us all. The compassionate person is never a burden on others, nor does he interfere with their efforts to find their own identity. In contrast, immature persons are jealous, burdensome, and interfering; they want more love than they are willing to give, and when they do give love it is always conditional and on their own terms.

Allport called the third criterion of psychological health "emotional security." A mature person is able to endure the inevitable frustrations and irritations of life without losing his poise. It is not that these people are particularly calm, cheerful, and optimistic—on the contrary, they are often temperamental pessimists. Rather, they have learned not to regard every contretemps as a disaster and every personal slight as ultimate rejection. An immature adult, in contrast, reacts to frustrations and reversals with complaints, accusations, rage, and self-pity; he often acts as though he has "cornered the market on misery." Through self-acceptance and emotional security, mature people achieve a sense of proportion that permits them to take in stride the social, political, and financial reversals that are inevitable in life.

The fourth criterion of personal soundness is functional intelligence or "common sense." The ordinary thoughts and perceptions of mature people are on the whole accurate and efficient. This raises a question about the relationship between personal soundness and intelligence. Those who are mature are usually above average in intelligence, but persons who are above average in intelligence are not necessarily mature (Terman & Oden, 1947). Mature persons not only have a good deal of practical intelligence but also have the ability to solve objective problems posed by their life tasks. Finally, mature people are problem-centered and have the capacity to lose themselves in their work; like Michelangelo, Freud, Rembrandt, and Beethoven, they are consumed by their self-appointed tasks. And, according to Allport, such absorption in one's work reflects the presence of functionally autonomous motives.

The fifth characteristic of mature people is self-insight. Everyone thinks he is insightful, but that is not the case. Allport defined self-insight as ". . . the relation of what a man thinks he is to what others (especially the psychologist who studies him) think he is (1961, p. 291)." Insightful people are aware of their own disagreeable qualities and try not to project them on others. They are also likeable, above average in intelligence, and good judges of other people. Perhaps the most important correlate of self-insight, however, is a sense of humor. A sense of humor—the ability to laugh at the things one loves (including oneself) and still love them—must be distinguished from the cruder sense of the comic. Almost everyone, including children, has a comic sense, a thinly disguised vehicle for sexual and aggressive impulses that typically leads to the degradation of someone else. Self-insight and the sense of humor ultimately rest on the capacity to be objective about oneself, on a sense of proportion about one's talents, ambitions, and goals. In contrast with he self-insight of the mature person, the immature person often appears pretentious and yet unaware that his posing is both obvious and unappealing. Everyone pretends to some degree to be something or someone he is not, but insight and humor are effective checks for such egotism.

Allport's final criterion for psychological health was anticipated by both Jung and McDougall: it is called *directedness*, a translation of the German term *Bestimmung*. It refers to the fact that the lives of mature persons are ". . . ordered or steered toward some selected goal or goals. Each person has something quite special to live for, a major intention (1961, pp. 294–95)." In Jung's terms, one who has *Bestimmung* has achieved self-hood; McDougall would explain directedness in terms of a hierarchy of values (sentiments) organized under a master sentiment. According to Allport, directedness comes from a unifying philosophy of life, under which one's values, goals, and intentions are organized. The most important source of a philosophy of life, according to Allport, is religion. Like Jung, he thought a religious sentiment was a universal trait in all adults. "The developed religious sentiment is the synthesis of . . . many . . . factors, all of which form a comprehensive attitude whose function it is to relate the individual to the whole of being (1955, p. 94)." Such a sense of relatedness to the "whole of being" is only possible in adulthood. Allport used the term religious sentiment very broadly. "Psychologically speaking we should point to the close analogy that exists between a religious orientation and all other high-level schemata that influence the course of becoming. Every man, whether he is religiously inclined or not, has his own ultimate presuppositions. He finds he cannot live his life without them, and for him they are true. Such presuppositions, whether they be called ideologies, philosophies, notions, or merely hunches about life, exert creative pressure upon all conduct that is subsidiary to them (which is to say, upon nearly *all* of a man's conduct) (1955, pp. 95–96)." Thus a well-developed code of moral conduct (that Allport called a "generic conscience") may also become a unifying philosophy of life.

To summarize this discussion of psychological health, Allport outlined six criteria of maturity that seem to contain the essence of previous research on the subject. These criteria were: *engagement* (self-extension), compassion, emotional security, functional intelligence, self-insight, and

directedness. Although no one individual will possess all these characteristics, together they convey the meaning of psychological health.

EVALUATION

It is appropriate at this point to offer an evaluation of Allport's
contribution to the personological tradition, beginning with some negative comments. First, Allport seems not to have understood the purpose
of science. For example, a major goal of the social sciences is to explain
social behavior. Allport thought the goal was to explain individuality.
This led him to the concept of the functional autonomy of adult motives, a notion that is logically circular and antiscientific in spirit. Science attempts to reduce events at one level of observation to events at
a different level. Reduction has to stop somewhere; but Allport's concept
of functional autonomy prevents it from ever getting started, since,
according to him, functionally autonomous motives cannot be traced
back to childhood experiences. The concept of functional autonomy
makes the search for causal variables underlying adult behavior meaningless in principle.

Allport's greatest strength—his humanism—was also his greatest
weakness and the source of a second flaw in his thinking. The essence
of humanism is the defense and celebration of the individual; the essence of science, however, is the search for generality. For the scientist,
the individual case is important only in so far as it provides information
about more universal principles. When science is used for the benefit of
the individual, it has humanistic consequences; but the goals of creative
science and traditional humanism are fundamentally incompatible. Thus,
Allport's criticism of the behavioristic psychology of the 1940s and 50s
stems from his desire to preserve the individual rather than from a
belief that such behaviorism would not advance psychological understanding.

Third, the clarity of Allport's writing paradoxically obscures some
real confusion in his thinking. As we noted earlier, he ignores the distinction between biogenic (instincts, drives) and psychogenic (values,
intentions) motives. He also confounds the meaning of the word *trait*.
Traits refer to things people do, or are likely to do, at repeated intervals;
they are labels for describing distinctive properties of people's behavior.
Yet Allport called them motives that arise from underlying neural mechanisms. He erroneously ascribed causal status to purely descriptive terms.
Moreover, although Allport thought through the problem of the self

with a great deal of scholarly energy, many of his distinctions overlap so that his stages are rather difficult to perceive clearly. Furthermore, he assigned motivational properties to the self-concept (e.g., propriate striving). Thus, in discussing motivation, Allport mixed together cognition, biology, physiology, the self-concept, and overt behavior, and in the end the term *motivation* had lost any distinctive conceptual properties.

On the positive side, Allport's position is unique with regard to four of the six root ideas. He has more to say about the self (proprium) than Freud, Jung, or McDougall. His ideas about motivation, particularly the notion of assigning causal status to cognitive variables and of functional autonomy, also contrast markedly with Freud and the tradition of depth psychology. Although Allport failed to discuss openly the concept of explanation, he implied an interesting solution to the problem in terms of values, intentions, and their organization, a solution that resembles that of McDougall. Finally, Allport's discussion of psychological health is the most sophisticated in the personological tradition.

Second, Allport maintained that values are the most stable, enduring, and determinative aspect of personality. Research in conjunction with the *Strong Vocational Interest Blank* (Strong, 1966), Holland's theory of vocational choice (Holland, 1966), and Allport's own *Study of Values* (Allport, Vernon, and Lindzey, 1970) strongly supports him in this claim. That is, values seem extraordinarily stable over time and permit one to make a wide range of predictions about various aspects of an individual's social performance (Hall and MacKinnon, 1969). Allport was unique in his insistence on the explanatory importance of values, and his insistence seems to have been well-founded.

Third, like McDougall, Allport clearly understood that, although theories of socialization since Freud leave the individual committed to the status quo, one must occasionally oppose the conventional norms of society. McDougall's observations on autonomy, however, were nonnormative; he merely observed that autonomous people exist from time to time. Allport's humanism insured that his observations would carry a normative thrust; the ideas of justice and democracy require autonomous people to preserve them from the encroachments of the technocracy. And Allport's many civil libertarian activities during his life suggest that he was part of that small group of teachers who use their theories as a basis for personal action.

In view of the criticisms raised above, one might ask how Allport became the dean of American personality psychology. Whatever his limitations as a systematic thinker, he was considerably better than his competition. He was a fine writer, a man of unusual learning and scholarship; and, perhaps more than any other person of his generation, he clearly saw that the major issues in the psychology of personality are motivation, the self-concept, socialization, the unconscious, explanation, and psychological health. At a time when American psychology was preoccupied with behaviorism and the experimental psychology of the white rat, Allport was almost alone in his attempt to call psychologists back to the study of the person. This fact seems to be a major and justifiable source of his subsequent reputation.

chapter eight

George Kelly

Three features of George Kelly's intellectual biography are distinctive. First, in contrast with Freud, Jung, and McDougall who were psychiatrists, and Gordon Allport who was a scholar, Kelly was a practicing clinical psychologist. Like many clinical psychologists in America, he rejected both the biological orientation of the medical tradition and the behaviorism that characterizes much academic psychology. Unlike many of his contemporaries, he took a markedly cognitive approach to the study of personality and social interaction.

Second, and in further contrast with Freud, Jung, McDougall and Allport, Kelly spent most of his life in the Midwest, removed from what is (sometimes incorrectly) seen as the mainstream of intellectual life in America. This partially explains his originality and the homely, down to earth tone of his writings; compared with Kelly's common sense, psychoanalysis seems effete and almost byzantine. On the other hand, Kelly sometimes resembles the character in Sartre's novel *Nausea* whose education consisted of reading his way through the public library from A to Z; at the time we meet him he has just reached the P's. There were gaps in Kelly's knowledge that, if filled, would have greatly strengthened his position; specifically, Kelly seemed unaware of the relationships

George Kelly
Photograph by Ralph Norman

between his ideas and those, for example, of George Herbert Mead and Georg Simmel. Recent Kelly enthusiasts claim to find parallels between Kelly's ideas and those of such diverse figures as Chomsky (1968), Vygotsky (1962), and Wittgenstein (1953) (Shotter, 1970). These parallels refer to Kelly's notion that each person develops a set of rules for thinking about the world and then uses these rules to organize his life.

Finally, in contrast with the prolific writing careers of Freud, Jung, McDougall, and Allport, Kelly's reputation rests almost exclusively on a single two-volume book, *The Psychology of Personal Constructs*, published in 1955. Bannister (1970, pp. vii–viii) comments on the book's reception:

> The fate of personal construct theory, since its formal presentation in 1955, has been strange in that it has had neither the kinds of acceptance nor the kinds of rejection that are customary for new ideas in the field. It has not, like "notions" such as cognitive dissonance . . . had any fashionable flowering. It has not, like learning theory, ingested a multitude of issues to seep on, contorted but vastly influential. It has not, like the Allportian psychology of the individual, stood admired and unused. Rather it has had a slow, almost unvarying momentum, such that uses of it and curiosity about it mount steadily.

In *The Psychology of Personal Constructs* Kelly proposed a theory of psychotherapy and personality designed to contrast as strongly as possible with psychoanalysis and traditional depth psychology; with his concept of "man the scientist" Kelly attempted nothing less than a complete reconstruction of his field. The theory is framed in terms of a peculiar vocabulary that he invented and presented in the form of some

115

of the most awkward prose since Carl Jung. Within the context of psychology in the 1950s, however, his theory is quite original. Unfortunately for the historian, Kelly's originality makes it difficult to trace the origins of his intellectual development. Two influences on his thought seem reasonably apparent, however: phenomenology and existentialism (to be discussed in greater detail in chapter 10). As Murphy and Kovach (1972) note, after World War II and particularly during the 1950s, "a great wave of phenomenology and existentialism" flooded the thinking of American psychiatrists and psychologists. Kelly developed his ideas during this period. His insistence that the therapist must understand his patient's world view, that the patient's life is not determined by his past, and his interest in Jacob Moreno (1934) and fixed role therapy clearly reveal his phenomenological and existentialist perspective (see also, Holland, 1970).

MOTIVATION

Kelly is perhaps best known for his repudiation of the concept of motivation. He criticized this concept for three reasons. First, he pointed out that many psychologists perceive man as inert unless a force of some sort acts upon him. These "special enlivening forces" are called *motives, needs,* or *drives.* But, Kelly argued, if we simply assume that man is active because he is alive, then motivational concepts that "explain" activity are pointless.

Kelly's second objection to the concept of motivation came from his experience as a practicing therapist. He concluded that it makes little difference, in terms of helping a client, whether or not one attributes a set of motives to him. Motivational concepts are interpretations that a therapist places on his patient's actions. They may be useful for *predicting* someone's behavior (e.g., Jack is lazy and, therefore, probably won't do his job), but they are useless for *understanding* and subsequently helping that person, because they reflect the way the therapist rather than the patient thinks about the world.

Finally, Kelly observed that motivational statements typically tell more about the speaker than about the person whose motives are in question. "When we find a person who is concerned about motives, he usually turns out to be one who is threatened by his fellowmen and wants to put them in their place (Kelly, 1969, p. 77)."

By repudiating the concept of motivation Kelly intended to be radical; however, he was unable to maintain this position consistently; and in fact he had an implicit theory of motivation. As Shotter (1970) observes, Kelly's model of man is that of a man with a model. For Kelly, the man on the street is a practicing scientist, attempting to understand certain aspects of his experience so that he can control them. As the biologist tries to conceptualize the mechanisms of genetic transmission, so the ordinary man tries to make sense of his social encounters. It follows that we wish to understand our environment, to formulate means for ordering the chaos around us. As Kelly observed, "Like the prototype of the scientist that he is, man seeks prediction. His structured network of pathways [conceptualizations of reality] leads toward the future so that he may anticipate it. This is the function it serves. Anticipation is both the push and the pull of the psychology of personal constructs... (1955, p. 49)." Thus, Kelly assumed that "man the scientist" needs structure, order, and predictability in his world.

Kelly's criticisms of conventional motivational theory (both of the biogenic and the psychogenic variety) seem well founded. Because man is naturally active the concept of motivation is redundant, motivational concepts are of little practical use in psychotherapy, and such concepts are typically used for polemical rather than therapeutic purposes. Nonetheless, Kelly was forced to include a minimal motivational consideration in his theory. Man *needs* to predict or anticipate what will happen to him. Man's construction of reality, the conceptual models of external events that he develops, give him this capability.

SOCIALIZATION AND THE SELF-CONCEPT

To understand Kelly's analysis of socialization and the self-concept, we must briefly review his theory of human thought. The theory is quite formal, and the key idea is "the construct," one's interpretation of his past experience that is then used to anticipate or predict future experience. "A construct is a way in which some things are construed as being alike and yet different from others (1955, p. 105)." Kelly's fundamental postulate states that what one does (one's "psychological processes") is determined ("channelized") by the constructs he has developed to predict recurring features of his experience. Kelly described the process of formulating constructs with eleven corollaries that can be summarized as follows. The individuality corollary refers to the fact that people usually interpret the same events differently; the Japanese play *Rashoman* dramatizes this corollary. The organizational corollary holds that people organize their constructs into hierarchies so that the more general constructs take in those that are more specific. Kelly's organizational corollary is similar to McDougall's notion of the hierarchical organization of sentiments. The next two corollaries maintain that constructs themselves are dichotomous, but each end of the dichotomy, however, is unique. If a patient perceives his father as hostile, this means that hostility is one pole of a construct that he uses to predict the behavior of others. The opposite pole of the hostility construct, however, must still be discovered; by calling his father hostile, we can infer only that the patient regards some people (possibly just himself) in other than hostile terms (e.g., benevolent, compassionate, rational).

In a seemingly arbitrary corollary, Kelly maintained that people typically act so as to extend and define their construct systems. But it is not clear why people should try to extend and define their ideas unless they have self-actualizing tendencies, a subject that Kelly never discussed.

Each construct has a specific set of events to which it best applies; each refers to a finite range of phenomena. Next, a person's constructs normally change as he interprets new experience. The permeability corollary states that the amount that a construct system will change, however, depends on the "permeability" of its constructs; that is, some constructs are more easily changed than others. Finally, people often use, in succession, constructs that are logically incompatible—the observer's logic is not the same as the logic of the observed. For the individual, mutually exclusive constructs can coexist nicely.

The preceding paragraphs summarize Kelly's nine corollaries regarding thought. His remaining two corollaries provide the key to the socialization process. The first, Kelly's commonality corollary, states that when people construe (interpret) their experiences similarly, their "psychological processes" (behavior) tend to be similar. Thus, if people interpret events in the same way, they will tend to respond alike.

Kelly's sociality corollary states that to interact effectively with another person one need not construe experience as the other does so much as one must construe his viewpoint and expectations. As Kelly remarked, "In order to play a constructive role in relation to another person one must not only . . . see eye to eye with him [share common constructs] but must . . . have an acceptance of him and his way of seeing things." Thus, ". . . social psychology must be a psychology of interpersonal understandings, not merely a psychology of common understandings (1955, p. 95)." His "sociality corollary" refers to the processes underlying social cohesion: organized society depends on people construing the outlooks of one another.

We may construe or anticipate the thoughts of others at several levels. Highway traffic is a social process that requires only superficial anticipation of other people's behavior. In order to live harmoniously with another person, mutual understanding must go much deeper.

This extended discussion is a means of introducing Kelly's most important concepts: the notions of role and role construct. In the earlier part of his career Kelly called his theory role theory. He later chose the title personal construct theory to avoid confusion with sociological role theory. For the sociologists a role is a unit of the social structure to which individuals are recruited (e.g., military officer, president, witch doctor). Kelly, however, defined a role as ". . . an ongoing pattern of behavior that follows from a person's understanding of how the others who are associated with him in his task think (1955, pp. 97–98)." Constructs that refer to the outlooks and expectations of other people are called *role constructs*, and whatever we do in the light of these role constructs (i.e., our understanding of the expectations of others) is called a *role*. The role is Kelly's unit of social interaction—social interaction proceeds in terms of roles—and socialization is defined in terms of the number of roles a person can play effectively.

Several points about Kelly's concept of role need further clarification. First, roles reflect a person's construct system, they are actions that are guided by one's understanding of the attitudes of one's associates, regardless of the accuracy of this understanding. Second, role playing is by definition social behavior, for it only occurs in a social context. Third, when two people interact, one may play a role (i.e., guide his actions in terms of his understanding of the other) while the other does not. The one who plays a role treats the other as a person; the one who does not play a role treats the other as an object and dehumanizes him. Finally, role-relationships depend not on commonality of construct systems but on mutual understanding. "To the extent that people understand each other . . . their activities in relation to each other may be called *roles,* a role being a course of activity which is played out in the light of one's understanding of the behavior of one or more people (1955, pp. 99–100)."

Although construing another person's viewpoint provides a basis for a role relationship, it does not necessarily mean that we will conform to that person's expectations. On the contrary, understanding another person's outlook also provides us with an opportunity to take advantage of him if we wish.

According to Kelly, the self-concept is also an interpretation of our experiences; it concerns how we are the same and how we differ from others, and it results in our seeing ourselves as distinct from other people. Because the self-construct is formed out of comparisons between ourselves and others, much of our social life is controlled by it. Consequently, as ". . . one construes other people, he [necessarily] formulates the construction system which governs his own behavior. . . . One cannot call another person a bastard without making bastardy a dimension of his life also (1955, p. 133)."

Kelly's discussion of social interaction seems, on the surface, quite commonsensical; productive relationships with other people require that we envision in advance the other person's outlook and guide our own actions accordingly. That is, in order to predict the behavior of others, we must anticipate their expectancies concerning ourselves. But this seemingly simple situation rapidly becomes complex, because other people's expectancies largely rest on their understanding of us. Thus, what we do often depends on what we think other people expect of us based on their image or construction of us. This immediately leads to a situation characterized by "I think that he thinks that I think, etc..." Role-playing therefore is a complex, double-contingency relationship.

We can now summarize Kelly's discussion of socialization. Socialization refers to the ability to play roles effectively, to take part in society. There are three requirements for full socialization. First, a person's construct system must be similar to those of the other members of his society; commonality of construct systems is one characteristic of socialization. Second, a socialized person understands the expectations of others, he can envision their outlooks: he has developed an adequate supply of role constructs. Third, a socialized person has developed a self-construct that controls his behavior *vis à vis* others. On the other hand, the construct system of a delinquent should differ markedly from those of nondelinquents. Delinquents have distorted self-constructs that ineffectively or incorrectly guide their behavior; but most importantly, the role systems of delinquents are underdeveloped, which means that they cannot construe the expectations of others. In this way they treat other persons as objects rather than subjects. Consider, for example, the attitudes of the American soldiers who took part in the My Lai massacre. From retrospective accounts it is clear that the soldiers involved considered the Vietnamese to be less than human—objects rather than subjects. This accounts for much of their behavior. Kelly once observed that a psychopath is like a stimulus-response psychologist who takes his theory seriously; i.e., psychopaths, like serious Skinnerians, attempt to manipulate others exclusively through rewards and punishments.

Thus, socialization consists of the ability to construe events as do the other members of one's culture, to make comparisons between oneself and others, and to interpret the outlooks of others. We may ask, however, why one would act in accordance with these socialized perceptions. Although we have described the characteristic features of socialization, we have said nothing about its dynamics. There are, according to Kelly, essentially two sets of pressures that produce socialized behavior. First, Kelly conceived modern society as a matrix of dependencies (1969, p. 191); people need one another, and the operation of society rests on these interdependencies. Relations among interdependent people break down, however, when they stop being concerned with one another's outlooks. Thus, socialized behavior is partially a function of the interdependencies of modern man; and people conform to socialized perceptions for pragmatic reasons—it is the only way they can live together productively.

But there is a more psychological reason for socialized conduct. According to Kelly, it is intrinsically satisfying to have one's predictions about other people confirmed. We have certain ideas about what others expect of us. When we act in accordance with these ideas and discover that we have correctly predicted the expectations of others, we are strongly encouraged toward further socialized behavior. Generally speaking then, Kelly felt that socialized conduct makes life more livable and predictable; such behavior is in a sense its own reward.

In contrast with most of the writers covered in this book, Kelly did not discuss the relationship between socialization and morality, an omission that is significant in itself. It seems reasonable to infer that he would regard the moral standards of a society as being defined in terms of the expectations of its members. Thus he would equate morality with social conventions and be left with an apparently unqualified commitment to the status quo.

EXPLANATION

Kelly handles the problem of explanation better than any writer since McDougall, and this may be his major contribution to the personological tradition. That this has not been more widely recognized reflects the degree to which both Kelly and the problem of explanation have been misunderstood.

Kelly explained the similarities in human conduct in terms of his implicit motivational assumption: we all need predictability and order in our lives. We are all alike in that we build conceptual models to represent our experience, test these models against further experience, and then use them to understand the world. Although the models will differ from person to person, the motives that produce them are apparently universal.

Individual differences arise because we all construe our experiences differently. Kelly, however, was not particularly concerned with explaining individual differences and considered people who were (e.g., Allport) as rather confused: "One cannot help but be reminded, at this point, of those psychologists and others who insist that everyone is an 'individual' and that we cannot understand one individual through understanding other individuals. Here is a form of conceptual distortion which seems to betray the particular scientist's deeply rooted confusion about what to do about 'people' (1955, p. 113)" Kelly also considered the idiographic-nomothetic problem that so preoccupied Allport to be a red herring: "Anyone who has tried very hard to understand the human personality has not spent much time wondering if people really are different from each other. For him the problem has been, rather, how to transcend the uniqueness of man in order to see him in terms of a comprehensive system simple enough to be understood (1969, p. 117)." Kelly felt any person could be adequately understood in terms of twenty-five or thirty constructs, only a few of which will be unique to that person.

Kelly explained specific actions in terms of roles and role constructs. According to him, social behavior proceeds in terms of role sequences and is explained in terms of role constructs—the role is the basic unit of analysis and the role construct is the basic explanatory concept.

Constructs are the rules that govern our social conduct; they explain our behavior by showing that it is intelligible. For Freud, social behavior is explained when it can be derived from (or interpreted in terms of) certain general psychoanalytic principles; for Kelly, however, behavior is explained when it is shown to be intelligible from the perspective of the individual actor.

Kelly's model of explanation, however, does not depend on intuition and nonempirical procedures. To explain a person's behavior the investigator must discover how that person construes his relations with others. Since people are often deceived about the reasons for their actions, and since they may try to deceive others as well, it may be very difficult to determine how a person actually views his interpersonal relations. The primary purpose of Kelly's theory as outlined in his two-volume book is to show how these determinations can be made. Kelly intended *The Psychology of Personal Constructs* to be a handbook for clinical psychologists; the theory of personality was almost an afterthought—it occupies only three of the book's twenty-two chapters. His book is a "guide to careful listening"; it shows the clinician what to look for in trying to discover why a person construes his experiences as he does.

Kelly's interpretive guidelines are too subtle to summarize here. Any remark of a client can be interpreted in several ways, and each interpretation is potentially of great importance for understanding that person. To determine the true meaning of a statement, the investigator must listen carefully and base his interpretations on what he knows about the way the speaker regards the world. Because each person has a unique construct system that cannot be clearly expressed, ". . . each study of an individual becomes a problem in concept formation for the psychologist. [Moreover, after] he has conceptualized each of his cases, he next has the task of further abstracting the individual constructs in order to produce constructs which underlie people in general (1955, p. 43)."

THE UNCONSCIOUS

Kelly thought Freud's concept of the unconscious was too imprecise to be useful for anything other than descriptive purposes. Instead he proposed that constructs can be arranged along a continuum of "cognitive awareness." Three kinds of constructs are characterized by low cognitive awareness and can be described as "unconscious." These are "preverbal constructs," constructs that have been "submerged," and those that have been "suspended."

Constructs are usually symbolized by words. As long as constructs are symbolized, they can be used, modified, and revised. Preverbal constructs, however, are formulated before a person has language; thus they typically involve such considerations as dependency, security, nurturance, that are most appropriate to young children. It is difficult to explain one's behavior if it is guided by preverbal constructs, because there are no words to symbolize the constructs that are in use. Consequently, preverbal constructs seem unconscious.

Every construct has two ends. "There is the *likeness* and the *contrast* end. Sometimes one of these two ends is less available than the other. When this is markedly true we may refer to the less available end as the *submerged* end (1955, p. 467)." It sometimes happens, according to Kelly, that people dwell obsessively on a theme (e.g., "Everyone has always been good to me") until one is forced to conclude that the other end of the construct (in this case the opposite of "goodness") is submerged; and submerged concepts seem to be unconscious.

The concept of *submergence* sounds like Freudian repression; however, Kelly referred to repression with the concept of *suspension*. If old ways of construing experience are replaced by new ones, the specific elements of the old construct system will be lost unless they have a place within the new system. "Our theory does not place the emphasis upon remembering what is pleasant or forgetting what is unpleasant; rather, it emphasizes that one remembers what is structured and forgets what is unstructured. In contrast with some notions of repression, suspension implies that the idea or element of experience is forgotten simply because the person can, at the moment, tolerate no structure within which the idea would have meaning. Once he can entertain such a structure the idea may become available within it (1955, p. 473)."

PSYCHOLOGICAL HEALTH

Kelly was primarily concerned with developing a theory of therapy; as a result, his ideas about psychological health must be inferred from his analysis of the causes of neurosis.

A major source of psychological stress comes from the interdependent nature of modern life; each of our friendships has a specialized function (e.g., we have friends with whom we play tennis, friends with whom we discuss politics, and so on). We in turn provide only specialized support to our friends. Thus, we are forced to be keenly aware of what we can offer to others in return for their support if our network of reciprocal supplies and demands is to operate effectively. "Yet so complex is the typical dependency matrix that rarely do two partners match themselves so well that each supplies all the wants of the other. What more often happens is that the reciprocal dependency breaks down, leaving one person clinging and wistful where the other is restless and impatient (1969, p. 191)."

It follows that dependencies are inevitable, and the manner in which they are handled is crucial. Generally speaking, neurotics do not handle their dependencies well; they tend to be either overly dependent or insensitive to the needs of others.

People typically consult psychotherapists because they are anxious and unhappy. Anxiety results when people are unable to comprehend experience in terms of their constructs. According to Kelly, anxiety is an important stimulus for reorganizing one's constructs. Since this is the primary goal of psychotherapy, anxiety should often be encouraged.

Persons who seem neurotic from a conventional psychiatric perspective have, according to Kelly, incorrectly interpreted or construed their social experience. Neurotics are like bad scientists: their predictions are wrong and they don't know why. Psychotherapy consists of persuading people to challenge, reformulate, and update their constructs. At the deepest level psychotherapy entails modifying and replacing "core constructs," those that are most central to the way one has interpreted his social experience. It won't do for the therapist to point out new ways of construing the world; the client must formulate the new constructs for himself. Kelly's method for helping his clients to develop and test new constructs is ingenious. They pretend to be someone else in their interactions with the therapist; in this way they may safely experiment with new roles. To the degree that thought follows behavior, new role constructs will tend to follow from different role performances. Kelly called this technique "fixed-role enactment." The role-playing session in psychotherapy provides an opportunity for a person to try out new roles without being criticized.

For Kelly one's personality is like a suit of clothes; if it does not fit one should try on a new one. It seems somewhat bizarre to imagine people taking on and shedding personalities to keep up with changes in their social circumstances, but there is an element of good sense in Kelly's method of therapy. If one wants to improve one's tennis game, for example, one can practice and/or take lessons before playing competitively. But what about one's social game—one's personality? When do we have a chance to practice or get coaching since we are always apparently playing for real? This was Kelly's insight—his clients were encouraged to try out new ways of presenting themselves, to experiment with new roles as a means of gaining perspective concerning their former roles. A meek and anxious person can practice being forceful, as the bumptious bigot can practice tolerance, achieving in the process some awareness concerning the inappropriate features of his role performances.

We now can discuss the characteristics of psychological health from Kelly's perspective. Healthy persons are willing to evaluate their constructs and to test the validity of their interpretations of other people. Such people test the predictions derived from their constructions. Second, healthy people are able to change their constructs and reorient their role systems when they appear invalid. In Kelly's terminology, their constructs are "permeable"; in ordinary language, they can admit when they are wrong. The third characteristic of psychological health is a desire to extend the range, scope, and coverage of one's construction system. In other words, healthy people are always open to possibilities for personal growth.

The final characteristic of personal soundness is a well-developed repertoire of roles; one is psychologically healthy if he can play many social roles and comprehend the perspectives of his counterplayers. Many people regard role-playing as dissembling, as somehow falsifying oneself. Kelly (1969, pp. 157–58) was amused by this attitude:

A good deal is said these days about being oneself ... While it is a little hard for me to understand how one could be anything else, I suppose what is meant is that one should not strive to become anything other than what he is. This strikes me as a very dull way of living ... There is another meaning that might be attached to this admonition to be oneself ... It is presumed that the person who faces the world barefaced is more spontaneous, that he expresses himself more fully, and that he has a better chance of developing all his resources if he assumes no disguises ... It might be helpful ... to ask ourselves a question about children at Halloween. Is the little youngster who comes to your door ... all dressed up in his costume and behind a mask ... disguising himself or is he revealing himself? Is he failing to be spontaneous? . . . Which is the *real* child—the child behind the mask or the barefaced child who must stand up in front of adults and say "please" and "thank you"?

There are two interesting contrasts between Kelly and Freud concerning psychological health. First, Freud's perspective was historical; unconscious emotions and events from one's past that remain active in the present are the cause of neurosis. Kelly's approach, however, was ahistorical: since one's interpretations of the world can always be revised, no one is a victim of his biography, and there are no infantile traumas to be "worked through." Second, for Freud a patient's symptoms can be interpreted best by his analyst; for Kelly, it is the patient who ultimately provides the interpretation—the therapist is merely a guide in the interpretive process.

EVALUATION

We now may appraise briefly George Kelly's contribution to the personological tradition. Three aspects of Kelly's overall discussion are problematical. First, his account of the dynamics of the socialization process is inadequate. As he observed, socialization depends in part on a disposition to construe the outlooks of other people, to anticipate their expectations about one's own conduct. But one must also be willing to do what he thinks others expect of him. The reasons Kelly gives for people complying with the expectations of others—because in the long run it is in their best interests to do so—are unconvincing. For example, most delinquents know their antisocial behavior is not in their best interests, and they don't care.

Second (and related to the first problem), Kelly assumed that people always act in their own best interests if given the opportunity to do so; maladaptive or self-destructive behavior is seen as the result of an honest mistake in the way the environment has been construed. Kelly's assumption ignores the problem of self-deception and the unconscious determinants of behavior that, as Freud and many others have suggested, lead almost everyone into occasional episodes of self-defeating conduct.

A third problem concerns Kelly's treatment of the concept of motivation. Although his criticisms of the concept are well-taken, his substantive contribution to the topic is inadequate. He uses the term in a vague and inconsistent manner; and, although understanding it, he routinely confounds the distinction between biogenic and psychogenic motives. Moreover, it is one thing to say man is always active; it is quite another thing to say he is always active for the same reasons.

Three aspects of Kelly's theory are particularly noteworthy. First, he was surprisingly successful in his attempt to be original. He formulated the root ideas, especially explanation and psychological health, in a unique and distinctive fashion. Moreover, his ideas (like those of McDougall) show almost no trace of Freud's influence—a remarkable accomplishment in view of the enormous influence of Freud's writing.

Second, Kelly was one of the few persons who has provided a fully psychological theory of psychopathology. With certain exceptions, theories of abnormal psychological functioning typically make use of such biological or physiological mechanisms as repressed instincts, neurophysiological anomalies, biochemical malfunctioning, and genetic predispositions. Kelly, however, derived the phenomena of neurotic symptoms from a purely psychological model of human thought.

Third, Kelly understood and analyzed the problem of explanation more clearly than anyone since McDougall, and this may be his most important contribution. He provided an entirely new model for understanding and explaining human conduct that assures him an important place in the personological tradition.

Granting the importance of Kelly's contribution, his writings nonetheless make me uncomfortable. My feelings about Kelly are expressed concisely in Bertrand Russell's (1945, p. 184) comment on Aristotle's ethics, presented below with suitable paraphrases:

> More generally, there is an emotional poverty in the [Psychology of Personal Constructs], which is not found in the earlier [writers]. There is something unduly smug and comfortable about [Kelly's] speculations on human affairs; everything that makes men feel a passionate interest in each other seems to be forgotten. Even his account of friendship is tepid. He shows no sign of having had any of those experiences which make it difficult to preserve sanity; all the more profound aspects of the moral life are apparently unknown to him. He leaves out, one may say, the whole sphere of human experience with which religion is concerned. What he has to say is what will be useful to comfortable men of weak passions; but he has nothing to say to those who are possessed by a god or a devil, or whom outward misfortune drives to despair.

Alternatively, these same considerations may account for the enduring appeal of Freud and Jung.

chapter nine

The Sociological Perspective

Sociology can be described as the study of social groups and their processes. Since most of what we do takes place within the context of these groups, and since most of our attitudes, values, and ideas are shaped by them (i.e., by our families, friends, etc.), the sociological perspective is clearly relevant to an analysis of the nature of personality. Psychologists tend to regard sociology with indifference. This indifference is not a function of subject matter, because psychology and sociology actually overlap a great deal; it seems to result from entirely different assumptions about the basic nature of man. Psychology primarily reflects an individualistic viewpoint. This perspective stems from a widespread reaction in seventeenth-century Europe against medieval culture; the reaction stressed rationalism, individualism, and progress, and it portrayed society as a collection of individual persons, each pursuing his own enlightened self-interest. According to this view, societies serve the purposes of self-determined individuals. People existed before there were societies and the individual is the irreducible unit on which they depend. Mechanisms of social control (culture) have evolved to limit the less agreeable aspects of human nature, but these mechanisms or social institutions are typically seen as necessary evils that promote the common good. Freud was an eloquent spokesman for this view of the relationship between man and society.

Sociology developed in the mid-nineteenth century in part as a reaction against the individualistic perspective that tends to characterize psychology; that is, against rationalism and the notion that a healthy society can emerge from an aggregate of individuals pursuing their enlightened self-interest. From a sociological perspective social institutions are not necessary evils; rather, they give meaning and purpose to human life. Self-development and personal fulfillment are only possible within the context of viable society.

Sociology is rooted in the philosophy of Georg Hegel. According to Hegel, the conceptual structure of nature can be defined in terms of the Absolute. The Absolute is like a transcendental or all-embracing mind (*objektiver Geist*) whose development is seen in the course of history, primarily in the history of the states. Individual men are creatures of the State and, indirectly, of the Absolute, whose evolution determines all human activity in advance. As a result Hegel was interested in individuals only to the degree that they reflect the world spirit or Absolute; the individual has no more significance for a (Hegelian) sociologist than a particular stone in an avalanche has for a geologist.

Emile Durkheim and George Herbert Mead—major figures in the sociological tradition—are representatives of that viewpoint. Durkheim was a French sociologist, Mead was an American philosopher, and both were strongly influenced by Hegel. They both regarded society as coming before individuals. They assumed that each person is born into an ongoing social process that controls the existence of individual minds, selves, and personalities.

From a psychological perspective, then, societies are created by individuals and exist for their benefit. For the sociologist, the individualism of psychology is symptomatic of advanced social decay. Man has a deep, organic need for his culture; culture does not exist for the convenience of individuals but gives form, meaning, and substance to an otherwise empty human existence. Consequently, the needs of society come before the needs of an individual, and an individual achieves meaning only within the context of society.

To clarify more fully the differences between a sociological and a psychological perspective on human nature, it would be useful to review the events that initially stimulated the study of sociology. Early sociological theory can be seen as a response to the French and Industrial Revolutions (Nisbet, 1966); and these two historical phenomena served extensively to promote modern individualism. The Industrial Revolution had three major consequences for Western societies. First, it transformed the basic nature of work. Craftsmen and farmers were turned into mere "hands"—anonymous workers filling slots at machines; their work was degraded, being taken out of the context of family and village where it had had meaning. For many people work became alienating because it was unrelated to the other aspects of their lives. Second, the Industrial Revolution transformed the basic social relationship between men from mutual trust and interdependency to self-interest and cash payment. Third, the Industrial Revolution destroyed the traditional associations between organized human communities and their territories. This happened primarily through the growth of urban industrial centers and their slums. People moved onto impersonal pieces of land that were (and are) incapable of inspiring the personal allegiance that leads to social stability; it was hard for people to identify with the backyard of a rowhouse in an industrial slum.

The French Revolution had an equally dramatic impact on the lives of western Europeans. The makers of the Revolution intended nothing less than a regeneration of the human race, that was to be accomplished through a manipulation of social institutions, a transformation of culture. This was done by attacking traditional sources of authority and social control. For example, the government weakened the power of the Catholic Church by making binding monastic vows illegal, by taking over its educational and charitable functions, by making bishops and priests elected officials who were required to take oaths of fidelity to the State, and by confiscating the Church's property. Guilds and trade unions were also abolished; this permitted freedom of occupation—but it also meant that people then had to choose their occupations. Moreover, the family was undermined by making divorces legal, by abolishing parental authority when children reached majority, by giving the State primary responsibility for all children, by changing inheritance laws, and by taking control of education away from the family. Napoleon, like many subsequent dictators, regarded education as a tool for producing efficient subjects.

The consequences of these two revolutions are still being felt. As the range of peoples' loyalties and social contacts broadened, they became progressively less able to relate to their fellows as concrete individuals. People began to think about one another in increasingly abstract terms: first as "students," "workers," and "politicians," and then later as "the working class," the "poor," and "the third world." Thus, the very categories of social thought were transformed from the personal and the familiar to the impersonal and the distant. For our purposes, however, the most important consequence of the two revolutions was the rediscovery by sociologists of the concept of "community"; Nisbet (1966, p. 47) regards this as "... unquestionably the most distinctive development in nineteenth-century social thought." Community refers to social relationships that are characterized by personal intimacy, emotional involvement, moral obligation, and a feeling that they are traditional and sanctioned by custom. Since the archetypal symbol of community is the family, almost every genuine community will be described in its terminology. Everything important in community contrasts with the noncommunal relations of competition, conflict, and contractual agreements that characterize modern society. The concept of community represents an ideal standard against which existing societies can be compared. And, according to the early sociologists, the history of the modern world since the eighteenth century can be described in terms of the loss of the sense of community; "community" has given way to "society," encouraged largely by the individualistic perspective that is reflected in modern psychological theory. Consequently, it should be clear that psychology and sociology are separated by entirely different assumptions about the relationship of the individual to society.

EXPLANATION

Emile Durkheim was determined to see the social sciences placed on a firm scientific footing. He thought the methods of the physical sciences should be applied rigorously to the social sciences; he seemed almost obsessed with showing that social facts are real, that they are as determinative in their effects as physical facts, and consequently must be treated as "things."

The existence of such social facts as family structures, political systems, and religious organizations is independent of the wishes or desires of any individual. As Durkheim noted, "The determining cause of a social fact should be sought among the social facts preceding it and not among the stages of individual consciousness (1964, p. 110)." This is so because, according to Durkheim, ". . . social facts have this characteristic. Far from being a product of the individual will, they determine it from without; they are like molds in which our actions are inevitably shaped (1964, p. 29)."

Rephrasing the point, for Durkheim society literally exists; it is not merely a collection of people, nor is it produced by the intersection of their individual interests; rather, it is substantive, it precedes the existence of individuals and shapes them accordingly. Everything in human nature beyond such purely physiological processes as digestion is caused by society. For Durkheim society actually becomes a kind of supreme being. Although this aspect of his thinking is foolish, his perspective also leads to an interesting insight concerning language, law, morality, religion, and personality: they may be social rather than biological phenomena as suggested by Freud, Jung, and McDougall.

Beginning with Durkheim, sociologists have thought through the problem of explanation with considerable scholarly energy, and to appreciate the subtlety and power of their analysis, most background is necessary. Let us first take as an example of a social fact the concept of social class. The members of every group of any complexity can be ranked (and can rank themselves) according to their prestige and power. Social classes —the natural end product of this process—can be defined as more or less homogeneous strata containing ". . . families of about equal prestige who are or would be acceptable to one another for 'social' interaction that is culturally regarded as more or less symbolic of equality (Johnson, 1960, p. 469)." Every social class tends to have its own life-style that sets it apart from the other classes in the same society.

The behavior of individuals can be predicted in terms of their social class membership to a remarkable degree. As Allport was fond of remarking, social class is correlated with everything of importance in personality. The following is merely a partial list of social behaviors that can be predicted from social class: quality and style of dress, personal hygiene, posture and physical mannerisms, speech habits (including grammar and vocabulary size), cognitive or intellectual style, type and location of house within one's community, amount and kind of education, annual income, child-rearing practices, diet, religious preferences and church attendance, reading tastes, political affiliations, standards of sexual conduct, kinds of illnesses and medical attention received, and life expectancy. The list can be extended almost indefinitely because social class and social conduct are so extensively interrelated. Because the class structure of a society typically precedes the existence of any individual member, and because a great deal of social behavior can be predicted on the basis of class membership, sociologists believe that much social behavior can also be explained in these terms.

The concept of social class can be broken down into two additional aspects of social structure that are of great interest to psychologists; norms and roles. Norms are social rules that set limits for behavior. The norms of a society tell its members what they may expect of one another; they codify the expectations within a social group. One's position in society is defined by the norms he must obey, and each social class has its own set of norms. Roles and norms are closely related: roles represent acceptable and routinized responses to social norms. Roles are typified responses to typified expectations; they are standard ways of responding to the norms of one's social group. Roles are denoted by such titles as mother, student, president, fireman, and lover; they represent functions that are necessary for a society's operations. By recruiting people to roles, society manufactures the staff it needs to keep itself going. We conduct our lives within matrices of roles and norms that surround us from birth and determine virtually our every move. Moreover, the notion that one's compliance with his roles is voluntary is always part of the official ideology of the State. Society in fact brings about our compliance through ridicule, abuse, opprobrium, economic sanctions and, ultimately, through violence. On the other hand, roles seem to produce their own commitment—with time people usually begin to take their roles seriously; in this way human nature serves the State as an agent of its own enslavement.

This sociological use of the word role differs considerably from George Kelly's usage. For Kelly a role is a pattern of behavior that follows from one's perception of what another person expects of him; thus, for Kelly a role is personal and highly idiosyncratic. For sociologists, on the other hand, a role is a pattern of behavior that is associated with a particular social position, and anyone who occupies that position should behave accordingly; thus, for sociologists a role is public and completely predictable. From Kelly's perspective a father's behavior, for example, would depend on his perception of his family's expectations. From a sociological perspective, however, a father's behavior is defined by the norms of his society, and all those who occupy the role of father should behave in a more or less standard way—provided, of course, that they are socialized.

The standard sociological model of explanation can be quickly stated now. Sociologists assume that explanation and prediction are the same. Since social facts can predict social behavior, they are assumed to explain it. As Nisbet (1966, p. 83) observes, "We have a kind of reversed reductionism, one that takes some of the deepest states of individuality ...and explains them in terms of what lies outside of the individual." It is an extremely deterministic form of environmentalism in which a set of social facts, uniquely organized for each social system, descends on people like a giant cookie cutter and stamps out the forms that individual lives will take in that system. Thus, we are born into societies whose "ways of existing" are predefined, and much of what we do is determined in advance by these preexisting social facts. The sociological concept of explanation fits in nicely with Hempel's model (see chapter two). That is, to explain a person's behavior, for example his going to college, we need to show only that college attendance is a general feature of a particular group and that the actor in question is a member of that group. If the actor's behavior can be predicted on the basis of his group membership, it is by definition explained.

Clearly then Durkheim believed people are all alike in no important ways. Those holding the same roles in the same or comparable groups are alike, but only because they experience the same social forces or influences. Sociology by definition has nothing to say about how people differ, nor about the explanation of specific, anomalous actions. The sociological perspective concerning these topics could be paraphrased as, "Individuality and uniqueness exist only in the cracks and chinks of the social structure."

SOCIALIZATION AND THE SELF-CONCEPT

Like Freud, Durkheim recognized that socialization is a central problem in the social process. In contrast with Freud, who thought the origins of morality were in the human unconscious (and especially in the Oedipus complex), Durkheim regarded morality as a social creation. "If there is one fact that history has irrefutably demonstrated, it is that the morality of each people is directly related to the social structure of the people practicing it (1961, p. 87)." Durkheim's ideas on socialization are presented most clearly in *Moral Education* (1925), which discusses in detail children's internalization of moral codes. According to Durkheim, moral development passes through three stages. Since moral conduct consists of conforming to preestablished norms, and since "the erratic, the undisciplined are morally incomplete," the first stage in moral development entails acquiring respect for social rules in themselves. Thus, Durkheim regarded moral conduct as initially arising from an unquestioning sense of duty to established norms. His view contrasts markedly with the view that people comply with social rules out of self-interest (i.e., moral conduct makes life more convenient). According to Durkheim, it is impossible for a strong society to be based on the self-interest of its members; people must first of all respect the rules themselves. The source of this respect is the sense of community.

Discipline, however, is not enough, because it says nothing about the goals of moral action. For conduct to be moral, it also must be oriented toward impersonal ends. Consequently, the second stage in moral development involves becoming a functioning member of society and adopting its ends as one's own. "Since . . . man is complete only as he belongs to several societies, morality itself is complete only to the extent that we feel identified with those different groups in which we are involved—family, union, business, club, political party, country, humanity (1961, p. 80)."

The third stage of moral development entails acting autonomously in accordance with the rules of society. For Durkheim, autonomy is a function of a clear understanding of the social and political reasons or justification for one's actions even though one's motives derive from a sense of duty and from identification with the goals of one's community. As Durkheim noted, "To act morally, it is not enough . . . to respect discipline and be committed to a group. Beyond this . . . we must have knowledge, as clear and complete an awareness as possible of the reasons for our conduct . . . Hence we can say that the third element of morality is the understanding of it (1961, p. 120)."

Durkheim simply assumed that social structures are able to influence people's behavior. As George Herbert Mead noted, Durkheim (and most other sociologists) ignored the problem of how the social structure exerts its power. Perhaps Mead's most important contribution was to analyze this process in detail, to describe how culture can influence personality.

From a sociological perspective socialization consists of internalizing roles; roles are sociology's units of socialization. As we previously noted, roles are composed of norms. Thus roles are also the units of cultural transmission: to the degree that one has internalized a role, he has internalized a set of cultural norms or expectations. Moreover, having roles to play gives one a self-concept or sense of identity (e.g., I am the one who leads the band). And a self-concept leads to an ability to view one's actions objectively, from a perspective outside oneself. As Mead phrased it, the most important feature of the self is that it can become an object to itself "How can an individual get outside himself (experientially) in such a way as to become an object to himself? This is the essential psychological problem of selfhood or of self-consciousness . . . (1934, p. 138)."

Mead then explained in detail how the capacity to view oneself from an external perspective develops. Young children invent imaginary companions, particularly while playing with dolls. A child may be heard speaking to himself in different voices, talking to himself as if he were the dolls or imaginary companions. Play of this type precedes organized games and ". . . is play at something. A child plays at being a mother, at being a teacher, at being a policeman; that is, it is taking different roles . . . (1934, p. 150)." This sort of play represents a child's first experience of adopting alternative perspectives with regard to himself, of seeing himself from the viewpoint of other roles.

In play a child moves through a ". . . succession of one role after another, a situation which is, of course, characteristic of the child's own personality. . . . He is not organized into a whole. The child has no definite character, no definite personality (1934, p. 159)." Games, however, are different because they require a child to adopt several perspectives simultaneously. Experience in games leads him to formulate a concept of "the other," a generalization based on the expectations of the other persons with whom he plays. The concept of "the other" is a stabilizing force in personality because it gives a child a consistent perspective from which to see himself. Thus, playing games promotes the inner coherence and organization of a child's personality as well as a self-concept and, ultimately, socialization. "What goes on in the game goes on in the life of the child all the time. . . . There are all sorts of social organizations . . . into which the child is entering, and he is playing a sort of social game in them. . . . That process . . . constitutes him a self-conscious member of the community to which he belongs (1934, p. 160)."

The self emerges in two stages from such role-taking experiences. In the first, it embodies the attitudes that others hold toward one in specific games and social interactions. In the second stage, the self reflects one's generalized notions about what others expect of one in the "game of "life." And once the self is formed it regulates one's behavior in accordance with the expectations of one's social groups.

To summarize Mead's discussion: through peer group experience, particularly in games, a child becomes sensitive to the expectations of others. He comes to see himself from the perspective of all those people with whom he interacts—this is called "taking the role of the generalized other." The generalized other represents the social structure or society in the round. Taking the role of the generalized other simultaneously makes a child self-conscious, gives coherence to his personality and social behavior, and serves to control it. To the degree that he can do this, a child has a self-concept; and socialization depends on a well-developed self-concept.

Consistent with his Hegelian perspective, Mead thought the development of socialization required that a child be securely enmeshed in an ongoing social process (usually a family). ". . . I want particularly to emphasize . . . the temporal and logical preexistence of the social process to the self-conscious individual that arises in it (1934, p. 186)."

It seems to me that Mead"s analysis of the origins of self-consciousness and individuality must be taken very seriously. At the close of his discussion he neatly compares his viewpoint with a psychological perspective on the same topic (*Mind, Self, and Society*, 1934, pp. 222–26), and the argument is worth repeating. Mead assumes a social process is the necessary precondition for the existence of the individual selves who are involved in that process. Psychologists assume individual selves are the precondition for the existence of the social process. According to Mead, the psychological perspective has two (apparently fatal) flaws. First, certain lower animals, especially bees and ants, produce complexly organized societies that do not in the least depend on the individual consciousness of the organisms that form them. Thus, social processes do not seem to depend on individual selves. Second, the psychological perspective can not explain the existence of selves, that it assumes as a precondition for society. On the other hand, Mead *can* explain an ongoing social process, that he sees as a precondition for the existence of individuals. This preexisting social process can be explained readily in terms of contemporary evolutionary theory (Hamilton, 1971), that suggests that social species always have an adaptive advantage over solitary species, that social living is a biological emergent, that societies in fact seem to come before individuals.

Unlike Mead, most sociologists tend to ignore the dynamics of socialization, because socialization is not a problem for most of them. Psychologists assume that culture is an alien force that is imposed on children. For psychologists, then, the problem of socialization entails explaining what must be done to an essentially asocial infant to fit him into society. The sociologists, however, try to explain what must be done to the fundamentally social infant to drive him out of society; normal socialization is taken for granted because people are assumed to be oriented toward social living from birth. Socialization is a natural and expected by-product of a healthy and viable social community. This perspective on socialization leads many sociologists to an interesting and perhaps counterintuitive view of criminal behavior. Psychologists consider delinquency to be the result of poor socialization; sociologists, however, consider delinquency to be the result of a person's being socialized into a life-style that is deviant from that of the majority of society. A favorite sociological example of this is the criminal families associated with the Mafia. From a sociological perspective these families are normal in every respect except the norms to which they have been socialized, that is, there are no valid grounds for rejecting Mafia norms in favor of the standard middle-class values of American society. It seems to me, however, the sociological analysis of delinquency reflects what seems to be an unwarranted degree of ethical relativism.

MOTIVATION AND THE UNCONSCIOUS

The Hegelian sociological notion that our behavior is determined by the social structure or culture into which we are born and socialized, implies an interesting concept of the unconscious. For Durkheim, community comes before the individual, and the essential elements of social control proceed from community. If so, then according to Durkheim we are more thoroughly and completely controlled by forces outside our awareness than Freud ever dreamed. For Freud the individual is real, for Durkheim the individual is a creature of the preexisting social process. Thus, from a sociological perspective the unconscious is a social unconscious: it is the totality of social facts existing outside our awareness that determines our behavior. And there are a very large number of these facts indeed.

Language is an example of the sociological unconscious. The language of one's culture is a social fact, and it seems to determine unconsciously the manner in which we perceive and think about the world. As Sapir (1929, p. 162) observed, "Language is a guide to 'social reality' ... it powerfully conditions all our thinking about social problems and processes ... the 'real world' is to a large extent unconsciously built up on the language habits of the group."

Another important form of the sociological unconscious is, of course, social class. Each social class represents a life-style, a set of values and preferences organized in terms of roles that are specific to that class. It takes an unusual degree of self-awareness to appreciate how much one's actions reflect one's socio-economic background. People typically develop class consciousness only by changing social class. If one spends his life within the same social class, he will tend to remain unconscious of its influence.

Sociologists tend not to discuss human motivation. Nonetheless, sociological theory is shot through with motivational assumptions, many of which are quite interesting. For example, sociologists assume that people need to feel that they belong to a particular geographical territory. As they note, one of the most alienating effects of the French and the Industrial Revolutions was to destroy the traditional European concept of property and the individual's sense of identification with his land. A sense of attachment to a geographical region is part of the idea of community and seems related to the territorial tendencies of some animals. The Czech term *ma vlast* and the French phrase *mon pays* reflect this apparently universal human disposition to feel an allegiance to a particular geographic region. William Faulkner's fondness for Mississippi and Albert Camus's love of Algeria further exemplify this point.

In describing the way that the Industrial Revolution degraded the value of individual labor, sociologists imply that man has a need to express himself through his work. The concept of craftsmanship suggests that the mastery and exercise of certain physical and mental skills is intrinsically rewarding and that the recognition of one's work by others is a major source of satisfaction in life. For example, during the demonstrations that took place at various colleges and universities in the late 1960s in America, the students frequently complained that their academic work lacked any intrinsic meaning, that the impersonal university system prevented them from taking pride in their work.

A third motivational idea implicit in sociological theory is that people need regularity and predictability in their lives. This motive is implicit in Max Weber's discussion of charismatic authority and the process of "rationalization." A charismatic leader is a person with enormous personal magnetism and the capacity to attract devoted followers. Examples are Jesus, Muhammad, Napoleon, and Adolf Hitler; charismatic leaders are often successful in organizing revolutionary movements.

Weber's concept of rationalization concerns the aftermath of the revolution and the fact that prophets are always followed by a priesthood, and revolutionaries by bureaucrats. Rationalization—one of the most important trends in human history—refers to the tendency for social organizations to become more standardized, consistent, organized, and bureaucratic over time. The process of rationalization is temporarily disrupted by revolutions but resumes its inexorable evolution immediately afterward. And the reason is that everyone, including revolutionary leaders, likes routine and hastens to implement it. Thus, in agreement with George Kelly, sociologists assume that people require structure and order in their everyday lives. As Berger and Luckmann (1966, p. 52) observe, "The inherent instability of the human organism makes it imperative that man ... provide a stable environment for his conduct. ... These biological facts serve as a necessary presupposition for the production of social order. In other words, although no existing social order can be derived from biological *data*, the necessity for social order as such stems from man's biological equipment." This need for order may in part explain the delight that children take in arguing about rules and the fascination that law, politics, and other games have for adults.

A fourth motivational assumption implicit in sociological theory is that people have innate religious needs. Psychologists tend to consider religious beliefs as irrational at best, as neurotic symptoms at worst. Religions for them are primitive attitudes and beliefs that should be eliminated through education and science. From a sociological perspective, however, religious impulses are built into human nature. The importance that sociology assigns to religion has nothing to do with the personal religious commitments of sociologists; rather it derives from their empirical observations concerning religion's role in human affairs. As Alexis de Tocqueville remarked, "Men cannot abandon their religious faith without a kind of aberration of intellect and a sort of violent distortion of their true nature; they are invincibly brought back to more pious sentiments. Unbelief is an accident, and faith is the only permanent state of mankind. If we consider religious institutions merely in a human point of view, they may be said to derive an inexhaustible element of strength from man himself, since they belong to one of the constituent principles of human nature (1945, p. 310)."

The power of religion has little to do with its ideas; rather it lies in two important functions that religion serves. On the one hand, it is a response to the problem of evil: it accounts for the inevitable discrepancy between merit and reward, for the undeserved suffering of the innocent— religion assigns a meaning to human misery. On the other hand, religion is a powerful mechanism of social integration: it is a source of unifying symbols of allegiance, of ritual and mystery that provide people with a sense of membership in society. Thus, as Durkheim observed, the essence of religion is not what it says about the world but what it does toward making life endurable. The point of this, however, is that the sociology of religion makes an assumption about human motivation. It assumes that man has a need for meaning, the motive—to which Jung referred when he spoke of an irrational commitment to an idea or entity, to a set of symbols that precedes and transcends us in time and space—is necessary for psychological health. The difference is that for Jung the symbols must be derived personally, while for Durkheim they are given socially.

The last motive from sociological theory that I will mention is also the most important—it is the conceptual pivot on which the notions of community and socialization turn. As we noted earlier, the feeling of community arises from human relationships characterized by intimacy, emotional depth, and moral commitment. Ultimately, the defining feature of community is phenomenological and subjective—it is the sense of being a member of a cohesive social unit. The concept of community therefore assumes a broad social motive: it assumes a need to be with and relate to one's fellow man in a noncompetitive, nonexploitive framework of trust, understanding, and mutuality of values and goals. This social motive is probably innate, and much sociological theory depends on it.

PSYCHOLOGICAL HEALTH

Durkheim and Mead were concerned with psychological unhealth, and they believed it results from a breakdown in the sense of community. Human welfare .necessarily presupposes a stable social order. To the degree that the social order is unstable, people feel isolated, estranged, and alienated from society. Durkheim used the term *anomie* to refer to these feelings of isolation and estrangement. From Durkheim's perspective the individualism prized by Freud and Jung is itself a reflection of the disintegration of modern society.

Anomie literally means normlessness; it denotes a condition in which people no longer respect the norms and traditions of their society. This loss of respect is, of course, caused by factors in the social structure. Of the many structural factors that produce anomie, two are particularly important. The first is role conflict: for example, talented women in America may experience anomie as a result of a conflict between the demands of a professional career and the traditional expectations associated with marriage and family. The second structural inducement to anomie occurs when many people in a group are required to pursue a goal but are at the same time denied access to means for attaining the goal.

In the United States, for example, competitive occupational success is part of the "American dream," and adults in the society are expected to become successful, to "make it." Nonetheless, there is only so much "room at the top," and a considerable proportion of those persons who take success seriously are doomed to frustration. The gap between the required goal of success and the possibilities available for achieving it should produce considerable anomie in the United States.

There are several responses to anomic conditions. People may simply withdraw from the social process; sociological examples of this include schizophrenics, hermits, drug addicts, and members of monastic religious orders. Alternatively, some people might become criminals, in an attempt to acquire culturally approved symbols of success by illegitimate means.

Social rules—by definition frustrating—inevitably entail contradictions. Consequently, everyone experiences anomie to some degree. There are, however, more subtle and passive ways of expressing anomie than by schizophrenia and drug addiction. One common example is overconformity. Bureaucrats, for example, show their alienation by conforming to organizational rules so rigidly that they prevent anyone, including themselves, from accomplishing the ends the rules were designed to achieve. A second passive expression of anomie is psychosomatic illness: ". . . many cases of sickness and injury should be considered in the sociology of deviant behavior. One obvious aspect of much sickness and injury is that it provides the patient with an acceptable excuse for not performing many of the duties he would otherwise be expected to perform (Johnson, 1960, p. 565)." In some cases a patient becomes sick in order to avoid his responsibilities; such passive expressions of anomie are termed *evasions.*

This analysis of deviancy reveals another interesting contrast between sociology and psychology. For sociologists deviant behavior results from disruptions in the social structure and deviants are people who have gotten out of step with an anomic society. Deviation is a predictable but undesirable response to anomic conditions, and society creates such professions as psychiatry, social work, and the police to control deviancy. Thus, from a psychological perspective psychiatrists serve the individual, but from a sociological perspective they are agents of the State.

Mead's definition of psychological unhealth also depends on Durkheim's concept of anomie. Because we have different relationships with different people, a multiple personality is in a sense normal, according to Mead. (The reader will remember that in the psychiatric tradition extending from Janet through McDougall, multiple personality is considered to be the primary form of neurosis.) Most of us are aware of and somewhat bothered by the inconsistencies that exist among our various social selves. Neurotics (hysterics) are persons who are unaware of these normal inconsistencies; "lines of cleavage" have developed between their various social selves.

We can now define psychological health from a sociological perspective. Psychological health requires that our various selves be as integrated as possible without at the same time ignoring necessary inconsistencies. But this integration is achieved neither by an act of will nor with the aid of an analyst. "The unity and structure of the complete self reflects the unity and structure of the social process as a whole (Mead, 1934, p. 144)." Deviant behavior occurs only when the sense of community breaks down. For a deviant to return to normalcy, he must feel identified ". . . with a collective existence which precedes him in time, which survives him, and which encompasses him at all points. If this occurs, he will no longer find the only aim of his conduct in himself; and, understanding that he is the instrument of a purpose greater than himself, he will see that he is not without significance. Life will resume meaning in his eyes, because it will recover its natural aim and orientation (Durkheim, 1961, p. 373)." Unfortunately, according to Durkheim, the net, tragic result of the Industrial and French Revolutions and all the trends of recent history has been to destroy this sense of community, to drive us apart, and to make it even more difficult to integrate our social roles.

EVALUATION

It is important to evaluate the contribution of the sociological perspective to the personological tradition. There are both positive and negative aspects to this contribution. One problem with sociological theory is that it depends on an extreme version of environmentalism. By explaining social action exclusively in terms of forces outside the individual, sociologists ignore biology and the problem of motivation. In so doing they make more reductive explanations of social behavior inapplicable and essentially mystify the social process.

The major problem with sociological theory, however, concerns its concept of explanation. From Durkheim to the present sociologists have confused the issue seriously—indeed, Durkheim's persuasive treatment of the problem may have been a major disaster for the social sciences. First, the manner that Hegelian sociologists assign causal status to the social structure shows faulty reasoning. Social structures literally exist somewhere in a nontemporal, nonspatial universe and govern the actions of their members. To talk this way, however, is very misleading because there is no such thing as a social structure that exists independently of individuals.

Second, sociologists from Durkheim to the present (e.g., Stinch-combe, 1968) equate explanation with prediction, assuming thereby that explanation in the physical and social sciences is identical. Explanation is clearly not prediction, nor is prediction explanation; for example, the ebb and flow of tides in the San Francisco Bay can be predicted quite nicely with U.S. Hydrographic Office tide tables, but surely this is not what is meant by an explanation of tidal flow. Furthermore, the explanation of social action must take into account the fact that people are capable of formulating plans and goals. These are irrelevant to the problem of explanation in the physical sciences, but they are essential for the ex-planation of social action. Most plans and goals can be stated in terms of rules that humans follow. Since social "... actions are guided by the agent's conception of rules, they can be explained in terms of those rules and the agent's construal of the situation confronting him... seen in this way, the study of thought-related human actions becomes a science that must use concepts and explanations different from those appropriate to the study of physical phenomena (Mischel, 1969, pp. 16–17)."

A third problem with the sociological model of explanation is that it cannot account for individual differences. From Durkheim's perspective a wastrel son of a Calvinist family, or a responsible boy in a delinquent neighborhood is an inexplicable phenomenon. For Durkheim, the more homogeneous the culture, the more similar will be its residents. But his assumption appears false; research concerning the relationship between culture and personality reveals, for example, that Tuscarora Indians differ as much from one another as they do from residents of Philadelphia (Wallace, 1961).

On the positive side, four aspects of sociological theory supplement in an important way the conventional perspective of psychology. First, sociology implicitly contains a very optimistic model of man. Man is not inherently wicked, aggressive, or immoral; rather he is ultimately per-fectable. There are no bad men, only bad societies. Greed, superstition, and man's inhumanity to man can all be eliminated by properly adjusting our social institutions.

Second, the sociologists have an interesting and valuable conception of the unconscious, one that does not depend on the concept of repression and makes a great deal of intuitive sense. The unconscious includes those aspects of a person's culture that affect one's behavior (e.g., one's lan-guage and social class) and are outside one's awareness.

Third, such sociological concepts as community, religion, and man's need for meaningful work point to important aspects of human motivation that typically have been ignored by psychologists. Psychological con-ceptions of motivation would be enriched greatly by considering the human needs implied in the notions of community, religion, charismatic leadership, and alienation. Indeed, these sociological conceptions may refer to motives that in the long run prove to be the most distinctively human.

Finally, the sociological discussion of morality, the self, and identity contains an insight into human nature that is often ignored by psychologists. Many psychologists believe that the major lesson to be derived from sociology is simply that behavior never takes place in a vacuum, that social action always occurs in a social context. But the sociological insight goes much deeper. Durkheim and Mead present an image of man as being defined by his existence in society. In their view each person is an undifferentiated biological organism that achieves a specific human identity only through taking part in society—through playing social roles. In fact each person *is* the sum of his roles. This perspective radically challenges the psychological assumption of the unity and continuity of personality across situations. "Looked at sociologically, the [personality] is no longer a solid, given entity that moves from one situation to another. It is rather a process, continuously created and recreated in each social situation that one enters, held together by the slender thread of memory (Berger, 1963, p. 106)." Moreover, as a result of socialization, society ". . . is not only something 'out there,' in the Durkheimian sense, but it is also 'in here,' part of our innermost being. . . . Society not only controls our movements, but shapes our identity, our thought and our emotions. The structures of society become the structures of our own consciousness (Berger, 1963, p. 121)."

If the sociological analysis of socialization and the self-concept is correct, then it is not enough simply to recognize that human action always occurs in a social context. The point is rather that human nature is at its very core social, that the expectations of our families, friends, and associates are reflected in every element of our conscious and unconscious psyches, that personality is socially defined. The sociological analysis of social conduct concludes that there is no stable core to personality, that our personality at any time is a reflection of the expectations of the other people with whom we are involved. This idea is a radical critique of the conventional wisdom of personality theory. For Freud, Jung, McDougall, Allport, and Kelly, personality is composed of inner structures that endure over time and across situations. The structures are variously defined—as id, ego, and superego, as master sentiments, cardinal traits, or core constructs—but each writer assumes that these structures are real and that they give stability and continuity to everyday social behavior. But the sociological perspective strikes at the heart of this assumption, saying that personality is in fact relative to the immediate social situation.

chapter ten

Existentialism

In chapter nine I tried to show that the sociological perspective contains a number of insights about human nature that psychology, with its commitment to an individualistic perspective, has overlooked. This sociological view poses a challenge to psychological theory that must be responded to in a straightforward and responsible manner. The remaining three chapters of this book present three approaches to the problems posed by sociological theory.

The first of these, existentialism, is a diffuse movement rather than a coherent theory. The term refers to a set of attitudes held in common by a particular group of philosophers and psychiatrists, attitudes developed in response to certain apparent changes in man's social and historical circumstances. Although existentialism dates back to the Old Testament and the Greek Stoic philosophers, the movement has three specifically modern roots. First, the existentialists were responding to the same historical changes that preoccupied such early sociologists as Durkheim, Marx, and Weber. They were disturbed by the declining sense of community in Western Europe, the emergence of mass culture and the dehumanization that seemed to accompany the growth of the modern industrial State. Science, in spite of its technological achievements, appeared to have made life actually more difficult by presenting the late nineteenth century with the image of a universe without any purpose. With the evolution of the modern technocracy, man has been alienated from his land, his community, his family, and his religion. But finally and perhaps most significantly, according to the existentialists, man has become alienated from himself. People have become identified with their social functions (e.g., their jobs, their roles), and the remainder of their being drops below the surface of consciousness; this loss of self and self-consciousness produces free-floating anxiety and despair. Thus, the existentialists and the sociologists agreed that the French and the Industrial Revolutions had transformed society and had produced widespread anomie; however, the existentialists rejected the sociological explanation of the cause of anomie, that individual states of consciousness are caused by forces outside the person.

The second source of modern existentialist thought was a vehement and somewhat irrational reaction against the implications of Hegelian philosophy in the study of man. Hegel stressed that what is highest in the realm of being is highest in the realm of abstraction, and that which is highest in the realm of abstraction is highest in the realm of value. Thus, for Hegel, the universal is more important than the particular, the abstract is more valuable than the concrete. A major, if not the major, thrust of existentialism is to reverse this Hegelian scale of values and to insist on the significance of the concrete, particular, and unique individual. Many writers regard Martin Heidegger's book, *Being and Time* (1927), as the source of modern existentialist thought; however, May (1958) suggests that the movement in fact began with a famous series of lectures given in Berlin by F. W. Schelling in 1841. These lectures attacked Hegel, who was enormously popular in Europe at the time; the distinguished audience included the revolutionaries Mikhail Bakunin and Friedrich Engels, Jacob Burckhardt, and Soren Kierkegaard, whose writing career began immediately upon his return to Denmark. Kierkegaard (1813–1855) and Friedrich Nietzsche (1844–1900) are probably the true founders of modern existentialism. Both were extremely critical of Hegelian philosophy and of the notion that the individual has no meaning beyond that provided by his membership in society.

The third root of modern existentialism comes from psychiatry in the form of a critique of Freud and psychoanalysis. The early existentialist psychiatrists (e.g., Binswanger, Minkowski) found several implications of psychoanalysis objectionable. First, in his preoccupation with biological drives, Freud suggested that a major problem in life is man's relationship to his own body. The existentialists point out that one's relationships with himself and others are equally problematical. Second, Freud was an advocate of scientism and technical reason. According to the existentialists, however, to analyze men in terms of technical reason leads precisely to the fragmentation that psychoanalysis was trying to cure. In this sense they regard Freud as an agent of the technocracy, as part of the problem rather than the cure. Third, psychoanalysis imposes interpretations on people; however, a responsible therapist must ask himself if he is seeing a patient as he really is, or if he is projecting his theories onto the patient. As May (1958, p. 5) points out, the early existentialist therapists, who were typically Freudian or Jungian in orientation,

> ...became disquieted over the fact that, although they were effecting cures... they could not, so long as they confined themselves to Freudian and Jungian assumptions, arrive at any clear understanding of why these cures did or did not occur... They likewise were unwilling to postulate unverifiable agents, such as "libido," or "censor"... or the various processes lumped under "transference," to explain what was going on. And they had particularly strong doubts about using the theory of the unconscious as a *carte blanche* on which almost any explanation could be written. They were aware... that the "unconscious ideas of the patient are more often than not the conscious theories of the therapist."

Although existentialism emerged in its present form as a protest movement, it has made substantive and methodological contributions to the personological tradition. The substantive contribution stems originally from Kierkegaard and Nietzsche, both of whom thought the anomie found in modern society was caused by man's inability to find a purpose for his existence. The central problem in existentialism is the meaning of life—and religion has historically supplied this meaning. Kierkegaard, however, was writing out of a world in which God was dying, and Nietzsche wrote in a time when God was dead. Both men sought some basis on which the essential worth of the individual could be reestablished. Thus, the point of existentialism is not to despair over a Godless world. Rather the movement recasts the problem of meaning in terms of the individual: each person must question radically the purpose of his life and see what answers emerge. The substantive contributions of Kierkegaard and Nietzsche can be summarized as follows. They argued that contemporary man feels alienated from society and himself. This alienation results from the failure of the Judeo-Christian tradition in industrial society; modern science in particular has undermined religion. As a result we are confronted with the problem of meaning, and the major task in life is to deal with this problem in a responsible way.

The existentialists use an analytical method known as phenomenology. It is important to be clear about the nature of this method, because phenomenology is to existentialism as dream analysis is to psychoanalysis. The phenomenological method can be attributed to the German philosopher, Edmund Husserl; it was introduced to the social sciences by his student, Max Scheler. Husserl's methodological admonition, *zurück zu den Sachen selbst* (back to the things themselves), suggests that philosophers and psychologists should adopt a form of radical empiricism, that they should reexamine the raw data of experience after purging themselves of their philosophical and metaphysical preconceptions. To adopt the phenomenological perspective is to say,

> Let us first look before we think; let us first observe before we theorize; let us first describe "what is there" in the world . . . from a natural standpoint before we set out to explain what it means from the unnatural standpoint of a scientific or philosophical theory. To say, then, that we look at the world from a natural [i.e., a phenomenological] standpoint means that we look at it naively, innocently, and freshly, that we try to describe and clarify what is there without prejudging it in terms of any fixed, conceptual categories—and blind spots. In this sense, the term "phenomenological" is practically equivalent to the term "descriptive" (Meyerhoff, 1959, p. 30).

Let us turn now to a discussion of what the existentialists find with their phenomenological method.

MOTIVATION

The phenomenological analysis of everyday social life provides a number of interesting insights into human affairs. Beginning with Heidegger, Husserl's most famous student, the existentialists distinguish between a form of existence that characterizes nonhuman objects (*Vorhandensein*) and one that is peculiar to human beings (*Dasein*). The difference is that objects (e.g., ships, stones, inkwells) are formed or created by forces outside themselves; man, however, must make himself. Man becomes what he makes of himself and nothing more. Heidegger's *Being and Time* is a phenomenological analysis of the structure of *Dasein*; his book strongly influenced the psychiatrist Ludwig Binswanger, whose viewpoint is called *Daseinanalyse* (existential analysis). Binswanger distinguished three modes of *Dasein*, three ways of "being in the world." The first is called *Umwelt*, a natural manner of living if one lacks self-awareness. *Umwelt* refers to man's physiological desires: "It is the world of natural law and natural cycles, of sleep and awakeness, of being born and dying, desire and relief, the world of finiteness and biological determinism, the 'thrown world' to which each of us must in some way adjust (May, 1958, p. 61)."

The existentialist school of psychiatry understands that biological reality sets fixed limits for us, yet it maintains that there is more to us than physiology. The second mode of *Dasein* is called the *Mitwelt*, the world of being with other people. The *Mitwelt* is the world of interpersonal relations; there are four existential modes in the *Mitwelt*. The first is called the dual mode; here relationships are characterized by warmth, trust, and personal intimacy—the sociological concept of community is an example of the dual mode of the *Mitwelt*. The dual mode is an existential ideal: it is the desired form of interpersonal relations. The second way of living in the *Mitwelt* is called the plural mode; this refers to formal interactions (e.g., lectures, wedding ceremonies) and to relationships characterized by competition and rivalry. The singular mode is a third way of being in the *Mitwelt*; the singular mode refers to all forms of narcissistic, self-oriented social behavior—masturbation and suicide are examples of the singular mode. Finally, the fourth existential mode is called anonymous. People adopt the anonymous mode when they want to avoid responsibility for their own lives; according to Binswanger, the anonymous mode is typical of soldiers and bureaucrats.

The third and final way of being in *Dasein* is called the *Eigenwelt*, or *own world* and refers to self-related, self-aware, self-actualizing ways of being. *Eigenwelt* is a way of understanding what things in the world mean explicitly for oneself and one's development.

Umwelt is defined almost entirely in terms of adjustment, adaptation, and accommodation—one adjusts to cold weather, hunger, and dirty air. *Eigenwelt* is a world made up almost exclusively of assimilation—the meaning of flowers, trees, or other people is grasped in terms of what they mean for oneself. *Mitwelt*, however, synthesizes *Umwelt* and *Eigenwelt*: it is a mode of being that contains a balance between adjustment and assimilation. The term that best characterizes *Mitwelt* is *relationship*. If I force others to adjust to me, to adapt themselves to my desires and expectations, I treat them as objects and dehumanize them; on the other hand, if I constantly adjust to the expectations of others, I dehumanize myself. A relationship is the ideal, dual mode of the *Mitwelt*, and is called an *encounter*—a relationship with another in which both participants are open to the possibilities of mutual influences and change. As May (1958, p. 38) observes, an "... encounter with the being of another person has the power to shake one profoundly and may potentially be very anxiety-arousing. It may also be joy-creating. In either case, it has the power to grasp and move one deeply."

Although each mode of *Dasein* refers to a distinctive style of being, it is important to remember that we live in all three modes simultaneously. Moreover, something is lost from our lives if we emphasize one mode of being to the exclusion of the others. Lives oriented primarily to pleasure, to social interaction, *or* to self-realization, are immature.

It was mentioned earlier that people differ from things primarily in that people define or create themselves. People are characterized by what Binswanger called *world-openness*, or the capacity for transcendence. This is related to one of the most important issues in existentialist thought: antideterminism. Man can achieve transcendence (and escape the bonds of determinism) in two ways. He can free himself from the constraints of his own thought processes—psychic reality—by becoming self-conscious about them; i.e., he can transcend psychic reality by making his mental processes the objects of psychological study. Man can free himself from physical reality through his capacity for world-openness; i.e., through his ability to restructure reality in his own terms. As Meyer-hoff (1961, pp. xxx–xxxi) notes, "Man not only lives in a world, he also . . . has the capacity for an unlimited 'openness' to, and detachment from, the natural world. It is this capacity which enables him to restructure this world in terms of abstract categories like substance and number, space and vacuum, time and causality, which are the theoretical foundations and basic tools for science and philosophy."

These two forms of detachment are necessary for transcendence; they provide the basis of human freedom and a means for critizing the absolute determinism of Freud and Hegel. Phenomenological analysis reveals that the human spirit overflows or transcends the bounds of psychical, physical, and historical causality through self-consciousness. Perhaps an example will clarify this rather abstract discussion. In the late 1950s a number of on-the-spot films of the Cuban revolution were shown on television in the United States. One filmed incident in particular struck me as a powerful example of transcendence. The revolutionary government had condemned the sheriff of a small provincial hamlet to die. The sheriff, however, was given the privilege of conducting his own execution. The scene was a small, open square on the edge of town. The sheriff, a tall black man dressed in khakis and wearing sun glasses, was standing in front of a ditch lined with bodies, nonchalantly smoking a cigarette. The firing squad, his former deputies, milled about uncertainly nearby. At the designated moment, the sheriff in a disdainful voice called them to attention, then marched them in tight formation to a position about ten yards in front of him, in a line parallel to the ditch. In the same voice he gave the orders for them to make ready and to take aim. He turned, casually flipped his cigarette into the ditch behind him, faced the group, and commanded them to fire. His attitude, at the moment the bullets hit his body, was one of indifference and contempt. And his scorn and refusal to be intimidated or otherwise influenced by the situation exemplifies transcendence.

A phenomenological analysis of everyday life also provides insight into human motivation. Blaise Pascal hinted at this in his *Pensées*: "When I consider the brief span of my life, swallowed up in the eternity before and behind it, the small space that I fill, or even see, engulfed in the immensity of spaces which I know not, and which know not me, I am afraid, and wonder to see myself here rather than there; for there is no reason why I should be here rather than there, now rather than then . . . (1946, p. 36)."

In contemporary existentialist terms Pascal was describing an encounter with the absurd. If we abandon our conventional religious and scientific preconceptions and ask why we exist, then from a phenomenological perspective there is no answer. As Camus observed, the inevitability of death makes life an empty charade. Man has been "thrown" into the world, a finite being, destined for death—and for no reason. Realization of this leads to a perception of the absurd, the condition that results when man, seeking happiness and purpose, confronts a meaningless universe—what Camus called the "unreasonable silence of the world."

The absurd is directly related to the problem of meaning that has been referred to earlier. It is another word for what Nietzsche saw as emerging nihilism, a problem produced by the collapse of the Judeo-Christian world view. People generally tend to avoid facing the problem of meaning; when they do, however, they tend to experience *Angst*, an emotion imperfectly translated by the words *anxiety* and *dread*. *Angst* is a subjective state in which a person is intensely aware of the possibility of nonbeing, of the fact that he can be destroyed. In his classic analysis of anxiety, Kierkegaard argued that people are never motivated by pleasure, happiness, or sex; they are motivated by dread, by anxiety over the possibility of nonbeing.

Two motivational ideas are central to the existentialist perspective. The first is *Angst*, man's innate response to his imminent nonbeing. The second (and closely related idea) is Nietzsche's concept of the *will to power*. The will to power contains a partial solution to the problem of meaning. It is a complex of biological energy that drives one not only to sustain life but also to go beyond it: man needs more from life than what is given on the strictly biological level. The will to power can be expressed in two ways. In the first, it is used to master the physical and social environment—this results in Science. In the second and more important case it is used to master oneself and mobilize one's powers to the highest degree compatible with sanity. Nietzsche called this the *will to truth*, the highest expression of the will to power and an indication of authentic being. The will to truth can lead to a destruction of life on the biological level; in the pursuit of self-knowledge one may ignore his physiological well-being. Truth in this Nietzchean sense is both absolute and entirely subjective; it is a function of one's life-style, and each person is true or false (authentic or inauthentic) in accordance with the degree of self-knowledge he has obtained.

To summarize this discussion, a phenomenological analysis of everyday life reveals three primary modes of being, denoted by the terms *Umwelt, Mitwelt,* and *Eigenwelt*; we live in these worlds simultaneously. Self-awareness produces in self-conscious persons the possibilities of transcendence and denial of scientific determinism. A phenomenological analysis also reveals that life is absurd. This insight produces *Angst,* one of existentialism's two major motivational concepts. The second concept, the will to power, refers to how one may deal authentically with *Angst* (i.e., by seeking self-knowledge). The will to power means that the pursuit of self-knowledge is prepared for biologically and required for authentic existence.

THE SELF-CONCEPT AND
THE UNCONSCIOUS

The *Angst* that results from the apparent purposelessness of human existence is more than most people can bear. Therefore, according to Kierkegaard and Nietzsche, most people choose not to ask about the meaning of their lives, and their resulting loss of self-awareness can be described as self-deception. Thus, most people are self-deceived, there are neurotic consequences that flow from this self-deception, and the cure is self-knowledge. The same theme is found in Heidegger who argued that the most authentic or "human" mode of Being was to be self-reflective. Those who are self-deceived are alienated from themselves; those who are self-aware are authentic.

For George Herbert Mead, the self-concept is defined socially; it is determined by the roles one plays and reflects how one sees himself from the perspective of his family and associates. The existentialists, however, distinguish between the self and the self-concept and define the former in terms of self-consciousness. The self is not the product of one's roles; rather it is the capacity to know that one is playing a role; it is the ability to see oneself in many roles. For the existentialists then, the self-concept in Mead's sense is something to be overcome. To the degree that one cannot step outside his social roles and see them in perspective, i.e., that one is identified with his self-concept or social roles, he is self-deceived; he has become an object because he is exogenously (socially) defined; he lives in "bad faith." The following passage from Sartre (1966, pp. 181–82) summarizes the relationship between self-awareness, transcendence, and self-deception: "Let us consider this waiter in the café. His movement is . . . a little too precise, a little too rapid. He comes toward the patrons with a step a little too quick. He bends forward a little too eagerly; his voice, his eyes express an interest a little too solicitous for the order of the customer. . . . All his behavior seems to us a game . . . He is playing, he is amusing himself. But what is he playing? We need not watch long before we can explain it; he is playing *at being* a waiter in a café." If Sartre's waiter sees himself exclusively in terms of his role, he denies the possibility of transcendence, he is self-deceived, and he lives inauthentically.

The topic of self-deception leads naturally to the existentialist conception of the unconscious. Among the existentialists Sartre has provided perhaps the most interesting analysis of this problem. He assumes first that consciousness is a "translucent sphere," that the contents of the mind are all potentially available to awareness. He then describes the phenomena that Freud called unconscious in terms of self-deception—in terms of the "inauthentic" as opposed to the "unknown."

From an existentialist perspective the first problem is to explain how self-deception or bad faith can occur given that consciousness is transparent and unified, that by definition there can be nothing unconscious in consciousness. According to Sartre, at the outset one does not decide to be self-deceived about a particular idea, memory, or wish; rather one falls into self-deception as one falls asleep and one remains in self-deception much as one dreams. If one thinks about falling asleep it is hard to do; and it is the same with self-deception. Self-deception represents, according to Sartre, a refusal to accept responsibility for one's actions; it is a failure (or refusal) to reflect on what one is doing. As Fingarette (1969, p. 99) observes, ". . . the core of self-deception is the disavowal of responsibility for, and the consequent refusal to reflect upon some project of consciousness."

For Sartre, unconscious neurotic symptoms are expressions of self-deception, they are behavior patterns on whose meaning the neurotic refuses to reflect. He illustrates this point with an example taken from Wilhelm Stekel's book, *La Femme Frigide*. Stekel regarded frigidity not as a neurosis but as a form of self-deception. In his clinical studies he observed repeatedly that pathologically frigid women seemed deliberately to distract themselves while making love in an effort to deny any enjoyment; many for example would, during the sexual act, think about their household chores and errands they had to run. "Yet if the frigid woman thus distracts her consciousness from the pleasure which she experiences, it is by no means cynically and in full agreement with herself; it is *in order to prove to herself* that she is frigid. (Sartre, 1966, p. 54)." And this is precisely what Sartre means by bad faith or self-deception.

If, as Sartre argues, manifestations of the Freudian unconscious (e.g., neurotic symptoms, lapses of memory) are actually examples of self-deception, what does this say about the psychoanalytic concept of repression? According to Freud, repression is unconscious; the neurotic is not conscious that he is engaged in repression. Moreover, the neurotic actively resists becoming aware of both his repression and the impulses that he has repressed. According to the existentialists, there are two serious problems with Freud's concept of repression. First, if the ego represses thoughts that originate in the id, how does it remain unaware of what it is doing? Does the ego defend itself against knowledge of its defensive activities, and if so, how can we explain this "second-level defense of keeping from consciousness the first-level defensive maneuver? This line of analysis obviously leads to an infinite regress. The second question concerns not *how* the ego remains unconscious of its defenses but *why*. Why should the ego strive to keep *anything* unconscious? That which characterizes psychoanalytic repression is that one hides something from oneself. But who, or what, is the object of this inner secretness?

> Is the impulse to be hidden from the id? This makes no sense, for it is the impulse *of* the id. Is it to be hidden from the superego? No, for it is typically the superego which perceives the emerging id derivatives, and which typically initiates the defence by inducing anxiety in the ego. Is the impulse to be hidden from the ego? Surely not, for the ego is by definition that "agency" which takes into account *both* the impulse and the conflicting superego demands, and which then designs and executes the defensive *manoeuvre*. Furthermore since the impulse remains active in the id, defence is a continuing process; the ego must therefore remain *continuously* cognizant of all relevant factors if defence is to succeed. However, if nothing relevant is "hidden" from id, ego, or superego, what is the point of keeping anything from being conscious? (Fingarette, 1969, p. 115).

For Sartre, then, ideas become unconscious through self-deception, whereas for Freud they become unconscious through repression. One might ask how Sartre has advanced our understanding of unconscious psychic phenomena by substituting self-deception for repression. It seems to me that there are three advantages to Sartre's conceptualization. First, it avoids the logical problems associated with the concept of repression; i.e., how the ego can repress a thought or memory without knowing what it is repressing. It might be recalled that McDougall also recognized this problem with the concept of repression and his analysis of the unconscious closely resembled that of Sartre.

Second, Sartre's notion of the unconscious as "that about which one is self-deceived" means that unconscious materials are potentially accessible to consciousness. For Freud, on the other hand, much of the unconscious is in principle inaccessible.

Third, Sartre's view adds an additional moral dimension to the analysis of the unconscious. That is, the individual in some sense chooses to be self-deceived and is therefore responsible for the contents of his unconscious. For Freud, however, the individual has no control over what does and does not become repressed, and he is allowed to avoid taking responsibility for an area of his life. Thus, Sartre concludes ironically, psychoanalysis "... substitutes for the notion of bad faith the idea of a lie without a liar.... It replaces the duality of the deceiver and the deceived ... by that of the 'id' and the 'ego' (1966, p. 92)."

A brief summary should clarify this discussion. It is necessary to distinguish between the self and the self-concept. The self-concept is defined in terms of one's social roles; the self is defined as the capacity to see oneself in one's roles, to view one's roles in perspective. To identify oneself with one's social roles is to deny the possibilities of transcendence and to be self-deceived. Thus, the socially-defined self is something to be overcome. For the existentialists, then, the self is defined as self-awareness—the more self-awareness, the more selfhood. But self-awareness is a state of being that can be attained only at a cost: the more one is self-aware the more one is faced with the problem of meaning. Thus, self-awareness produces anxiety and dread. On the other hand, if one refuses to face the absurd, one lives in bad faith. The choice then is between *Angst* and inauthentic existence, between dread and self-deception; the choice, as J. S. Mill observed, is whether one wishes to be a satisfied pig or a dissatisfied Socrates. Finally, the existentialists equate the unconscious with self-deception and bad faith. Unconscious thoughts, motives, and wishes are regarded as mental elements about which one has deceived oneself.

SOCIALIZATION

The existentialist description of socialization closely resembles G. H. Mead's analysis of the same topic. When we enter a social situation, expectations greet us that require us to respond in a specific way. As we pass through various social situations in the course of a day, we are met with different expectations associated with the different areas of our lives. When we respond appropriately to these demands, we play a role—a typified response to a typified expectation—required by the situation. Thus, for example, when a student enters a classroom he or she knows the expectations that prevail there and begins to play the role of a student. But by playing a role we tend to become committed to it, that is, we become sad because we cry and patriotic because we act like soldiers.

Futhermore, people reflect on this process only rarely. As Berger (1963, p. 97) notes, "Even very intelligent people, when faced with doubt about their roles in society, will involve themselves even more in the doubted activity rather than withdraw into reflection." Moreover, such involvement is understandable because a life of pure pretense is impossible to sustain.

We each develop a repertoire of roles and our lives come to resemble an extended sequence of stage performance, some of which require profound changes of costume and demeanor. Socialization is, of course, equated with the internalization of these roles. The more intensely one has internalized his roles, the more one is socialized. Roles often conflict, producing inconsistencies in one's performances from time to time. To avoid anxiety over these inconsistencies, people commonly dissociate or segregate their consciousness as well as their roles. They don't *repress* awareness of role inconsistencies, because the concept of repression makes no sense from an existentialist perspective; rather they *redirect* their attention. Thus, most people are sincere as they play their roles because, once again, sincerity is easier to maintain than self-awareness. Sincerity is the psychological state of one who believes his own act.

But one lives in bad faith if he plays his roles with sincerity and inner identification; one lacks self-awareness and is self-deceived. Human dignity requires role distance, an inner detachment from one's social situation; it requires self-awareness. Thus, for the existentialists, conventional socialization, like the socially-defined self-concept, is something to be overcome.

In spite of their concern with values and their hostility toward conventional socialization, existentialist writers are rather vague concerning the process of socialization. Although it is very sketchy, perhaps the best discussion was provided by Kierkegaard (1941). Kierkegaard identified three levels of socialization or stages in life that have clear developmental overtones. The first, the aesthetic stage, is characteristic of children: the aesthete lives solely for the pleasure or pain of the moment. For Kierkegaard intellectuals and academicians stand outside life as detached observers, and are another variety of aesthete. He treats the aesthete with sympathy but concludes that such a life ultimately leads to despair. The second level of existence is called the ethical. Here one commits oneself to a goal in life and binds oneself to universal moral norms. Such a person is truly just and moral, but his development is nonetheless incomplete. At some point, according to Kierkegaard, one must perform a "teleological suspension of the ethical" in order to form an absolute relationship with a particular absolute. This level of existence is called the religious. Kierkegaard's example is Abraham, who agrees to violate a universal moral norm (i.e., to sacrifice his son Isaac) for no discernable reason other than that it seems to be required by his God. This final stage of development requires a leap of faith, a complete suspension of analytical reason. It is important to emphasize, however, that religion for Kierkegaard did not mean the Church. The Christianity of average churchgoers was for him inauthentic and an unspeakable abomination.

EXPLANATION

Existentialists are in agreement concerning the problem of explanation. They distinguish between the form of explanation appropriate to objects and that appropriate to people. Human behavior can be predicted using considerations drawn from biology and physiology (*das Umwelt*) and in terms of roles and social class (*das Mitwelt*). However, to the degree that a person's behavior actually can be explained in terms of his physiology or his social class he has given up the possibilities of transcendence and is less than human.

According to the existentialists, similarities in human nature (personality as *Personalität*) arise from man's need for meaning and purpose in life. Realization that the traditional sources of meaning (e.g., religion) are no longer valid produces *Angst*. And the universal human response to *Angst* is a flight into self-deception by immersing oneself in one's social roles (Jung called this a regressive restoration of the personna). Thus, people are alike in that they need meaning and they respond to the lack of meaning with *Angst* and self-deception.

Differences among people (personality as *Persönlichkeit*) are explained in terms of the choices a person has made about his life. Choice is fundamental because, from an existentialist perspective, choice literally makes the man; a person becomes what he chooses. At any point in a person's life he has a character, an essence, a personal meaning that is the sum of the choices he has made up to that point. This sum, however, is constantly being added to as a result of new choices. The past, consequently, does not determine the future of one who chooses—nothing does. Each person is entirely on his own, whether or not he wants to be. One must chose without external guidance; to do so is to live authentically but in anguish.

Most people, however, do not make authentic choices. Rather they choose in accordance with habits and custom, or they excuse themselves on the grounds that history, society, or human nature forces them in a particular direction. The existentialists regard this as an evasion: by not choosing one still makes a choice and it is to be self-deceived. One simply cannot be guided by decisions other than one's own and still live authentically. Thus, for the existentialists the differences among people are explained in terms of the pattern of each person's choices. Existential analysis, according to Sartre, is a method designed to illuminate in an objective fashion the subjective choices by which each person makes himself a person.

The existentialists treat the explanation of specific actions in an interesting way. The early phenomenologists (e.g., Dilthey, Windelband) distinguished between the natural sciences (*Naturwissenschaften*) and the social sciences (*Geisteswissenschaften*). They argued that objects can be analyzed, but people must be understood. Individuals and individual conduct cannot, in principle, be explained using explanatory models taken from the natural sciences. Each person, they argued, must be understood as a concrete and unique particular. Although with their emphasis on uniqueness these phenomenologists tended to anti-intellectual nonsense (see chapter seven, p. 111), they also hinted at a useful explanatory notion. In particular, they believed that each person should be regarded as located somewhere on the trajectory toward his life's goal; each person is in the process of becoming something that he has chosen to become. If the psychologist can determine a person's goals (his values) and can unravel his pattern of choices, then any particular action can be interpreted or understood in terms of these goals and choices. Although the vocabulary differs, there is considerable agreement among McDougall, Allport, Kelly, and the existentialists concerning the explanation of particular acts. They all stress values, the person's orientation to the future, and the particular sentiments, motives, constructs, or choices the person has evolved in order to reach his goals.

PSYCHOLOGICAL HEALTH

To understand the existentialist concept of psychological health we must first review their discussion of neurosis. From an existentialist perspective anxiety and guilt are never undesirable *per se*. Because intellectual honesty inevitably leads to the problem of meaning and an encounter with the absurd, *Angst* is the first sign of intellectual awakening. *Angst* may subsequently serve as a stimulus for personal growth. Therefore psychological health is not defined by an absence of anxiety but rather by using the proper means to deal with it.

The existentialists distinguish between *Angst*, normal guilt, and neurotic guilt. *Angst* results from the problem of meaning; guilt on the other hand is a product of one's life-style. Normal guilt arises when a person denies his potentialities or fails to fulfill them. Neurotic guilt arises from a failure to acknowledge normal guilt, from a refusal to deal with it in a responsible way. For the existentialists neurotic and psychotic symptoms are seen as techniques for reducing neurotic guilt. Typically these symptoms have the effect of allowing one to avoid responsibility for his own life.

Neurotic symptoms are always somewhat effective in that they allow a neurotic to preserve his sense of personal worth. According to Rollo May, (1958), sickness is precisely the method the neurotic uses to preserve his own being. Because the existentialists feel modern society is dehumanizing, they tend to be sympathetic with their clients. Often a neurotic life-style is the best that a person can manage, given his life circumstances. Moreover, people are changing constantly, and one must continually adapt to the demands of life. Thus happiness now is no guarantee of happiness later; in a real sense, life consists of one crisis of existence after another—as H.L. Mencken said, "Life is just one damned thing after another."

Although the existentialists have some sympathy for neurotics, their predominant attitude is actually more ambivalent. In *The Sickness Unto Death*, Kierkegaard suggested two general principles concerning neurosis. First, we never feel anxiety or despair over external objects but always over ourselves; i.e., we don't despair over the loss of a job but over the image we have of ourselves as jobless. Second, what we call neurosis is actually a form of sinfulness. There is a tendency to regard morally deficient people as sick, mentally ill, or neurotic. The closer we get to any neurotic, the more we are struck by his perversity and willful disagreeableness. In Sartre's terms a neurotic, one who has undergone a "mental breakdown," is in fact self-deceived; he is a coward who flees from self-awareness and personal responsibility. Nietzsche referred to neurotics as "pale felons," as would-be villains who do not have the courage of their immoral convictions; they lack sufficient nerve to affirm their existence as great scoundrels and are content with perpetrating petty crimes on other people—by being late for appointments, forgetting to return items they borrow, being unreasonably moody, etc.

If neurotics are victims of mental disease, then our proper response should be pity and compassion. If, however, neurotics are self-deceived, then our response should be the same as that which we have toward any other form of cowardice. As Fingarette (1969, p. 143) observes, "What the self-deceiver lacks is not concern or integrity but some combination of courage and a way of seeing how to approach his dilemma without probable disaster to himself." The neurotic must be led firmly but tactfully to self-awareness; he must be persuaded to confront as much reality as his courage will bear. If neurotics are self-deceived cowards, then psychotherapy becomes a moral rather than a medical enterprise.

Drawing on all the material presented above, there seem to be five criteria that, from an existentialist perspective, define psychological health. First, as May (1958) observes, neurotics are overconcerned with the *Umwelt* and underconcerned with the *Eigenwelt*. Thus the healthy person is one who has established a proper balance among the three modes of *Dasein*. In particular, psychological health is denoted by the capacity for significant interpersonal relationships: it is the capacity to live in the dual mode of the *Mitwelt*.

Second, as Allport noted, psychological health requires *engagement*, a commitment to life and the pursuit of certain personally chosen goals therein. Camus (1959) remarked that the only important philosophical question was whether or not to commit suicide. The fact that a person does not shoot himself means that he has made an affirmation. He then has a responsibility to live up to that affirmation by making a commitment to life. Consequently, we must pursue our goals as vigorously as possible, realizing that they are quite arbitrary but must be pursued nonetheless.

A third criterion of psychological health is the capacity to assume responsibility for one's life. Sartre's refusal to accept the Nobel prize for literature is perhaps an example of this. Sartre claimed that he refused the prize in part because he felt the Nobel committee, in offering it to him, was also offering to forgive him for some of the ideas and actions of his youth. Sartre maintained that his youthful behavior had seemed valid at the time and, although he had subsequently changed his mind, he would not disavow those earlier actions in the present. He had meant them at the time, they were part of him, and to deny them now would be an evasion. Thus, the existentialist notion of responsibility is quite stern; it is not a concept for the faint-hearted or the conventionally ambitious.

A fourth criterion of psychological health is a unified or integrated personality. As stated several times in this book, integration is a problem that psychoanalysis ignores. Fingarette (1969) suggests that Freud acknowledged this in his last, posthumous, paper entitled "The splitting of the ego and the process of defence." In that paper Freud confessed that he had been "clearly at fault" to "take for granted the synthetic (i.e., integrative) nature of the processes of the ego (Fingarette, 1969, p. 131)." For the existentialists, dissociation (or lack of integration) results from self-deception. The cure for self-deception is self-awareness. According to Nietzsche, this becomes possible through sublimation, the only defense mechanism that strengthens man. Through sublimation we withdraw biological energy (the will to power) from immediate use and direct it toward personal integration, control, and organization. The will to truth, the highest expression of the will to power, results in self-awareness, the necessary precondition for integration. In direct contrast with the cult of self-expression that seems so prevalent in parts of our society, the existentialists, along with Freud and the ancient Greeks, argue that self-actualization depends on suppression and self-discipline; only those who are willing to be hard on themselves can attain self-awareness.

Finally, psychological health is characterized by self-consciousness, self-awareness, and a willingness to be an individual, to affirm one's own existence, to avoid the anonymous mode of *Dasein*. Because the self-aware individual is capable of transcendence, he is free.

However, psychological health does not mean happiness; it means living with the knowledge that one's being has no ultimate justification or purpose. In "The Myth of Sisyphus" Camus develops an inspired metaphor for man's fate. Sisyphus is condemned to spend eternity pushing a huge boulder up a high hill; each time he reaches the top the boulder rolls back down to the underworld. Similarly, each person struggles through life only to die. Yet Sisyphus *does* have a task to complete. And during those brief moments he spends at the crest of the hill he can enjoy the breeze and his momentary view from the summit. For these reasons, Camus concludes, we must consider Sisyphus content. Life's final lack of meaning can be transcended by a self-conscious affirmation of an otherwise arbitrary goal.

EVALUATION

At this point it is appropriate to attempt an assessment of the existentialist contribution to the personological tradition. The movement has some distinctive strengths and weaknesses. Looking first at the shortcomings, existentialist writers express themselves in terms of the most inconsistent and ambiguous language in philosophy or psychology. This undisciplined language reflects to some degree the literary origins of the movement, but for the most part it is intentional and deliberate, a self-conscious repudiation of technical reason and scientific discourse. Although their hostility to scientism is understandable, their murky language is a poor instrument of intellectual reform.

Second, the level of self-awareness required to live in good faith is itself unrealistic. According to Sartre, the structure of consciousness is such that people are by definition self-deceived. As he remarks, ". . . human reality, in its most immediate being, in the inner structure of the prereflective *cogito*, must be what it is not and not be what it is" (1966, p. 201). Sartre means that there can be no such thing as conscious self-identity, that we can know ourselves as objects of knowledge only as we have existed in the past; the free self of the immediate present is not a possible object of experience. "Thus we find at the base of sincerity a continual game of mirror and reflection, a perpetual passage from the being which is what it is, to the being which is not what it is and inversely from the being which is not what it is to the being which is what it is (1966, p. 198)". According to Sartre, then, self-deception is built into the nature of consciousness. The most we can accomplish with diligent self-scrutiny is to narrow the gap between the unknowable free self and the self known by introspection. Self-awareness is an unattainable goal that we are nonetheless morally obligated to pursue. Thus, the existentialists risk trivializing an important issue—the problem of the relationship between self-awareness and self-deception—for the sake of scoring an ironic point.

A third difficulty with existentialism is that its reply to the problem set by Hegel and the sociological perspective simply misses the point. The problem, in a nutshell, is to indicate how there can be a stable core to personality given the overwhelming evidence for social and historical determinism that the sociologists can bring forward. A proper response would be a careful examination of the mechanisms of social influence and cultural transmission, a close look at the points of contact between the individual and his society. The existentialist response, however, is on the one hand to deny the validity of sociological data and, on the other hand, to assert a radical form of individualism. Most particularly, the existentialists fail to grasp that authentic existence is only possible within a social context. Authenticity is defined in terms of *how* one plays one's social role; the question of whether or not to play a role is irrelevant. In view of the fact that authenticity itself is defined socially, the existentialist response to Hegel and sociology seems naive.

A fourth problem with existentialism is that the movement is essentially leaderless. This chapter seriously misrepresents the organization and structure of existentialism, which in fact is an unstructured gathering of loosely related viewpoints. Moreover, the movement has long since passed from the hands of the substantive thinkers who founded it—Kierkegaard, Nietzsche, Heidegger, and Sartre—into the control of a group of writers whose work (with the exception of Merleau-Ponty) is derivative and superficial. The fate of every revolution, political or intellectual, seems to be the same: the initial inspiration is dissipated in the hands of the faceless functionaries who subsequently gain control.

There is a final irony about existentialism that is worth noting. Although the movement professes to be a philosophy of the common man and to deal with concrete reality, it is in fact a terribly abstract and esoteric viewpoint whose appeal is primarily to the academic elite it claims to spurn.

On the positive side, four contributions of existentialism are noteworthy. First, the phenomenological method, its analytical methodology, is a major contribution whose importance American psychologists are now beginning to recognize. Phenomenology is an important antidote to the experimental methodology to which American psychology seems wedded. Moreover, in the hands of such investigators as Jean Piaget, Kurt Lewin, Gustav Ichheiser, and Fritz Heider, the phenomenological method has made and will continue to make substantive contributions to psychological knowledge.

Second, the existentialist critique of the psychoanalytic concept of repression seems essentially correct. Inasmuch as Freud regarded the concept of repression to be the "keystone of the psychoanalytic arch," the existentialists seem to have delivered psychoanalysis a heavy blow. Moreover, by unraveling the concept of repression the existentialists simultaneously point out that the integration of consciousness is also problematical. In the concept of self-awareness they suggest a means of resolving this problem: consistent with the tradition in psychiatry represented by Pierre Janet and William McDougall, the existentialists argue that dissociation rather than repression is the central feature in neurosis. But they go beyond Janet and McDougall by attempting to specify the mechanisms (self-awareness) by which dissociation can be resolved.

Third, along with Jung, the existentialists deserve credit for calling attention to the problem of meaning. There seems to be a wide range of individual differences in sensitivity to this problem. Freud, for example, thought concern over the problem of meaning was in itself a neurotic symptom. Artists, on the other hand, seem particularly sensitive to it, and their sensitivity seems to drive them to produce and create. Thus the problem of meaning is of some importance, and a psychology that ignores it may be impoverished as a result.

Finally, along with Freud, the existentialists present us with a tragic view of life, a view that seems neither sustained nor understood by the other contributors to the personological tradition. For the existentialists as for Freud happiness is not possible; indeed, there is something a bit odd about those who pursue it. Life is pointless, death a certainty, and within those two unassailable realities one must find a meaning for himself. The emphasis is on action despite the fact that such action is inevitably futile. The moral response to the certainty of death is not to redirect one's attention to other affairs; nor is a languid melancholy appropriate. Rather the will to truth calls for defiance and affirmation; the poet Dylan Thomas caught the mood when he wrote:

Do not go gentle into that good night
Rage, rage against the dying of the light.

chapter eleven

Erik Erikson

Judged in terms of the scope and originality of his ideas and the depth of his insight, Erik Erikson is appropriately regarded as a peer of Freud, Jung, and McDougall. Moreover, he is the finest writer in the personological tradition since Gordon Allport; Erikson's book, *Gandhi's Truth*, was awarded both a Pulitzer Prize and a National Book Award. Thus, his ideas have outgrown the limits of academic psychology and have become part of the broader intellectual climate of America.

I argued in chapter nine that the sociological perspective poses a major challenge to the conventional assumptions of psychology, and that future progress in understanding the social nature of man depends in part on how well psychological theory can incorporate these sociological insights. Chapter ten presented one solution: the existentialists essentially deny the challenge exists. On the other hand, Erikson confronts the problem directly in his attempt to show, specifically and in detail, how culture can influence personality. In contrast with those who study the parent-child and environmental conditions that destroy individual competence, Erikson is also concerned with how social organization supports and promotes personal effectiveness.

The origins of Erikson's thought can be traced quickly. His back-

Erik Erikson
Harvard University News Office

ground, first of all, is nonacademic. A painter whose formal education ended with the German equivalent of high school, Erikson began his professional career almost accidentally when, at age twenty-five, he became employed as a tutor by one of Freud's patients in Vienna. Almost casually, he began a training analysis with Anna Freud; after completing his training in 1933, Erikson moved to Boston, where he entered private practice as a child analyst. The primary influence in Erikson's intellectual development, then, was psychoanalysis, as reflected by Anna Freud.

A second major influence on Erikson's thought was his exposure to ethnology. After arriving in America, he became acquainted with such prominent anthropologists as Margaret Mead, Skudder McKeel, and Alfred Kroeber and later made field trips to study the Sioux and Yurok Indians of North America. Among the great psychologists only McDougall had more anthropological field experience than Erikson. This familiarity with anthropological theory and practice helps account for Erikson's broad perspective and awareness of the role of social factors in individual development.

One of the most interesting themes in Erikson's writings is his attempt to define his relationship to orthodox psychoanalysis. Erikson regards himself as squarely in the mainstream of psychoanalytic thought. Robert Coles remarks that "... Erikson can be called a strict Freudian because he is loyal to the essential principles that Freud declared to be the core of psychoanalytic work, and because he is very much like Freud— a writer, a man at home in history and philosophy, a clinician who won't let go of the world outside of the office (1970, pp. 267–68)."

His own protestations (and those of his interpreters) notwithstanding, Erikson deviates from classic psychoanalysis in a number of ways:

by broadening Freud's conception of mental dynamics to include more than the conflicts between the id and the ego, and by insisting that the sexual and moral conflicts of children be placed within their socio-economic, historical, and ethnic context. Thus Erikson criticizes the psychoanalytic attitude that people can exist independently and without social organization. This individualistic perspective lacks empirical support and threatens to isolate psychoanalytic theory from modern biology (Erikson, 1964, p. 150). Moreover, as Coles (1970, p. 168) observes, Erikson doubts that "... psychoanalysts [will] someday find some 'level' of mental activity that is ultimately 'deep' and, as it were, *sui generis*, that is, removed from the social and cultural 'conditions' that strike both analysts and nonanalysts of common sense as important." That is, Erikson agrees with Mead and Durkheim that thought is social rather than instinctual in origin. Finally, Erikson criticizes orthodox psychoanalysis for its "originology," the attempt to explain later stages of life in terms of childhood experience. This originology contradicts common sense and is a major conceptual difficulty with psychoanalysis.

SOCIALIZATION AND THE SELF-CONCEPT

Erikson describes the socialization process in terms of eight crises in "psychosocial development"; the resolution of these crises permanently alters a person's self-image and has profound consequences for further personal development. Generally speaking, Erikson's discussion of "the eight stages of man" is his most original and important contribution to personality theory.

The developmental sequence that Erikson describes parallels the classic Freudian stages of psychosexual development. Erikson's discussion, however, extends far beyond the Freudian stages to span the entire human life cycle. Erikson, therefore, is one of the few personality theorists since Carl Jung to discuss in detail the period in life—from age sixteen or eighteen onward—that psychoanalysts treat under the single concept of genital maturity. Each of the eight phases in the human life cycle is characterized by a "phase-specific" developmental task, a problem in social development that must be dealt with conclusively at that time. The solution to this problem, however, has been prepared for during the previous stages of development, and it in turn will have ramifications in the later stages. The problem that defines each stage in development must be resolved before a person can move on to the next. Thus, for Erikson, life proceeds in terms of a series of psychosocial crises, and personality is a function of their outcome.

Consistent with the tradition of ego psychology with which he is identified, Erikson assumes that every child is born "preadapted" to an "average expectable" human (and social) environment. Consistent with his background in anthropology, Erikson feels that in every society there is a "crucial coordination" between the developing individual and the human environment. This coordination is expressed by what he calls "a cogwheeling of the life cycles," a law of reciprocal development that insures that the caretakers in society are most fit to provide care and support at the time when a developing individual needs it most. Thus, in Erikson's terms, the needs and capacities of the generations interwine. He denotes this complex pattern of interdependence between the generations with the term *mutuality*.

Erikson's concepts of mutuality and the cogwheeling of the life cycles reflects his belief that every society has institutions appropriate for our needs during each phase in our psychosocial development. The society into which each of us is born makes us its member by influencing, through these institutions, the manner in which we solve the tasks posed by the various phases of psychosocial development. Thus, these institutions insure that the developing individual will be viable within his society and, at the same time, the society will be renewed and enriched by the contributions of its members.

Erikson considers the eight psychosocial stages he has identified to be universal, common to mankind as a species across societies and throughout history. Although the sequence of developmental phases is universal, the solutions to the problems present within each stage vary from society to society as directed by the prevailing institutions. Erikson therefore shares with Freud a belief that development can be characterized in terms of a limited set of universally valid and formally equivalent stages. He differs from Freud, however, in his belief that socialization neither begins nor ends with the Oedipal crisis. Rather, socialization is progressively advanced yet qualitatively transformed with the resolution of each developmental crisis. It is as if there were a morality appropriate to each stage of development; in an essay entitled "Human Strength and the Cycle of Generations," Erikson in fact argues that certain basic human qualities that he calls virtues, are the expectable end products of the successful completion of each developmental stage.

Erikson's analysis of socialization and the self-concept can be presented best by describing the distinctive features of the eight stages of psychosocial development.

Trust versus Mistrust

In the first stage, which extends roughly through the first year of life, the problem involves developing a firm sense of trust. Feelings of trust are closely tied to forms of maternal care. Specifically, a sense of trust does not depend on the amount of food or demonstrations of affection the infant receives; rather, it seems related to the mother's ability to give her child a sense of familiarity, consistency, continuity, and sameness of experience. "The infant's first social achievement, then, is his willingness to let the mother out of sight without undue anxiety or rage, because she has become an inner certainty as well as an outer predictability (1950, p. 247)."

A child who receives maternal nurturance and care will naturally develop a sense of trust and in later life will be able to provide the same care to his children. The reverse also holds true: inadequate mothering leads to deep, prevading feelings of suspicion and mistrust concerning the world. Erikson feels the absence of basic trust is the primary dynamic in the development of schizophrenia; whether or not this speculation is valid, it seems to be the case that failures at this first stage are rarely overcome in later life, that they produce a tendency toward low self-esteem, depression, and social withdrawal.

The first year of life corresponds to Freud's oral stage. Teeth appear at this time, and the infant must learn to endure the discomfort of teething without biting the source of his food. To experience pleasure while enduring pain, however, is the prototype of masochistic behavior, just as experiencing pleasure while giving pain (i.e., biting) is the forerunner of sadism.

At the level of society the counterpart to the individual's sense of trust is the institution of religion. Religion is both a reflection of man's residual immaturity (i.e., his need to be taken care of) and a source of support and stability in his life. Nor are religions merely delusional systems; as Erikson notes, religions have always recognized (as science and technology tend to forget) "... the abysmal alienations—from the self and from others—which are the human lot (1964, p. 154)."

In his characteristically realistic fashion Erikson makes a final point about the first stage of the life cycle that, it seems to me, many psychoanalytically inspired writers tend to overlook: we should avoid making a Utopia out of the "mother-child relationship." Infancy is only the first, temporary stage of life, and the lessons learned there are rarely of much help in adulthood.

Autonomy versus Shame and Doubt

During the second stage, which corresponds roughly to ages one to three, the problem for the developing child is to achieve a sense of autonomy and self-control. "From a sense of self-control without loss of self-esteem comes a lasting sense of good will and pride; from a sense of loss of self-control and of foreign overcontrol comes a lasting propensity for doubt and shame (Erikson, 1950, p. 254)." A sense of autonomy and self-control is closely related to patterns of parental guidance and control. The parents must exercise enough firmness to protect the child from himself and from meaningless experiences of failure (produced by infantile incompetence). If, however, the child is not allowed to develop a sense of autonomy and free choice (and if his feelings of trust are weak), he will develop a precocious conscience and, thereafter, overcontrol himself. Parental restrictiveness, therefore, may produce a pedantic and compulsively moralistic child.

This second period corresponds to Freud's anal stage; in addition to gaining control of its body and musculature, a child must learn to regulate his bowels. Here, in interaction with his parents during toilet training, a child discovers the difference between holding as a form of caring and holding as a cruel and destructive form of restraint. Conversely, he also learns to distinguish between letting go as a form of destructive releasing, and letting go in the sense of a relaxed tolerance.

The societal counterpart of the child's sense of self-control is the institution of law and order. Legal institutions serve simultaneously to safeguard the feelings of autonomy and will of each person while at the same time coordinating the willfulness of all, thereby allowing the social process to continue. Eventually the sense of autonomy and self-control in childhood develops into a sense of justice in adulthood, in conjunction with the institution of law and order.

Initiative versus Guilt

The third stage begins around age three and concerns the child's problem of learning what kind of person he can become, of defining the limits of the permissible. This is a time of walking, exploring, and dawning sexual curiosity. The child "... is apt to develop an untiring curiosity about differences in sizes in general, and sexual differences in particular. ... His learning is now eminently intrusive and vigorous: it leads away from his own limitations and into future possibilities (1959, p. 76)." This stage is encouraged to a large degree by a child's ability to move around more freely, by his newly found language ability that permits him to ask questions of his parents, and by a radically expanded imagination that allows him to speculate beyond the information actually given. Once again, the manner in which parents deal with a child's exploratory curiosity during this period is critical for later development. The problem concerns mutual regulation, not merely in eating and bowel control, but in social behavior more broadly defined.

This third period corresponds to Freud's phallic stage which, as we know, culminates in the Oedipal crisis. This is the time when the child ostensibly fears his genitals will be harmed as punishment for erotic fantasies. It is also the time of conscience development when parental dictates are internalized and set up in opposition to instinctual demands. The danger of this stage, according to Erikson, is that a child may feel guilty about the goals that—out of sheer exuberance over his newly-developed abilities—he has set for himself. This guilt will blunt his sense of initiative. Moreover, the conscience that develops at the end of the Oedipal crisis is, at best, harsh, punitive, and immature. Thus, further development requires that this conscience be outgrown.

A failure of trust in the first stage may lead to schizophrenia, a failure of autonomy in the second stage may lead to obsessive-compulsive disorders, and the guilt caused by a failure of initiative in the third stage appears in adulthood as hysterical neuroses, as impotence and frigidity, as a form of showing off that overcompensates for low self-esteem, and as various forms of psychosomatic illnesses.

The social institution coordinated with this third stage is economics. The economic ethos of a culture is absorbed, according to Erikson, when a child, through identification with his parents, ties the fantasied aspirations of childhood to the socially permissible goals of adulthood.

Industry versus Inferiority

In the fourth stage, which encompasses the school years and corresponds to the latency period in psychoanalysis, a child is concerned with doing things, alone and with others. As Erikson observes, ". . . before the child, psychologically already a rudimentary parent, can become a biological parent, he must begin to be a worker and potential provider (1950, p. 258)." Thus, during the latency period a child learns to seek recognition and praise by producing things; by adjusting himself to the impersonal laws of tools and craftsmanship, a child develops a sense of industry, a capacity for productive and self-expressive work.

In all cultures children at this age are taught the roles of adulthood and the techniques of economic survival in an organized and didactic fashion. In the modern industrial state, however, these tutorial practices have become overblown. The goals of modern technology are considerably removed from the necessities for survival and are thus diffuse and ill-defined. Adult roles have also become ill-defined. The education process is no longer tied to the concrete goals of individual economic survival; education has become an end in itself, a self-contained enterprise divorced from social reality.

Erikson does not comment on the sort of parent-child relationship necessary to promote a sense of industry. He is, however, clear about the consequences of failure at this stage. If a child fails to develop a sense of industry, he will have feelings of inadequacy concerning his tool-using skills, sense of craftsmanship, and status among his co-workers. He may lose confidence in his ability to take part in the working world. Thus one's self-image as a competent, productive, and capable worker is closely tied to the outcome of the tutorial years.

The social institution that corresponds to this stage in human development is a culture's technology, and it is during this fourth stage that a child acquires a sense of the technological ethos of his culture. One should identify with this ethos, but not to an exaggerated degree. If a person ". . . accepts work as his only obligation, and 'what works' as his only criterion of worthwhileness, he may become the conformist and thoughtless slave of his technology and of those who are in a position to exploit it (1950, p. 261)."

Identity versus Identity Diffusion

Freud considered instinctual repression to be the major psychological problem of the Victorian period; Erikson argues, however, that the central conflict for twentieth-century Americans is one of establishing a sense of personal identity. Although the problem of identity seems particularly acute today, it has always been a critical stage in the life cycle. Erikson is perhaps best known for his discussion of this topic; it is as central to his writing as sexuality was to Freud and functional autonomy was to Allport.

This stage is the culmination of one's childhood experiences; the first seventeen or eighteen years of life are, in a sense, designed to prepare one to handle this crisis. The problem of identity emerges when, after completing one's training in the technology and technological ethos of one's culture, one has to choose a mate and an occupation. If the first four developmental crises have been successfully resolved, and if the society itself is reasonably structured, then the identity crisis can be dealt with in a relatively effortless manner.

In his most explicit essay on the subject, Erikson defines identity as follows: "The conscious feeling of having a *personal identity* is based on two simultaneous observations: the immediate perception of one's self-samedness and continuity in time; and the simultaneous perception of the fact that others recognize one's samedness and continuity (1959, p. 23)." According to Erikson, then, in order to achieve a sense of identity ". . . the young individual must learn to be most himself where he means most to others—those others, to be sure, who have come to mean most to him (1959, p. 102)."

A sense of identity depends on the presence of certain environmental as well as psychological conditions. That is, an identity can be complete only when there is a congruence between a person's biological drives, his personal abilities, and his social opportunities. The structure of society, therefore, is a major determinant of the form of the identity crisis. The social institution most important in this regard is an ideology. An ideology, according to Erikson, is an unconscious set of values and assumptions underlying the religious, scientific, and political thought of a culture; the purpose of an ideology is ". . . to create a world image convincing enough to support the collective and the individual sense of identity (1958, p. 22)." Ideologies offer young people overly simplified but definite answers to those basic questions associated with identity conflict (e.g., "Who am I?" "Where am I going?", etc.). Ideologies often direct youth into activities that challenge the established procedures of a culture—into rebellion, riots, and revolutions. In the name of ideology youth also seeks hardship and discipline, found by wandering and exploring frontiers, by physical training and intellectual concentration. Ideologies then are a primary tool for mobilizing and directing the energies of youth—and this energy can be used for sinister as well as benevolent purposes, as Hitler's youth movement and John Kennedy's Peace Corps indicate.

One's sense of identity is normally unconscious; we become aware of its presence (or absence) only during moments of crisis. It is more typically experienced as a sense of psychosocial well-being, as ". . . a feeling of being at home in one's body, a sense of 'knowing where one is going,' and an inner assuredness of anticipated recognition from those who count (1959, p. 118)." A sense of identity, however, is never permanently gained or maintained. Rather, it is periodically lost and regained, although more enduring and efficient methods of identity maintenance and restoration are developed in late adolescence.

It frequently happens that, upon reaching the age when a choice of identity is necessary, a young person is unable to do so. At this point a person may take what Erikson calls a psychosocial moratorium, "a prolongation of the interval between youth and adulthood," during which time the young person lives somewhat purposelessly, waiting to find himself. In the United States, the psychosocial moratorium has been institutionalized in the form of a system of higher education that allows young people to forestall the identity crisis until their middle twenties.

As we have seen, Erikson departs from orthodox psychoanalysis by suggesting that socialization is progressively advanced and transformed at each stage in the life cycle. He further departs from Freud in maintaining that each successive developmental crisis bestows on a person a characteristic self-image. At the end of the first stage of development, for example, a child may see himself as one who is (or is not) worth caring about. At the end of the second stage the self-image might be that of one who will go far or as one who might go too far. In the third stage, self-images depend on the scope of a child's aspirations and whether they are maintained in a confident or a guilty fashion. These self-perceptions are critical because, taken together, they prepare one's sense of identity. If the various self-images are too inconsistent with one another, then a firm sense of identity will not develop.

This discussion of self-image can be summarized in terms of three points. First, a characteristic self-image emerges from each stage of psychosocial development. Second, these self-images are socially bestowed: they depend on the interaction between a child, his caretakers, and the culture in which they live. Third, a sense of identity depends on one's having an integrated set of self-images derived from the first four stages of the life cycle.

Implicit in Erikson's concept of identity is his analysis of the mechanisms by which culture influences personality. To show how this analysis works, let us start with Erikson's observation that psychosocial development can stop at the stage of identity formation for two reasons. Development will be arrested in the first case if a person fails to resolve any of the earlier developmental crises. In the second case, development stops because the identity the person achieves is not viable within the larger context of society. This happens, for example, when the healthy identity attained by a member of an ethnic minority is incompatible with the adult identity required by the overclass.

Erikson uses as an example of this point the fate of many Sioux Indians who now live on the large reservation in South Dakota. As he observes, child-rearing practices change more slowly than social circumstances (because the parents of each generation tend to raise their children as they themselves were). For centuries the Sioux survived by following the buffalo herds roaming the great central prairies of North America. Sioux mothers, consequently, evolved a set of child-rearing practices designed to produce buffalo hunters. Each stage of psychosocial development was handled so as to encourage male Sioux children to be self-confident, resourceful, independent, personally courageous, and, on demand, murderously aggressive. Within the community every possible educational device was used to develop maximum self-confidence in the boys. They were extensively indulged by their mothers, and their right to autonomy and duty of initiative were constantly emphasized. As a result the boys learned to direct all their hostility outward into the pursuit of game and the enemy, or inward against themselves in the pursuit of spiritual power. As Erikson notes, although this system worked well for the Sioux man, "... one cannot help feeling that the woman was exploited for the sake of the hunter's unbroken 'spirit'; and, indeed, it is said that suicides were not uncommon among Sioux women, although unknown among men (1950, p. 144)."

Certain general character traits were necessary for the Sioux to exploit successfully the buffalo economy. Specifically, competition within the group had to be ruthlessly suppressed and redirected toward other groups—primarily, the buffalo and generally the external environment. Moreover, because the tribes were constantly on the move, acquisitive and hoarding tendencies would threaten the group's mobility. Thus, the accumulation of material goods (i.e., anal retentiveness) was discouraged.

The combination of ferocious independence, high spirituality, ingroup solidarity, a refusal to compete within the tribe, and the absence of acquisitive tendencies add up to a character structure that is the antithesis of American middle class identity. Thus, a young Sioux with a well-established sense of Sioux identity will be, by definition, out of step with American society.

The power of Erikson's analysis can be appreciated further if it is applied to the life of Malcolm X, the great American black leader of the 1950s and 60s. Born Malcolm Little, the son of Earl Little, a Baptist minister and militant supporter of Marcus Garvey's black separatist movement, Malcolm was a big, bright, talented boy who seems to have been the favorite of both his parents. Although his childhood was traumatic by middle class standards, Malcolm X apparently resolved the first four psychosocial crises in an acceptable fashion. By late adolescence he was an excellent student, the president of his class, and ready to confront the choice of an identity. "And then one day ... something happened which was to become the first major turning point of my life. Somehow, I happened to be alone in the classroom with Mr. Ostrowski, my English teacher ... He was a natural-born 'advisor' ... who said ... 'Malcolm, you ought to be thinking about a career. Have you been giving it any thought?' " (Malcolm X, 1964, pp. 35–36). When Malcolm said he would like to be a lawyer, his white advisor told him the choice was unrealistic, that he should think instead of becoming a carpenter. "The more I thought afterwards about what he said, the more uneasy it made me. It just kept treading around in my mind ... I realized that whatever I wasn't, I *was* smarter than nearly all those white kids. But apparently I was still not intelligent enough in their eyes, to become whatever *I* wanted to be (1964, pp. 36–37)."

When faced with the identity crisis, this otherwise well-integrated youngster discovered that the overclass—white society—had prepared an identity for him that was utterly unacceptable. And, according to Erikson,

"... should a child feel that the environment tries to deprive him too radically of all the forms of expression which permit him to integrate the next step in his ego identity, he will resist with the astonishing strength encountered in animals who are suddenly forced to defend their lives. Indeed, in the social jungle of human existence, there is no feeling of being alive without a sense of identity (1950, p. 24)."

Thus, Malcolm X developed a negative identity: he became a "hoodlum, thief, dope peddler, pimp", the antithesis of the "Uncle Tom" identity that white society demanded. It was several years later, through his experience with the Black Muslin movement, that he was able to assume the identity that his childhood membership in a minority culture had prepared him for: that of a militant, semireligious, moral leader of an oppressed minority.

Intimacy versus Isolation

At the resolution of the identity crisis a person leaves childhood and moves into the trajectory of his life. If there is a generation gap, then this is where it occurs. This first stage of adulthood concerns the problem of intimacy and parallels the Freudian concept of genitality. Intimacy is possible only when based on a firm sense of identity; one must know clearly who he is before he can risk losing himself in another person.

According to Erikson, genitality must include mutuality of orgasm with a loved partner of the opposite sex, with whom one shares a mutual trust, regulates the continuing cycles of work, procreation, and recreation, and provides one's children with everything necessary for their satisfactory development. Erikson's concept of genitality, then, bears little relation to a free love ethic or the notion that maturity is simply the capacity for good orgasms.

Erikson qualifies the Freudian concept of genitality in two additional ways. First, he acknowledges that psychoanalysts are wrong if they believe that genitality is a universal cure for the problems of society. Second, he further maintains that the psychoanalytic notion of genitality carries a strong social class bias—the kind of mutuality of orgasm that psychoanalysis has in mind is most readily attained by classes and cultures that have enough leisure time to devote themselves to the pursuit of such goals. But most of the world's people have neither the time nor the resources for such pursuits. Erikson argues then that genitality entails only the potentiality for orgasm, but includes as well the capacity to withstand genital frustrations without serious regression.

At a more abstract level, genitality includes a willingness to fuse one's identity with others, to commit oneself to lasting affiliations and social obligations, and to honor these commitments even if they require personal sacrifice. The social institution that is coordinated with this phase of the life cycle is ethics: an ethical sense evolves as one recognizes the areas of adult duty, as one learns with whom he must and must not compete.

In a later essay, Erikson (1964) suggests that moral development passes through three necessary stages: the Oedipal stage wherein one acquires moralizing tendencies; the stage of identity, wherein one perceives the universal good in ideological terms; and finally, the stage of intimacy wherein a truly ethical sense develops.

People who fail to develop a capacity for intimacy come to avoid intimate contacts; they withdraw into themselves, feel isolated, and besome self-absorbed. This can lead to severe "character disorders;" i.e., to people who lack any ethical sense. Only when people have a capacity for intimacy can they face the next stage in development.

Generativity versus Stagnation

In the second and socially the most important stage of adulthood the problem involves generativity, a concern with "establishing and guiding the next generation." The concept of generativity includes the more ordinary terms of productivity and creativity.

The ability to lose oneself in others through a meeting of bodies *and* minds produces an expansion of interests that may include ever larger sections of the community. Merely to want or to have children is not evidence of generativity. On the contrary, many people who are parents have not reached this stage, because of failures at any of the preceding stages. In any case, when people fail to achieve a sense of generativity, they may regress to an obsessive need for pseudo-intimacy. "Individuals, then, often begin to indulge themselves as if they were their own—or one another's—one and only child (1950, p. 267)." There is no one single social institution that parallels the problem of generativity; it is broadly associated with education, art, and science.

Integrity versus Despair

In the integrity crisis one returns again to "the portals of nothingness." The problem here concerns how to grow old with integrity and how in death to give meaning to life. Integrity is possible only for those who have been productive in work, in parenthood, or both and who have some idea of the successes and failures inherent in adulthood. Integrity is characterized by the feeling that subsequent crises in living can be managed, a feeling that life is somehow worthwhile in spite of the sufferings it contains, and a sense that one's life was as it had to be. Integrity includes an awareness of the relativity of life-styles, yet a readiness to defend one's own against "all physical and economic threats."

Every viable culture or civilization develops a unique style of integrity in which those who are able participate. Nonetheless, persons of integrity have a good deal in common regardless of their cultural origins. Those who are unable to deal with the integrity crisis experience despair and the fear of death. Despair reflects the person's feeling that there is no time to begin another life, to seek a better path. It also indicates that the person is unwilling to affirm the one life he has lived.

All the great cultural institutions of a civilization are relevant to this last stage of human development: economics, politics, philosophy, and religion. To achieve integrity, a person must be a follower of and a participant in one of these institutions.

Finally, with this stage, the two endpoints of the life cycle come together. According to Erikson, the development of trust in children depends on the integrity of their fathers: "... healthy children will not fear life if their elders have integrity enough not to fear death (1950, p. 269)."

The theme underlying the rather lengthy foregoing discussion of socialization and the self-concept is that, in viable societies, there is a reciprocal interplay between social institutions and human development. Socialization is advanced and transformed by the resolution of the crisis that defines each stage in the life cycle. Moreover, the resolution of each stage confers on a developing individual a particular self-image; these self-images together produce a sense of identity and the various forms of adult personality. I mentioned earlier that Erikson's most significant contribution may be his analysis of how culture can influence personality. It seems appropriate to close this section with a summary of that analysis.

Each human society is located within a specific and concrete set of historical, economic, and geographical circumstances. In response to the pressures and demands of their environment, the members of each community, individually and collectively, develop a particular set of attitudes, values, and behaviors. The long term survival of the group depends on: (1) the degree to which its institutionalized attitudes, values, and behaviors are appropriate to the demands of the environment; and (2) the degree to which these are effectively transmitted to the next generation.

Thus, the mothers of a culture unconsciously develop a particular set of child-rearing practices, that tend to produce the adult character types best adapted to deal with the historical, economic, and geographic concerns of that group. If, as in the case of the Sioux, the contingencies change, then the institutionalized child-rearing practices must also change in order for the culture to remain viable. The point here, however, is that there is no direct relationship between culture and personality. Rather, cultures develop as responses to environmental demands. An important element of each culture is its child-rearing practices. And it is through the specific child-training behavior of each set of parents in a society that culture makes its mark on personality.

MOTIVATION

Erikson has been concerned primarily with understanding human development and its relationship to supporting social institutions. Consequently he has focused on the concepts of socialization, the self-concept, and psychological health, and the other root ideas receive only glancing treatment. A discussion of Erikson's concepts of motivation, the unconscious, and explanation must therefore be somewhat speculative.

Like Freud and McDougall, Erikson takes the biological substrates of social behavior seriously. He feels that a discussion of human development must begin by describing the processes "inherent in the organism"; these processes are, of course, instincts, that in animals are "... relatively inborn, relatively early, ready-to-use ways of interacting with a segment of nature ... (1950, p. 94)." Man's instincts are unreliable and incomplete guides to behavior and must be given form and structure by the social process: "Man's 'inborn instincts' are drive fragments to be assembled, given meaning, and organized during a prolonged childhood by methods of child training and schooling which vary from culture to culture and are determined by tradition (1950, p. 98)." Thus, the socialization process elaborates the infant's innate fragmentary drives, integrating them into conscience and tradition.

Implicit in Erikson's developmental model are four fragmentary drives that must be harnessed and directed by socialization; these drives represent Erikson's theory of motivation. The first is, of course, sex, which seems to emerge most prominently at stage three (Initiative), but which is fully articulated during stage six (Intimacy). In contrast with Freud, who often spoke as if people exist for their libido, Erikson argues that one must place sexuality in its proper context: there is more to human motivation than the search for sexual release. The dynamics of psychosocial development suggest the presence of three additional drive fragments.

The emphasis Erikson puts on stage one (basic trust) as critical for later development is justified by a series of empirical investigations known collectively as "maternal deprivation studies." Children who are deprived of maternal contact and attention—mothering—during the first portion of their lives often experience severe psychological trauma, and in some cases may even die (Spitz, 1945). Ainsworth (1969) and Bowlby (1969), the most important modern students of this phenomenon, describe it in terms of "attachment." But whether it is called trust or attachment, this early infant requirement seems to rest on a need for positive, friendly attention and social interaction, a need that persists in a modified but undiminished form in adults. Commenting on this motivational theme in Erikson's work, Coles observes, "We are born with the need for someone to do more than feed us. We need to be held, recognized, and affirmed (1970, p. 287)." Erikson's second drive fragment, then, seems to be a need for social attention. It appears at the beginning of psychosocial development and remains a persistent theme throughout the rest of development, although it is particularly important during the identity crisis.

The motivational assumption implicit in the crises of autonomy, initiative, industry, and generativity is something like a need for competence—a need to master oneself and the environment—that in adult life is expressed in occupational choice. Erikson remarks in *Young Man Luther* (p. 17) that "... the most neglected problem in psychoanalysis is the problem of work." The need for competence (White, 1959) includes self-mastery, self-expression, and imposing one's will on the environment; it resembles aggression as defined by James, McDougall, and more recently by Lorenz (1967) and Ardrey (1970). A need for competence is implicit in four of Erikson's eight stages and seems to play a central role in his motivational theory.

Erikson's final motivational assumption, implicit in stage five (identity) is a need for structure and order in one's social affairs. With an ideology a young person acquires a pervasive meaning system, a conceptual overlay that renders the world predictable and orderly. Here Erikson makes a substantial contribution, it seems to me, to the psychological analysis of religion. He suggests that people do not have religious needs per se; rather they seek religion for many purposes, especially to give meaning and order to their lives.

THE UNCONSCIOUS

Erikson often uses the concept of the unconscious in a manner consistent with Freud's usage—as referring to mental elements that have been repressed as a defense against anxiety. But Erikson goes beyond Freud: he feels that the personal unconscious contains unconscious expectations and anticipations left over from each stage in the life cycle. Thus, the personal unconscious includes a person's attitudes toward the basic issues of trust, autonomy, initiative, etc. These unconscious expectations determine a large part of one's interactions with others, and they remain unconscious primarily through repression.

In most cases, however, Erikson seems more concerned with analyzing the sociological unconscious—those aspects of one's culture and social class that influence one's behavior but lie outside of one's awareness. Indeed, if the fundamental thrust of Freud's work is seen as an exploration of the *personal unconscious,* and Jung's primary goal is interpreted as an analysis of the *collective unconscious,* then much of Erikson's writing can be regarded as a description of how the *sociological unconscious* operates in everyday life.

The culture into which we are born provides us with a set of values and a world view or metaphysic—usually a religion. Culture also gives us prototypical images of good and evil, usually embodied in heroic legends, folk songs, and myths. These world views, values, and heroic and evil images are absorbed very early in life and are important parts of one's identity. Thus, identity formation itself rests on the sociological unconscious. "While the end of adolescence . . . is the stage of an overt identity *crisis,* identity *formation* neither begins nor ends with adolescence: it is a lifelong development largely unconscious to the individual and to his society (Erikson, 1959, p. 113)."

The following is one Erikson's many examples of how the sociological unconscious functions in everyday life. A German soldier moved to the United States to escape Nazism. His son was quite young when the family left Germany and was quickly "Americanized." Over time, however, he developed a violent, neurotic reaction to authority that Erikson described as an "unconscious one-boy-Hitler-youth rebellion," a reaction typical of many German boys his age. The parents sent the boy to a military school, a move that might have seriously exacerbated the boy's already neurotic authority problems. According to Erikson, however, the moment the boy was handed a uniform a marked change came over him: he was transformed into an unconscious Hitler youth—an adolescent member of the *Wehrmacht*—disguised as an American military schoolboy. At this point the father became a mere civilian and his son's rebellion disappeared. Somehow, Erikson observes, this father, and his male relatives and friends—probably in talking about the exploits of the German army in World War I—had unconsciously established in the boy "the military prototype" that, in the German mind is "one of the few thor-

Erik Erikson   **181**

oughly German and highly developed identities (Erikson, 1959, p. 27)."
As might be expected, the unconscious identity emerged in spite of the
boy's changed cultural circumstances.

Through his subtle and skillful analyses of the unconscious work-
ings of culture in the individual mind, Erikson has expanded and enriched significantly the concept of the unconscious.

EXPLANATION

Erikson explains the similarities in human nature in terms of man's
common biology. We are all impelled by drive fragments that have been
described here as needs for social attention, sexual release, order and
predictability, and competence. We are also similar in that we all pass
through the same psychosocial crises that serve to modify and control our
biology. Erikson explains individual differences within a particular society
or culture in terms of a person's biography, giving special attention to the
outcome of each psychosocial crisis; i.e., people differ from one another to
the extent that they have developed a sense of trust, autonomy, initiative,
and industry.

Finally, Erikson explains particular symptoms, anomalous behavior,
and dreams through interpretation, using his considerable knowledge of
history, ethnographic material, and sensitivity to language. These interpretations are combined with psychoanalysis and common sense to produce complex thematic patterns within which the action in question is
seen to be overdetermined. And how does Erikson know if an interpretation is correct? An aesthetic judgment certainly forms part of the answer,
and Erikson is also pleased if the patient agrees with it. Most importantly, however, ". . . the proof lies in the way in which the com-
munication between therapist and patient 'keeps moving,' leading to new
and surprising insights and to the patient's greater assumption of responsibility for himself (1964, p. 75)."

PSYCHOLOGICAL HEALTH

If the unconscious is Freud's "god term"—his primary explanatory
concept, denoting a powerful but ineffable agency responsible for most
of man's misery—then the ego is the god term for Erikson and the ego
psychologists. Psychological health for Erikson is basically a function of
the strength of one's ego. The ego is a concept that indicates man's

capacity to unify his experience and actions in an adaptive fashion. The ego "... guards the coherence and individuality of experience ... by enabling [the person] to anticipate inner as well as outer dangers; and by integrating endowments and social opportunities (1950, p. 35)." Thus, for Erikson, the ego is an inner-psychic regulator that organizes experience and subsequently protects us from pressures arising in both the id and the superego. He believes that the "... ego in psychoanalysis, then, is analogous to what it was in philosophy in earlier usage: a selective, integrating, coherent and persistent agency central to personality formation (1964, p. 147)."

As we noted earlier, Erikson has been largely concerned with examining the manner in which social organization supports the development of the individual ego. But Erikson is sensitive to the same theme that preoccupied the early sociologists and existentialists: the increasing alienation and fragmentation that seem to characterize modern industrial society. Because societal institutions no longer cohere, the resolution of the identity conflict will be more difficult for developing persons within a given culture. Thus, according to Erikson, the identity conflict has become the prototypical form of neurosis among the young in modern society. What are the symptoms of an identity crisis? They include a disturbance in the experience of time—feelings of urgency followed by a sense that time is already lost and is therefore irrelevant. There also can be a disrupted sense of workmanship, resulting from an inability to concentrate or from a self-defeating preoccupation with very specific, usually irrelevant pursuits. Related symptoms include excessive self-awareness and an abhorrence of competition. All these symptoms can combine to produce, as in the case of the young Malcom X, a negative identity that leads to a contempt for one's own family and ethnic history and an overvaluation of themes from foreign cultures.

It is clear from Erikson's theory of psychosocial development that proper human development requires not one but a series of basic environments, each tailored to a separate stage of the life cycle. When social institutions and human development are properly coordinated, certain strengths emerge from each psychosocial stage. Psychological health can be defined in terms of these strengths. The strength or virtue associated with earliest infancy is *hope,* that arises from early experiences with trustworthy maternal persons. Hope is reflected in a lifelong, usually unconscious, belief that one's most fervent wishes are attainable. The opposite of this is, of course, hopelessness, a state that typifies most forms of mental illness.

The virtue appropriate to the second stage of development is *will,* a resolute determination to make one's own choices, to exercise both free will and self-restraint. "Will is the basis for the acceptance of law and necessity, and it is rooted in the judiciousness of parents guided by the spirit of the law (1964, p. 119)." The opposite of will, for Erikson, is a sense of having been defeated.

The third stage in life gives rise to a sense of *purpose*, the capacity to project goals for oneself and pursue them. Purpose begins in childhood play, its mature form depends on the ability to tell the difference between "playing around" and purposeful activity. Purpose is closely related to conscience development.

The fourth virtue or human strength, *competence*, eventually characterizes workmanship. It is the ability to exercise one's physical and mental skills without their being impaired by an infantile sense of inferiority.

The virtue that emerges from adolescence is called *fidelity*, the ability to sustain and maintain freely given commitments. Fidelity is the basis of identity and is rooted in youthful ideologies. It is manifested in a sense of duty, in accuracy, and the desire to portray reality accurately. It also appears as truthfulness, sincerity, genuineness, and authenticity, as a sense of fairness in rule-governed contexts, and finally, as a sense of devotion.

The virtue that characterizes the sixth psychosocial stage is *love*, that Erikson calls "the greatest of human virtues." Although love comes in many forms, it is most appropriately defined, according to Erikson, as "the mutuality of mates and partners in a shared identity."

In the generative phase of the life cycle the critical virtue is *care*, in which human adults must extend their personal involvements (McDougall's self-regarding sentiment) over the "long, parallel and overlapping childhoods" of youngsters in their own homes and in their community. One important aspect of care is teaching; "... man *needs* to teach, not only for the sake of those who need to be taught, and not only for the fulfillment of his identity, but because facts are kept alive by being told, logic by being demonstrated, truth by being professed (1964, p. 131)." All mature adults are (or should be) teachers.

The virtue appropriate to the final stage of life is *wisdom*, a detached concern with life in the face of death. Erikson argues that the final stage of life must be lived with vigor and intelligence so that the coming generations may have an example of the closure of a life-style.

For Erikson, then, psychological health can be defined in terms of the degree to which one possesses the virtues appropriate to his point in the life cycle. In another context Erikson provides a much briefer formulation of the distinctive characteristics of psychological health: "Man, to take his place in society, must acquire a 'conflict-free,' habitual use of a dominant *faculty*, to be elaborated in an occupation; a limitless *resource*, a feedback, as it were, from the immediate exercise of this occupation; and finally, an intelligible *theory* of the processes of life ... (1959, p. 110)."

EVALUATION

We turn now to an evaluation of Erikson's contribution to the personological tradition, beginning with some critical observations. First, although Erikson has advanced significantly our understanding of the socialization process, there is an important residual ambiguity in his discussion. It is never clear what it is that child-rearing practices transmit, to the children of a particular culture. Does child-training instill values, that then persist because others expect the child to have them? Or, alternatively, does child-training produce behavioral traits that are subsequently rationalized by adult values? Do children, in response to parental treatment, develop traits, learn values, or acquire expectations? One is never sure what Erikson intends on this point.

Second, a recurrent theme in Erikson's discussion of child-rearing is that, given certain minimal environment supports, human development will essentially unfold in a prosocial fashion; caretakers can, under reasonably normal conditions, expect children to develop properly. This amounts to recommending permissiveness in child-rearing. Yet common sense and personal experience suggest that some children need considerably more control and guidance than others. Most parents are probably not capable of exercising permissiveness and trust with Erikson's judiciousness. Finally, empirical evidence suggests that after the first year of life permissive child-rearing practices may produce insecure, hostile, and impulsive children (Baumrind, 1971).

Third, Erikson shares the usual psychoanalytic hostility toward conventional morality—that the truly moral person will ignore the conventional rules of his society when it seems appropriate. For Erikson the proper standard for social conduct is a combination of the Golden Rule, Freud's ethic of honesty (minimum self-deception), and Gandhi's concept of Satyagraha (nonviolence). Although Erikson's version of the Golden Rule is an appealing formulation of a psychologically-based categorical imperative, his standard seems far too ambitious to be a guide for practical action; few people are capable of governing their lives with such lofty principles. On the other hand, if we could enforce on a universal basis a few simple dictates of conventional morality—such as telling the truth and not murdering babies—we could significantly reduce the total amount of human suffering in the world. The tendency of social scientists (including Erikson) to regard the conventional rules of a society as having only questionable moral justification derives from an overly optimistic view of man's capacity for benevolent self-restraint.

Fourth, although Erikson takes great pains to express his admiration for and fidelity to Freudian theory, his best ideas are essentially unrelated to the main body of orthodox psychoanalysis. As Yankelovich and Barrett (1971, p. 121) observe, ". . . however skillful [he is] in blurring the divergence between him and the official theory, the fact remains that . . . the logic of Erikson's thought creates a yawning gap between him and the prevailing orthodoxy." Thus, ". . . Erikson affords us the curious picture of a prominent psychonanalytic theorist who ignores four-fifths of Freud's metapsychology and uses the remainder idiosyncratically (p. 153)." The following is merely a partial list of Erikson's disagreements with Freud: Erikson has a sympathetic understanding of the role of ideologies in promoting psychological health (Freud thought ideological commitment was itself a sign of neurosis); he regards the superego as a biological given rather than an imposition of civilization; he feels that neurosis must be understood from the perspective of what it means to be healthy rather than the reverse; he rejects Freud's "originology"—for example, a sense of identity cannot be reduced to infantile sexuality; he uses the self-concept in a fashion precisely analogous to G.H. Mead (Erikson, 1959, p. 147) whereas Freud never uses the term; and he regards society as supporting rather than frustrating biological development. But perhaps the most telling sign of how far Erikson has deviated from Freudian orthodoxy is that the most important parts of his classic studies of Martin Luther and Gandhi—the manner in which these men resolved their respective identity crises—has nothing to do with psychoanalysis. Erikson, therefore, should be regarded as an original and important thinker in his own right and not merely as an ego psychologist and a Freudian apologist.

The foregoing paragraph conveys some indication of Erikson's originality. Three additional points should be mentioned as a means of summarizing his positive contribution. First, more than any other psychologist in the personological tradition, Erikson understands the common man. The model of man that forms the data base for a great deal of psychological theory is that of a bright, well-to-do, articulate, and socially-skilled undergraduate; it is, consequently, a profoundly distorted image in that it represents only a small fraction of mankind. In contrast, Erikson's brilliant essays on American, German, Russian, Sioux, and Yurok identities reveal that he has an extraordinary knack for understanding and sympathetically portraying the mentality of common folk in America and other cultures. This talent gives Erikson's work a scope and generality rarely found in psychological theory.

Second, other than Carl Jung, Erikson is the only great psychologist to suggest that human development occurs over the course of the entire life cycle. Moreover, Erikson's epigenetic theory represents a substantial improvement over Jung's primitive developmental model. In view of the still prevalent tendency among Freudians to equate developmental psychology with the study of infants, Erikson seems to have outstripped psychoanalytic theory in yet another area.

Finally, Erikson has provided the most explicit, detailed, and convincing answer thus far to the question of how culture influences personality. In his discussion of the manner in which the needs and capacities of the generations are interrelated, and of how groups find ways to support human development while ensuring that the developing person will be viable within that group, Erikson has suggested a conceptual means by which psychology can begin to take account of the empirical contributions of sociology and anthropology. Thus he has offered a potential solution to the problem posed by sociological theory—one of the most important problems in the social sciences. In view of this contribution one can sympathize with Yankelovich and Barrett's view that Erikson is probably among the great minds of his age.

chapter twelve

Psychological
Role
Theory

This chapter outlines a third possible response to the challenge of the sociological perspective. The viewpoint—primarily my own—draws heavily on contemporary approaches to the study of social behavior, most particularly on the ethological perspective of Lorenz and Tinbergen, on anthropological research, and on role theory as exemplified by Cottrell (1942), Goffman (1959), and Sarbin (Sarbin and Allen, 1968). The chapter makes use of two metaphors: society as a game of games, and man as a rule-following animal. According to a recently emerging perspective in the philosophy of science, social interaction occurs in rule-governed episodes; man's self-consciousness and playfulness tend to turn these episodes into games (whose outcomes, however, are often very serious); social life consists of moving from one game to another; in each game people invent roles to play; roles are sets of rules; and social action is explained in terms of the rules an actor is following. (Harré and Secord, 1973; Hogan and Henley, 1970).

The *Oxford Dictionary of the English Language* defines the word *role* in two ways. On the one hand, role refers to a part in a play to which individuals are recruited if the play is to be performed—this is how the word is used by sociologists, except that they substitute *social process* for the word *play*. On the other hand, role refers to a self-constructed performance that one puts on, usually for the benefit of others, to achieve some personal goal—this is how the word will be used in this chapter.

Roles may be the natural units of social behavior. Three considerations prompt this conclusion. First, perceptive nonpsychologists from Shakespeare to the present have tended to describe social relations in role-theoretical terms. Consider the following from the novelist John Barth (1958, pp. 27–28):

> "I'm a cad," I agreed readily, and rose to leave ... The game was spoiled now, of course: I had assigned to Miss Rankin the role of Forty-Year-Old Pickup ... I had no interest whatever in the quite complex (and no doubt interesting, from another point of view) human being she might be apart from that role. What she should have done, it seems to me ... was assign me a role gratifying to her own vanity—say, The Fresh But Unintelligent Young Man Whose Body One Uses for One's Pleasure Without Otherwise Taking Him Seriously—and then we could have pursued our business with no wounds inflicted on either side. As it was, my present feeling ... was essentially the same feeling one has when a filling-station attendant or cab driver launches into his life story: as a rule ... one wishes the man to be nothing more difficult than The Obliging Filling-Station Attendant or the Adroit Cab driver. These are essences you have assigned them, at least temporarily, for your own purposes, as a taleteller makes a man The Handsome Young Poet or the Jealous Old Husband; and while you know very well that no historical human being was ever *just* an Obliging Filling-Station Attendant or a Handsome Young Poet, you are nevertheless prepared to ignore your man's charming complexities— *must* ignore them, in fact, if you are to get things done according to schedule ... we are all casting directors a great deal of the time, if not always; and he is wise who realizes that his role-assigning is at best an arbitrary distortion of the actors' personalities; but he is even wiser who sees in addition that his arbitrariness is probably inevitable, and at any rate is apparently necessary if one would reach the ends he desires.

A second reason for regarding roles as the natural unit of social behavior is that ethologists find the term useful for describing animal behavior. According to McBride (1971) for example, animal social behavior has three levels of organization: the caste, the role, and the interaction. Caste depends primarily on age and sex. Roles depend on social rank within a particular caste; dominant animals have the most distinctive roles. Various roles combine to form the basic interactional repertoire of castes. Crook (1971, p. 250) analyzes primate social behavior in role-theoretical terms; peer interaction in primates produces an "... individual style of behavior for each animal. The style adopted by an animal ... defines the animal's social position." Thus, in gregarious animals roles are a major unit of social interaction, role behavior is the product, McBride suggests, of natural selection, and roles determine the nature of interaction among animals.

Third, research by myself and my colleagues further suggests that roles are a natural social unit because role (and rule)-governed interactions begin so early in life. For example, children as young as three and a half show a remarkable ability to invent roles and use them to structure their play. They find role-play intrinsically enjoyable and become visibly upset when their playmates refuse to honor reasonable role expectation. Moreover, they seem to have little to say to one another outside of their simple but spontaneous roles. Role-playing is important in the social conduct of nonhuman primates, as well as young children and presumably adults. With roles as our functional unit of analysis, we may turn to a discussion of motivation.

MOTIVATION

Let us postulate five hypothetical biological motives. These motives, *theoretical primitives*, are based on the key metaphors of the chapter—society as a game of games and man as a rule-following animal; they should be considered as theoretical assumptions necessary to begin the discussion rather than as rigorously defensible propositions about biological reality.

I call these motives *psychomotive forces* (pmf's) in order to parallel them with the physical concept of electromotive force (emf). The first category of pmf's are biological urges with immediate survival relevance: hunger, thirst, air, sex, elimination, and sleep. The existence and importance of this class of pmf's need no defense.

Class II pmf's produce a need for social interaction—for recognition, approval, affiliation, and positive, friendly attention. The notion that man has a built-in need for social attention and approval seems reasonable in view of his evolutionary history as a group-living animal, research concerning the effects of maternal deprivation (e.g., Harlow, 1958; Spitz, 1945), and attachment theory (e.g., Ainsworth, 1969; Bowlby, 1969). Class II pmf's do not determine the form of social interaction, but they make its occurrence inevitable.

Class III pmf's produce a need for interaction with the nonsocial environment. People need to look at trees and sunsets, to interact with nature. As the Ehrlichs observe:

> Physically and genetically, we appear best adapted to a tropical savanna
> ... For thousands of years we have tried in our houses to imitate not

only the climate, but the setting of our evolutionary past: warm, humid air, green plants and even animal companions ... The specific physiological reactions to natural beauty and diversity, to the shapes and colors of nature (especially to green), to the motions and sounds of other animals, such as birds, we as yet do not comprehend. But it is evident that nature in our daily life should be thought of as a part of the biological need (Ehrlich and Ehrlich, 1972).

The manner in which this pmf is expressed will vary with cultural contexts. Nonetheless, we see its effects whenever we observe people gardening, camping, sailing, sunbathing, and taking nature walks. Class III pmf's may underlie many conservationist activities and are probably related to aesthetic impulses.

Class IV pmf's generate a need for structure and order in everyday affairs. Most people need to predict, anticipate, and understand their environments. Hebb (1954), for example, argues that man is more emotionally upset by strangeness and unpredictability than any other animal; he suggests that a major function of culture is to reduce the range of unfamiliar stimuli man must experience. Similarly, the Nobel laureate geneticist Jacques Monod (1971) considers man's need for structure and order to be biologically given. Such a pmf is an unstated assumption in the work of George Kelly and the Swiss developmental psychologist, Jean Piaget. Class IV pmf's underlie much systematizing and scholarly activity and promote the rule-following tendencies necessary for the maintenance of culture.

The first four categories of pmf's are, in Allport's terms, deficit motives (see chapter seven). Class V pmf's on the other hand produce a need for exercise, self-expression, and the desire to impose one's will on the external environment; they correspond to an aggressive or competitive instinct (Lorenz, 1967). When properly socialized, aggression promotes friendly competition, personal achievement, and self-expression; unsocialized aggression, however, leads to violence and brutality. In most cases, then, class V pmf's generate a need for exercise, a drive to develop one's talents, to seek challenges, and to match one's skills against those of others.

The next question concerns how the pmf's are related to social behavior. *Homo Ludens* by the Dutch historian Johan Huizinga (1955) provides a possible answer. According to Huizinga, play is a fundamental category of behavior in all animals and especially man; it is "... a voluntary activity or occupation executed within certain fixed limits of time and space, according to rules freely accepted but absolutely binding, having its aim in itself and accompanied by a feeling of tension, joy, and the consciousness that it is 'different' from ordinary life ... We venture to call the category 'play' one of the most fundamental in life (p. 28)." There is a slight but systematic ambiguity in Huizinga's use of the word play; he seems to mean something like gaming or game-playing, and that is the sense in which the word will be used here.

Huizinga argues that game-playing was a major stimulus for the development of culture, that art, law, religion, scholarship, and all the other distinguishing features of our culture and civilization originated in games. His argument is persuasive in itself, but gains further significance in view of the fact that the biological evolution of man is closely tied to the evolution of culture (Mayr, 1963). As Fox (1971, p. 291) observes, "Man took the cultural way before he was clearly distinguishable from the animals, and in consequence found himself stuck with this mode of adaptation . . . Those animals, therefore, that were best able to be cultural were favored in the struggle for existence. Man's anatomy, physiology, and behavior . . . are in large part the result of culture . . . Our uniqueness is a biological uniqueness and . . . culture does not in some mysterious sense represent a break with biology." We are not simply producers of institutions such as the family, science, language, religion, warfare, kinship systems, and exogamy: we are also their products. Man's culture, game-playing tendencies, and biology seem, then, to be related fundamentally.

All animals play, but it appears that man in particular evolved as a game-playing, and concomitantly as a rule-following and culture-bearing, animal. This raises two further questions that Huizinga ignores. First, what makes games so central to human activity; second, what function do they serve?

With regard to the first question, game-playing seems over-determined, because games provide an optimal solution to the demands posed by the pmf's: game-playing satisfies most of the requirements of the human motivational system. Consider, for example, Class V pmf's. Competence at almost any game requires precise control over a number of mental and physical skills. Games provide a structured opportunity for acquiring mastery over one's body and a limited aspect of the physical environment. It feels good to exercise and it feels good to beat a worthy opponent after a period of intense competition. Thus, games are a vehicle *par excellence* for the expression of class V pmf's.

Playing games also satisfies man's need for order (class IV pmf's). As Huizinga notes, "Inside the playground an absolute and peculiar order reigns. Here we come across another, very positive feature of play: it creates order, *is* order. Into an imperfect world and into the confusion of life it brings a temporary, a limited perfection. Play demands order absolute and supreme. The least deviation from it 'spoils the game,' robs it of its character and makes it worthless. The profound affinity between play and order is perhaps the reason why play . . . seems to lie to such a large extent in the field of aesthetics (1950, p. 10)."

Games also match the requirements posed by the class III pmf's. Most games (e.g., tennis, skiing, soccer, sailing, and hunting) bring one into contact with nature and the elementary reassurances it can provide. Concerning the importance of these reassurances, Camus (1955, pp. 14–15) remarked:

> Of whom and of what indeed can I say: "I know that!" . . . This world I can touch, and I likewise judge that it exists. There ends my knowledge and the rest is construction . . . here are trees and I know their gnarled surface, water and I feel its tastes. These scents of grass and stars at night, certain evenings when the heart relaxes—how shall I negate this world whose power and strength I feel? [In contrast with these immediate sensory perceptions] . . . all the knowledge on earth will give me nothing to assure me that this world is mine. You describe it to me and you teach me to classify it . . . You take apart its mechanisms and my hope increases. At the final stage . . . you tell me of an invisible planetary system in which electrons gravitate around a nucleus. You explain this world to me with an image. I realize then that you have been reduced to poetry . . . So that science that was to teach me everything ends up in a hypothesis, that lucidity founders in metaphor, that uncertainty is resolved in a work of art. What need had I of so many efforts? The soft lines of these hills and the hand of evening on this troubled heart teach me much more. I have returned to my beginning.

Finally, and most importantly, games provide man's primary outlet for social interaction: they furnish a structured and orderly framework within which the requirements of class II pmf's can be met. Although people need to get together, simple coexistence can be boring. Moreover, people—both children and adults—have surprisingly little to say to one another that requires serious attention and concentration. Consequently, they must get together and do something: play touch football, poker, or dolls. In addition, if one becomes skilled at a game one may then be asked to play before an audience, and that provides further social stimulation. It is enormously satisfying to play on the center court at Wimbledon, to argue a case before the Supreme Court, or to debate one's political opponent on national television. Finally, it can be very rewarding to be part of a cohesive team or closely knit group that is in close competition with other groups. Thus, games are well suited to provide social rewards and interaction.

Generally speaking, then, man can be seen as a game-playing (and at a deeper level a rule-following) animal, which tendencies are rooted in his biological nature.

The next question concerns the functions of game playing, and two come immediately to mind. First, games ritualize and thereby detoxify aggression, always a potentially disruptive force in society. Games are a socialized means of expressing class V pmf's; thus conventionalized competition controls aggression. Second, as Huizinga suggests, participation in games—particularly within the peer group—stimulates the feelings of social cohesion that bind society together.

The foregoing discussion of motivation can be summarized as follows. Man's evolutionary history and innate instinctual endowment make him a group-living, culture-bearing, norm-respecting animal; thus man has a deep organic need for his culture. Man is simultaneously an attention-seeker and a rule-follower; he tends to cast his activities into game-like, rule-governed frameworks, as seen especially in social interaction. Roles, the means we use to play the social game, are our primary vehicle for social interaction.

Most role theorists ignore the biological or motivational substrates of social behavior; they study instead the determinants of socially-defined regularities in conduct (e.g., norms and social roles) and how these are transmitted from person to person. In such approaches the regularities in social interaction are seen as relative to the circumstances in which they occur. In contrast, the present role-theoretical perspective suggests that although social interaction may seem to be relative to a particular situation, at a deep level the functions that it serves and the forms that it takes are universal.

THE SELF-CONCEPT

As Mead noted, roles and the self-concept are closely related. For Mead the self-concept is a function of one's roles; the present view suggests, however, that roles are a function of one's self-concept.

The notion that man needs social interaction within a rule-governed framework (i.e., needs to play the social game) suggests that a primary goal for each person in the interpersonal situation is to maximize the amount of positive, friendly attention he receives, and to minimize hostile, negative rejection. This is typically done by impression management (Goffman, 1959). We develop a set of "lines" or roles used to foster and maintain the image that we would like others to accept as true of ourselves. This image is the self-concept, and it is designed to gain the approval or minimize the disapproval of our counterplayers in the social game. And we have no choice as to whether we should engage in role playing for, as Goffman observes: "Regardless of whether a person intends to take a line, he will find that he has done so in effect. The other participants will assume that he has more or less willfully taken a stand, so that if he is to deal with their responses to him he must take into consideration the impression they have possibly formed of him (1967, p. 5)."

There are two ethical principles associated with these interpersonal performances; Goffman calls them the rule of considerateness and the rule of self-respect. "Any individual who possesses certain social characteristics has a moral right to expect that others will value and treat him in a appropriate way. Connected with this principle is a second, namely that an individual ... who signifies that he has certain characteristics ought in fact to be what he claims he is (1958, p. 13)." Thus, the rule of considerateness requires that in general we tolerate and support others in their roles. The rule of self-respect on the other hand states that if a person adopts a role, "... he will be expected to live up to it ... he will be required to show self-respect, abjuring certain actions because they are above or beneath him, while forcing himself to perform others even though they cost him dearly (1967, p. 9)."

The assumption that people need rule-governed social interaction also implies that recurring social encounters tend quickly to stabilize and become ritualized. For example, the second time two people meet they tend to repeat the pattern of their first interaction. They do so partly as a matter of convenience and partly because the rules of considerateness and self-respect promote this sort of interactional stability. As they begin to repeat the interaction on their third meeting, they may experience a sense of "Here we go again!" Thus, social routines as simple as the morning cup of coffee quickly tend to become ritualized and resistant to change. But more importantly, these rituals stimulate the development of roles—typified ways of presenting oneself in social situations that facilitate interaction and ward off social disapproval.

Roles reflect one's self-concept—the image that we would like others to accept as true of ourselves—and can be directly observed in everyday life. Under the guidance of our self-concept we invent the roles necessary to express our image of ourselves; other people perceive us in terms of the roles we are playing and make inferences about the self-images that produced these roles.

Role performances fall naturally into one of two broad categories that represent alternative strategies for gaining attention and avoiding social disapproval. These strategies are reflected in such contrasting terms as individual status and group solidarity, egocentrism and altruism, competition and affiliation, the outgroup and the ingroup. Goffman (1967) describes these strategies in his analysis of "defensive" and "aggressive" facework. In aggressive facework or role performances the actor tries to "make points" at another person's expense; in a defensive performance the actors behave so as mutually to protect and support the lines that each has adopted. Aggressive facework promotes status at the expense of others whereas defensive facework leads to solidarity among the actors at the expense of their individual status. Huizinga, in a similar fashion, distinguishes between festal contests and sacred performances. Festal contests produce status orderings, whereas sacred performances foster feelings of group solidarity.

These two strategies—competition and affiliation—seem to pervade every aspect of social life and may reflect an important feature of man's evolutionary heritage. As Campbell (1965) and Hamilton (1971) suggest, man has been exposed to selection pressures that allow the individual to survive at the expense of others, *and* tendencies that promote the survival of one group at the expense of other groups. These selection pressures are manifested in man as a fundamental ambivalence between egocentrism and altruism, one that is unique in most social animals. This ambivalence is reflected in the presence of contradictory values in the same moral code (e.g., "T'is better to give than receive," versus "Charity begins at home"). However, it is probably adaptive; that is, when each of two opposing tendencies has survival value, the optimal biological solution seems to be an alternation in the expression of each, rather than a consistent expression of an intermediate state.

Once a person has developed a set of roles, he uses them in accordance with his perceptions or beliefs about specific situational requirements (e.g., what is fitting, or what he thinks others expect of him in a given situation). It should be emphasized that many of these roles are defensive in nature, designed to ward off criticism and abuse. As we have noted, from the perspective of this chapter one's self-concept is the image that lies behind one's role performances. (Actually, as William James (1890) remarked, one may have several self-concepts, each appropriate to a different audience.) It follows that self-images provide the context for role performances; any single action can be interpreted only by taking account of the self-image a person is attempting to put across. Thus, the kind of son, daughter, student, or teacher one becomes depends to a large degree on the self-image that lies behind that role.

In late adolescence or early adulthood some people begin to implement for themselves a life-style, an idealized pattern of living that may subsequently organize their self-concepts and role performances. Life-styles, therefore, provide a context for the expression of particular self-images. Roles, self-concepts, and life-styles are usually conscious and are normally expressed in overt behavior. Because roles and self-concepts reflect the demands of particular social situations, and because social expectations vary with these contexts, one's role performances will change from situation to situation.

Roles, self-concepts, and life styles form a set of more or less coherent cognitive schemas that may be called *role structure*. Role structure is one of two major psychic structures underlying personality. Although role structure *may* reflect the influence of one's family, it results primarily from peer group experience—from one's efforts to gain the approval (or avoid the disapproval) of one's age mates. The second major structure—*character structure*—is formed in response to one's parents and family in childhood and will be described in the next section. Douvan and Adelson (1966) highlight the importance of this distinction between role and character structure by pointing out, for example, that our style of dress and speech habits (elements of role structure) are influenced by our peers, but our political and religious beliefs (elements of character structure) are primarily influenced by our families.

Six essential points characterize the preceding discussion of the self-concept. First, in response to the demands set by the pmf's, man is disposed to seek social interaction within a structured or rule-governed framework—i.e., to play the social game. Second, one plays the social game by developing a set of roles that are designed to foster and support an image that one would like others to accept as true of oneself. Third, this image is the self-concept; it organizes or provides the context for role performances. Fourth, for Mead the self-concept is a function of one's roles; here, however, roles are seen as a function of one's self-concept. Fifth, role performances are a primary means by which we gain the approval and avoid the criticism of our counterplayers. Although the number of possible roles that one can develop is indefinitely large, any given role serves either an aggressive/competitive or an affiliative purpose—i.e., is either egocentric or altruistic. Sixth, self-concepts, their associated roles, and their organizing life-styles make up role structure, the first of two psychic structures necessary to explain personality.

SOCIALIZATION

A good deal of everyday social conduct can be explained in terms of role performances guided by what we believe others expect of us and what we would like them to believe about us. Nonetheless, our social behavior is rarely if ever a simple function of the social situation: it is also determined from within by the residue of our reactions to the demands and expectations of parents and family. Through the various processes of identification, imitation, and unconscious suggestion, each child accommodates himself to the rules, values, and conventional wisdom of his parents, ethnic heritage, cultural and religious history. This usually unconscious accommodation makes up character structure, the second psychic structure necessary to understand personality. From the perspective of this chapter then, socialization is equivalent to the development of character structure.

Culture in humans regulates many of the actions formerly guided by instinct; consequently, it is difficult to overemphasize the importance of culture and (at the individual level) character structure as a determinant of social behavior. As Fox (1971, p. 293) observes for example, "Even if a species shed its dependence on instincts, it still has to do the same things instincts were designed to do ... [Thus,] one had to make cultural behavior in many ways like instinctive behavior. It had to be unconscious so that it did not require thought for its operation, it had to be 'automatic' so that certain stimuli would automatically produce it, and it had to be common to all members of the population."

Kardiner (1939) provided an early discussion of the function of character structure in promoting human survival. For Kardiner, each culture occupies a particular environmental and ecological niche. The environment poses certain challenges to which each culture must respond if it is to survive. Assuming that the adults of a culture have worked out an appropriate response to their particular environmental challenge, it will be encoded in terms of their rules, values, and conventional wisdom. This cultural response is passed on through the child-rearing practices of the group; when the process of transmission is successful, it promotes the group's continued existence. Erikson (1950) makes the same point, although phrased somewhat differently. He suggests that the mothers of a culture unconsciously develop a set of child-rearing practices that yield the character type most appropriate to the survival demands facing that culture.

The form of character structure is largely determined by one's early interactions with parents and family. It tends to be stable and enduring, but covert and unconscious; unlike role structure, character structure is reflected only indirectly in peer interaction and everyday social behavior.

Many middle-class Americans keep their character and role structures separate through a kind of segregation of consciousness. That is, much of what one does during a normal day tends to be unrelated to one's character structure. For example, the reader might compare his feelings and behavior at a traditional family holiday celebration in his childhood with his feelings and behavior at an office cocktail party. The resulting discrepancy will suggest the degree to which he has segregated these two aspects of his personality. Obviously, some people are closer to one, as others are to the other of these psychic structures.

Character structure is reflected in a person's primarily unconscious but characteristic ways of selecting, using, justifying, and enforcing the rules and values of his culture. The development of character structure can be conceptualized in terms of three dimensions—compliance, empathy, and autonomy (Hogan, 1973)—that are related to Durkheim's earlier discussion of socialization broadly defined (see chapter nine).

Durkheim suggested that the first critical stage in socialization involves developing a sense of respect for (and complying with) the rules of one's culture. More recently, Erikson (1950) and Waddington (1967) have argued that children are innately predisposed to comply with adult authority and this compliance is elicited by the proper parent-child relationship. This sense of respect for social rules produces a qualitative transformation in character structure: for the first time the child becomes capable of true (rule-governed and nonegocentric) social interaction. In the absence of further developmental changes, it also produces a tendency to act as if rules are sacred and immutable, valuable for their own sake.

As Durkheim further suggested, the second stage in character development entails adopting impersonal ends for one's actions. This happens, he argued, when one becomes identified with the social groups of which he is a member. This sense of identification is promoted by the development of empathy, that brings about a second transformation in character structure. Empathy serves to humanize and qualify the rule-bound compliance of the preceding stage. It heightens a child's sensitivity to social expectations; and it allows a child to think in terms of the "spirit of the game," to understand the concept of fairness that seems to evolve into the adult notion of justice. Too much empathy, however, is as bad as too little—one can be concerned with the expectations of others at the expense of one's own legitimate plans and aspirations. Thus, empathy can lead to indecisiveness and a kind of morbid moral oversensitivity as well as tact, sympathy, and ultimate concern.

Durkheim considered autonomous rule compliance to be the final feature of the moral man. The development of an autonomous sense of moral obligation produces a final transformation in the structure of moral character. A compliant person upholds social norms because he regards them as personally binding and, at a deeper level perhaps, out of respect for authority. An empathic person respects social norms because he is sensitive to the expectations of others; the unconscious motive here may be fear of social disapproval. An autonomous person, however, complies with social norms because that is simply the sort of person he is; the unconscious motive for the autonomous person is fear of self-disapproval. Such a person understands that ultimately one must be able to live with oneself.

In conjunction with high compliance and high empathy, autonomy produces moral maturity, a statistically rare character type. In company with high compliance and low empathy, it will tend to produce a stern, patriarchal old testament moralist such as Melville's Captain Ahab and

Dickens's Madame LeFarge. Together with low empathy *and* low compliance, autonomy tends to produce such strong, effective, resolute, unyielding scoundrels as Shakespeare's Richard III.

The foregoing discussion made four primary points. First, culture controls aspects of human behavior that were formerly regulated by instinct. Consequently, the accommodation that each person makes to his culture has important implications for his social behavior. Second, this accommodation is symbolized by the term character structure; socialization is defined as the development of character structure; character structure and role structure are the major psychic determinants of social conduct. Third, the degree to which character structure and role structure are integrated within any given person must be empirically determined; in most people, however, they tend to be somewhat dissociated. Finally, character structure (and socialization) can be conceptualized in terms of three dimensions (compliance, empathy, and autonomy), and various character types can be defined in terms of differential development along these dimensions.

THE UNCONSCIOUS

From the present role-theoretical perspective, the term unconscious refers to three phenomena: actions about which the actor has deceived himself; the influence of the pmf's; and character structure. With regard to the problem of self-deception, Goffman (1959) remarks that it occurs when the roles of performer and audience coexist in the same individual. If a person puts on a performance for his own benefit, he must conceal from himself the discreditable aspects of his performance; ". . . in everyday terms, there will be things he knows . . . that he will not be able to tell himself. This intricate maneuver of self-delusion constantly occurs; psychoanalysts have provided us with beautiful field data of this kind under the heading of repression . . . (p. 81)." Role theory substitutes the concept of self-deception for repression. Although the two terms refer to the same phenomena, they entail differing explanations; i.e., deliberate redirection of one's attention versus being influenced by an unconscious censor. The concept of self-deception avoids the logical difficulties associated with the concept of repression, moreover, self-deception can be corrected by self-examination but repression cannot.

Since the actions of the pmf's cannot be analyzed by introspection, they must also be unconscious. Although man's needs for social contact, natural beauty, predictability, and aggressive self-expression are unconscious, they are also insistent, and each person must work out a response to their demands.

Finally, character structure like the Freudian superego tends to be unconscious and persists into adulthood, often with very little change. Character structure is unconscious because it is part of a world that exists largely in the past and is rarely called into question. Freud's analysis of superego formation, however, seems inadequate in three respects. First, character structure (or in his words the superego) is not a single agency; it is a multidimensional concept—the evolution of empathy and autonomy, for example, are as important for character development as compliance with parental sanctions. Second, character structure is not something forced upon the child from the outside by a necessarily coercive society; rather, it is rooted in human biology, and most people effortlessly acquire a stable set of values. Third, character structure is not harsh, primitive, and life-denying; it is a key to man's evolutionary success and tends to facilitate rather than impede human social development. Freud was probably correct, however, in suggesting that professional assistance is necessary to make the contents of character structure conscious.

EXPLANATION

The manner in which people are all alike can be explained in terms of the pmf's: people are similar in that they need predictability and order, they need to express themselves, and most importantly they need to interact with others and their environment. We are also all alike in our tendency to play games and to evolve rule-governed frameworks for social interaction. Finally, we all resemble each other in our tendency to develop roles, self-images, life-styles and an unconscious character structure. Personality as *Personalität*, therefore, is explained in terms of a universal set of pmf's and the development of role and character structure—much of which is unconscious.

Differences among people can be explained partially in terms of individual differences in the strengths of the various pmf's; these appear as differences in temperament (Thomas et al., 1963). Individual differences can be explained further in terms of the roles that people develop to accomplish their social goals. These roles depend on a person's developmental history, social circumstances, and peer group experience. Finally, people differ in terms of the accommodations they have made to parental demands. Thus, personality as *Persönlichkeit* can be explained in terms of differences in temperament and in the development of role and character structure within each person.

Enigmatic and anomalous actions must be explained through interpretation. Any purposeful act can be regarded as a portion of a role

performance that must be interpreted in terms of the actor's self-concept
—the image he is trying to present to his intended audience. The individual's self-concept, however, can often be understood only within the
context of his life-style—the total pattern of values and goals that provide
a basis for social behavior. Thus, a particular puzzling action is explained
if it can be interpreted in terms of what we know about a person's values
and goals, what he thinks his audience expects of him, what he wants the
audience to believe concerning himself, and the strategies or roles that he
has evolved to deal with these problems.

PSYCHOLOGICAL HEALTH

Personality research since World War II indicates that psychological health may be unrelated to childhood trauma (MacKinnon, 1960).
Moreover, Barron (1963) notes that highly creative persons are frequently
both saner and more neurotic than less creative persons. The reader
might also recall that Aristotle thought neurosis and psychological health
were independent phenomena; neurosis was produced by disturbances in
one's biochemistry and psychological health reflected the degree to which
one had developed his capacity for reason. All this suggests that we should
distinguish between neurosis on the one hand and psychological health
on the other.

The origins of neurosis may be relatively specific. A series of laboratory and natural experiments over the last eighty years—including research by the Russian physiologist Pavlov and the experiences of the crew
of the U.S.S. Pueblo, captured by the North Koreans in 1968—suggest that
when animals or people are placed in situations where they must perform
but where feedback concerning their performance is ambiguous and
where success is rewarded inconsistently, they tend to break down. They
display all the usual signs of neurosis—anxiety, perseveration, overdriven
behavior, etc. The experience of being rewarded and punished on a random basis seems in itself quite stressful. Several members of the Pueblo
crew reported, for example, that they didn't mind the beatings they received so much as the fact that they never knew when the beatings would
occur. A similar situation would confront a child trying to cope with erratic parents who hand out rewards and punishments in an unpredictable
manner. The stress involved is a major cause of neurosis, but people also
seem to differ considerably in their ability to withstand it. It seems likely
that a tendency to break down under such stress is, in the long run,
genetically determined. When Freud, toward the end of his life, was
asked why not everyone who lives in stressful circumstances falls ill, he

replied that apparently some people are born with the capacity to withstand stress.

As suggested above, people also vary along a dimension of psychological health that is unrelated to neurosis. This second dimension reflects an increasing scale of maturity. At the high end, psychological health is defined by two characteristics. The first is self-awareness—Goffman calls this "role distance"—the ability to view oneself from a detached, external perspective. Too much self-awareness, however, can inhibit effective action: as Hamlet remarked, "thus conscience doth make cowards of us all." On the other hand, too little self-awareness leads to dissociation. Psychological health requires self-awareness only in the proper degree. The second element of psychological health—personal integration—was discussed earlier by Jung, McDougall, and Allport. Psychological health is a function of integration, produced by self-awareness in conjunction with a far-reaching goal, purpose, or task in life—such as the pursuit of knowledge, religious faith, revenge, or the desire to leave one's mark on the world.

The opposite or low end of this dimension of psychological health is characterized by dissociation. In the development of personality there are three points at which dissociation can occur. Consider first the development of role structure. In the absence of a well-defined self-concept, a person's role performances will be disconnected, unpredictable, and inconsistent. He will flit from role to role and seem shallow, changeable, and superficial—as was once said about a presidential candidate whose dissociative tendencies were pretty well-known, "He always sounds like the last person he talked to." In the absence of a well-defined life-style, the larger segments of a person's life will also lack organization: he will drift from job to job·and hobby to hobby in a seemingly random fashion.

Dissociation can also occur in the development of character structure. Ideally, the rules and values that one adopts in childhood are a response to a homogenous set of family and cultural demands, integrated under a more encompassing ideology—a religion, a family tradition, or a political perspective. If a child is exposed to contradictory sets of values, or if a comprehensive ideology is unavailable to him, he may then be subject to unconscious dissociation and conflict. For example, a talented and insightful man I know had a mother who was overly concerned that he be a "good boy." However, this woman obviously idolized her wastrel brother. She apparently endorsed one set of values and acted in accordance with a second; as a result her son developed a dissociated character structure.

A third source of dissociation is a product of inconsistencies between role and character structure. Under ideal circumstances the two are compatible: the kinds of behavior one's parents expected of one will be consistent with the kinds of behavior one exhibits before one's peers. But many if not most of us resemble only slightly either the person our parents thought they were raising, or the person we actually became under the pressure of their expectations and guidance. As a result our everyday behavior is often unrelated to the Calvinist, Catholic, Jewish, or other character structure that we acquired while very young—and that is still with us when our intellectual and emotional defenses are down. D.H. Lawrence was a good example of this form of dissociation. A coal miner's son, in adulthood he was lionized by upper-middle-class British intellectuals whom he despised, and was miserable in the glow of their attention. As Goffman (1959) observes, ". . . to the degree that the individual maintains a show before others that he himself does not believe, he can come to experience a special kind of alienation from self and a special kind of wariness of others (p. 232)." Personal integration requires that one's sense of right and wrong correspond to one's sense of what is socially appropriate. Dissociation may result from social roles that are too discrepant with one's character structure.

Let us close this section by noting two contrasts with psychoanalysis. First, according to psychological role theory, the origins of neurosis can be traced to man's needs for order and social approval rather than to his sexual and aggressive needs. More specifically, neurosis does not result from a conflict between the demands of man's instincts and his culture. In fact, conflict seems to have little to do with neurosis. Rather, it seems primarily to result from an inability to establish acceptable and dependable sources of social attention and approval in conjunction with an innate inability to withstand stress. Second, and in agreement with Rieff (1959), Freud's most important insight may have been that conscience rather than instinct is the ultimate source of unhappiness in our lives. Freud seems to have erred, however, in his notion that character structure (or the superego) is pathogenic *per se*, because it is unconscious. Rather, character structure is dangerous only when it is dissociated.

EVALUATION

Some final comments on psychological role theory will serve as a provisional evaluation of the model described in this chapter. First, a major weakness of the perspective is that it does not account for man's irrational and ambivalent relationship to authority. Freud seems to have been correct in his observation (in *Totem and Taboo*) that a portion of our social behavior is rooted in our unconscious reactions to father surrogates and other symbols of adult authority. Although psychological role theory compares unfavorably to psychoanalysis in this regard, the comparison is ironic because, as was noted in chapter four, this aspect of Freud's thinking has been generally ignored.

Second, the model proposes a solution to the central paradox of the social sciences, first formulated by Auguste Comte: how man can be both the cause and the consequence of society. Man's evolutionary heritage— the pmf's—generates rule-governed, ritualized, social interaction. Social behavior emerges inexorably from man's biological endowment. Once ritualized and institutionalized, these patterns of social conduct determine how we think about ourselves, others, and the world in general. The situation is similar to the ontogenesis of cognition as described by Vygotsky (1962): at some point in early life a child's capacity for thought (which is initially independent of language) and language (which is initially independent of thought) come together and both capacities are irrevocably transformed. Similarly, in the ontogenesis of social behavior a child's instinctual tendencies come together with arbitrary social requirements and both are transformed—the biologically generated behavior dispositions are socialized, and the arbitrary social forms are given biological significance. For psychological role theory then, social behavior inevitably emerges from human biology. In contrast with psychoanalysis, however, there is no necessary conflict between man's biology and his culture; rather, rule-governed social interaction is seen as an optimal solution to the demands set by the pmf's.

Third, many people are troubled by role-theoretical analyses of social behavior, feeling that those who "play" roles are in some ways insincere. Common sense, they argue, requires that we distinguish between real and contrived social performances. Close examination reveals, however, that a distinction between real and contrived performances is difficult to maintain. For example, when a person wants to convey his authenticity (e.g., a doctor his concern, a lover his fidelity, a professor his expertise), he must choose carefully the right expressions and avoid doing anything that might discredit the impression he is trying to foster—he must not yawn when he is supposed to be interested. In fact most of us actually seem to play our roles with a mixture of cynicism and belief, and the line between phoniness and sincerity is very difficult to discern. As Goffman observes, "All the world is not, of course, a stage, but the crucial ways in which it isn't are not easy to specify (1959, p. 72)."

It is also worth noting that performances that begin as mere shows have a tendency to become sincere over time; as Park states (1950, pp. 249–50),

> It is probably no mere historical accident that the word person, in its first meaning, is a mask. It is rather a recognition of the fact that everyone is always and everywhere, more or less consciously, playing a role . . .

It is in these roles that we know each other; it is in these roles that we know ourselves ... In a sense, and in so far as this mask represents the conception we have formed of ourselves—the role we are striving to live up to—this mask is our truer self, the self we would like to be. In the end, our conception of our role becomes second nature and an integral part of our personality.

Finally, a general problem with role-theoretical accounts of personality is that they strongly suggest that the sources of our unhappiness are amenable to rational solution. The implication is that if we think clearly enough about our roles, our values, and their interrelationships we can somehow solve our problems. However, there are fixed limits to the amount of happiness attainable in life, because of certain constraints built into human nature. The first is an adaptation level problem. We are only happy when the amount of social approval we are receiving exceeds that which we normally expect, and we are unhappy when we receive less. But each new level of approval quickly becomes the norm, and our subsequent unhappiness is inevitable. Second, if society is a game, then we have no choice but to enter and to give up our lives to competing and affiliating, to defending against loss of status and social rejection. But many people are temperamentally unable to play the game and, consequently, are doomed from the outset to failure. Third, a fundamental part of man's nature and a key to his evolutionary success is his need for meaning and order. We all need to feel that there is meaning and purpose in the universe, but there does not seem to be any—at least any that can be known in the normally accepted sense of the word knowledge. Finally, man's built-in aggressive and competitive tendencies guarantee that no matter what we do, no matter how kindly we are, in spite of all the benevolence and charity that we may display toward our brother man, there will always be someone trying to put his foot on our necks.

These considerations suggest that Freud was right in his meliorist attitude: the most we can do is control some of the sources of our unhappiness. At a slightly later point in history, Camus suggested that the proper response to this problem is scorn and defiance. Similarly, when T.E. Lawrence was asked how he could bear to put out slowly a lighted match with his fingers he replied that the secret is in not paying any attention. On this point then, psychological role theory, Freud, Camus, and Lawrence appear to agree.

Bibliography

AINSWORTH, M. D. S. 1969. Object relations, dependency, and attachment: A theoretical review of the infant-mother relationship. *Child Development,* 40, 969–1025.

ALLPORT, G. W. 1955. *Becoming.* New Haven: Yale University Press.

ALLPORT, G. W. 1960. *Personality and social encounter.* Boston: Beacon Press.

ALLPORT, G. W. 1961. *Pattern and growth in personality.* New York: Holt, Rinehart, and Winston.

ALLPORT, G. W. 1968. *The person in psychology.* Boston: Beacon Press.

ALLPORT, G. W., VERNON, P. E., AND LINDZEY, G. 1960. *A study of values.* 3rd ed. Boston: Houghton Mifflin.

ARDREY, R. 1970. *The social contract.* New York: Atheneum.

BALDWIN, J. M. 1902. *Development and evolution.* New York: Macmillan.

BANNISTER, D., ed. 1970. *Perspectives in personal construct theory.* New York: Academic.

BARKER, R. G., AND WRIGHT, H. F. 1951. *One boy's day.* New York: Harper & Row.

BARRON, F. 1963. *Creativity and psychological health.* Princeton, N.J.: Van Nostrand.

BARTH, J. 1958. *The end of the road.* New York: Doubleday.

BAUMRIND, D. 1971. Current patterns of parental authority. *Developmental Psychology,* 4, Pt. 2.

BERGER, P. L. 1963. *Invitation to sociology.* New York: Doubleday.

BERGER, P. L., AND LUCKMANN, T. 1966. *The social construction of reality.* New York: Doubleday.

BOWLBY, J. 1969. *Attachment and loss,* vol. I, Attachment. New York: Basic Books.

CAMPBELL, D. G. 1965. Ethnocentric and other altruistic motives. In *Nebraska symposium on motivation,* ed., D. Levine. Lincoln: University of Nebraska Press.

CAMUS, A. 1955. *The myth of sisyphus and other essays.* New York: Random House.

CHOMSKY, N. 1968. *Language and mind.* New York: Harcourt Brace Jovanovich.

CLAUSEN, J., ed 1968. *Socialization and society.* Boston: Little, Brown.

COLES, R. 1970. *Erik Erikson: The growth of his work.* Boston: Little, Brown.

COTTRELL, L. S. 1942. The analysis of situational fields in social psychology. *American Sociological Review,* 7, 370–82.

CROOK, J. H. 1971. Sources of cooperation in animals and man. In *Man and beast: Comparative social behavior,* ed. J. F. Eisenberg and W. S. Dillon, pp. 235–60. Washington, D.C.: Smithsonian Institution Press.

DE TOCQUEVILLE, A. 1945. *Democracy in America.* Phillips Bradley, ed. New York: Knopf.

DOLLARD, J., AND MILLER, N. E. 1950. *Personality and psychotherapy.* New York: McGraw-Hill.

DOUVAN, E. A., AND ADELSON, J. 1966. *The adolescent experience.* New York: John Wiley.

DURKHEIM, E. 1961. *Moral education.* New York: Free Press.

DURKHEIM, E. 1964. *The rules of sociological method.* New York: Free Press.

EHRLICH, P., AND EHRLICH, A. 1972. *Populations, resources, environment.* San Francisco: W. H. Freeman.

ELLENBERGER, H. 1970. *The discovery of the unconscious.* New York: Basic Books.

ERIKSON, E. H. 1950. *Childhood and society.* New York: Norton.

ERIKSON, E. H. 1958. *Young man Luther.* New York: Norton

ERIKSON, E. H. 1959. Identity and the life cycle. In *Psychological issues,* ed. G. S. Klein, pp. 1–171. New York: International Universities Press.

ERIKSON, E. H. 1964. *Insight and responsibility.* New York: Norton.

ERIKSON, E. H. 1969. *Gandhi's truth.* New York: Norton.

FINGARETTE, H. 1969. *Self-deception.* London: Routledge & Kegan Paul.

FOX, R. 1971. The cultural animal. In *Man and beast: Comparative social behavior,* ed. J. F. Eisenberg and W. S. Dillon, pp. 273–98. Washington, D.C.: Smithsonian Institution Press.

FREUD, S. 1950. *Totem and taboo.* New York: Norton.

FREUD, S. 1953. *A general introduction to psychoanalysis.* Garden City, N. Y.: Doubleday.

FREUD, S. 1960. *Group psychology and the analysis of the ego.* New York: Bantam.

FREUD, S. 1960. *The ego and the id.* New York: Norton.

FREUD, S. 1961. *Civilization and its discontents.* New York: Norton.

FREUD, S. 1963. *Dora—An analysis of a case of hysteria.* New York: Collier.

FREUD, S. 1965. *The interpretation of dreams.* New York: Avon Books.

FREUD, S. 1965. *New introductory lectures.* New York: Norton.

GALL, F. J. 1835. *On the functions of the brain and each of its parts,* etc. Vol. I. Boston: Marsh, Capen, and Lyon.

GLASSER, W. 1965. *Reality therapy.* New York: Harper & Row.

GOFFMAN, E. 1959. *The presentation of self in everyday life.* Garden City, N. Y.: Doubleday.

GOFFMAN, E. 1967. *Interaction ritual.* Garden City, N. Y.: Doubleday.

GOLDFARB, W. 1945. Psychological privation in infancy and subsequent adjustment. *American Journal of Orthopsychiatry,* 15:247–55.

GRODDECK, G. 1928. *The book of the it.* New York: Nervous and Mental Diseases Monograph.

HALL, W. B., AND MACKINNON, D. W. 1969. Personality inventory correlates of creativity among architects. *Journal of Applied Psychology,* 53:322–26.

HAMILTON, W. D. 1971. The selection of selfish and altrustic behavior in some extreme models. In *Man and beast: Comparative social behavior,* ed. J. F. Eisenberg, and W. S. Dillon pp. 59–91. Washington, D.C.: Smithsonian Institution Press.

HANCHER, M. 1970. The science of interpretation and the art of interpretation. *Modern Language Notes,* 85:791–802.

HARLOW, H. F. 1958. The nature of love. *American Psychologist.* 13:673–85.

HARRÉ, H. AND SECORD, P. F. 1973. *The explanation of social behavior.* Totowa, New Jersey: Littlefield Adams.

HARTMAN, H. 1939. *Ego psychology and the problem of adaptation.* New York: International Universities Press.

HEBB, D. O., AND THOMPSON, W. R. 1954. The social significance of animal studies. In *The handbook of social psychology,* ed. G. Lindzey pp. 532–62. Reading, Mass.: Addison-Wesley.

HEIDEGGER, M. 1949. Being and time. In *Existence and being,* ed. W. Brock. Chicago: Henry Regnery.

HEMPEL, C. G. 1965. *Aspects of scientific explanation.* New York: Free Press.

HENDERSON, J. L. 1964. Ancient myths and modern man. In *Man and his symbols,* ed. C. G. Jung, pp. 95–156. New York: Dell.

HILGARD, E. R. 1973. Dissociation revisited. In *Historical conceptions of psychology,* eds. M. Henle, J. Jaynes, and J. Sullivan, pp. 205–19. New York: Springer-Verlag.

HOGAN, R. 1973. Moral conduct and moral character. *Psychological Bulletin.* 79:217–32.

HOGAN, R., AND HENLEY, N. 1970. Nomotics: The science of human rule systems. *Law and Society Review.* 5:135–46.

HOLLAND, J. 1966. *The psychology of vocational choice.* Waltham, Mass.: Blaisdell.

HOLLAND, R. 1970. George Kelly: Constructive innocent and reluctant existentialist. In *Perspectives in personal construct theory,* ed. D. Bannister. New York: Academic.

HOMANS, G. C. 1967. *The nature of social science.* New York: Harcourt Brace Jovanovich.

HUGHES, H. S. 1958. *Consciousness and society.* New York: Random House.

HUIZINGA, J. 1955. *Homo ludens.* Boston: Beacon Press.

JAMES, W. 1890. *Principles of psychology.* New York: Holt, Rinehart & Winston.

JAMES, W. 1962. *Psychology: A briefer course.* London: Crowell-Collier.

JAMES, W. 1958. *Varieties of religious experience.* New York: New American Library.

JEBB, R. C. 1909. *The characters of theophrastus.* London: Macmillan.

JOHNSON, H. M. 1960. *Sociology: A systematic introduction.* New York: Harcourt Brace Jovanovich.

JOURARD, S. M. 1971. *The transparent self.* New York: Van Nostrand Reinhold.

JUNG, C. G. 1933. *Modern man in search of a soul.* New York: Harcourt Brace Jovanovich.

JUNG, C. G. 1933. *Psychological types.* New York: Harcourt Brace Jovanovich.

JUNG, C. G. 1956. *Two essays on analytical psychology.* New York: Meridian Books.

JUNG, C. G. 1961. *Memories, dreams, reflections.* New York: Vintage.

KARDINER, A. 1939. *The individual and his society.* New York: Columbia University Press.

KELLY, G. A. 1955. *The psychology of personal constructs.* New York: Norton.

KELLY, G. A. 1963. *A theory of personality.* New York: Norton. (A shortened paperback edition of previous entry.)

KELLY, G. A. 1969. *Clinical psychology and personality.* B. Mather, ed. New York: John Wiley.

KIERKEGAARD, S. 1941. *Fear and trembling.* Princeton: Princeton University Press.

LORENZ, K. 1967. *On aggression.* New York: Harcourt Brace Jovanovich.

MACKINNON, D. W. 1944. The structure of personality. In *Personality and the behavior disorders,* ed. J. McV. Hunt, pp. 3–48. New York: Ronald Press.

MACKINNON, D. W. 1960. The highly effective individual. *Teachers College Record* 61:367–78.

MALCOLM X, AND HALEY, A. 1964. *Autobiography of Malcolm X.* New York: Grove Press.

MARCUSE, H. 1955. *Eros and civilization.* New York: Random House.

MAY, R. 1958. The origins and significance of the existential movement in psychology. In *Existence,* eds. R. May, E. Angel, and H. F. Ellenberger, pp. 3–36. New York: Simon & Schuster.

MAY, R. 1958. Contributions of existential psychotherapy. In *Existence,* eds. R. May, E. Angel, and H. F. Ellenberger, pp. 37–91. New York: Simon & Schuster.

MAYR, E. 1963. *Populations, species, and evolution.* Cambridge, Mass.: Harvard University Press.

McBRIDE, G. 1971. The nature-nurture problem in social evolution. In *Man and beast: Comparative social behavior,* eds. J. F. Eisenberg and W. S. Dillon, pp. 35–36. Washington, D.C.: Smithsonian Institution Press.

McDougall, W. 1908. *Social psychology.* London: Methuen.

McDougall, W. 1923. *Outline of psychology.* New York: Scribner's.

McDougall, W. 1926. *Outline of abnormal psychology.* New York: Scribner's.

McDougall, W. 1930. William McDougall. In *A history of psychology in auto-biography,* Vol. 1, ed. C. Murchison, pp. 191–224. Worcester, Mass.: Clark University Press.

McDougall, W. 1932. *The energies of men.* London: Methuen.

Mead, G. H. 1934. *Mind, self, and society. Chicago:* University of Chicago Press.

Meyerhoff, H. 1959. The return to the concrete. *Chicago Review.* 13:27–38.

Meyerhoff, H. 1961. Translator's introduction. In *Man's place in nature,* Scheler, M., pp. vii–xxx. New York: Farrar, Strauss, and Cudahy.

Mischel, T. 1969. Scientific and philosophical psychology. In *Human action,* ed. T. Mischel, pp. 1–40. New York: Academic Press.

Monod, J. 1971. *Chance and necessity.* New York: Random House.

Moreno, J. L. 1934. *Who shall survive?* Washington, D.C.: Nervous and Mental Disease Publishing.

Murphy, G., and Kovach, J. K. 1972. *Historical introduction to modern psychology.* New York: Harcourt Brace Jovanovich.

Nisbet, R. A. 1966. *The sociological tradition.* New York: Basic Books.

Park, R. E. 1950. *Race and culture.* Glencoe, Ill.: Free Press.

Pascal, B. 1946. *Pensees of Pascal.* New York: Peter Pauper Press.

Peters, R. S. ed. 1962. *Brett's history of psychology.* Cambridge, Mass.: MIT Press.

Piaget, J. 1964. *The moral judgment of the child.* New York: Free Press.

Rieff, P. 1959. *Freud: The mind of the moralist.* New York: Doubleday.

Russell, B. 1945. *A history of western philosophy.* New York: Simon & Schuster.

Rychlak, J. F. 1968. *A philosophy of science for personality theory.* Boston: Houghton Mifflin.

Sapir, E. 1929. The status of linguistics as a science. *Language.* 1929: 5, 207–14.

Sarbin, T. R., and Allen, V. L. 1968. Role theory. In *The handbook of social psychology,* Vol. I, eds. G. Lindzey and E. Aronson, pp. 488–567. Reading, Mass.: Addison-Wesley.

Sartre, J-P. 1966. *Being and nothingness.* New York: Washington Square Press.

Scriven, M. 1964. Views of human nature. In *Behaviorism and phenomenology,* ed. T. W. Wann, pp. 163–90. Chicago: University of Chicago Press.

Sheldon, W., Stevens, S. S., and Tucker, W. B. 1940. *The variety of human physique: An introduction to constitutional psychology.* New York: Harper & Row.

Shotter, J. 1970. Men, the man-makers: George Kelly and the psychology of personal constructs. In *Perspectives in personal construct theory,* ed. D. Bannister. New York: Academic.

Snell, B. 1960. *The discovery of mind.* New York: Harper & Row.

Spitz, R. A. 1945. Hospitalism: An enquiry into the genesis of psychiatric conditions in early childhood. *Psychoanalytic Study of the Child.* 1:53–74.

STINCHCOMBE, A. L. 1968. *Constructing social theories.* New York: Harcourt Brace Jovanovich.

STRONG, E. K. Jr. 1966. *Manual, Strong vocational interest blanks.* Stanford, Calif.: Stanford University Press.

TERMAN, L. M., AND ODEN, M. H. 1947. *The gifted child grows up.* Stanford, Calif.: Stanford University Press.

THOMAS, A., BIRCH, H. G., CHESS, S., HERTZIG, M. E., AND KORN, S. 1963. *Behavioral individuality in early childhood.* New York: New York University Press.

VYGOTSKY, L. 1962. *Thought and language.* Cambridge, Mass.: MIT Press.

WADDINGTON, C. H. 1967. *The ethical animal.* Chicago: University of Chicago Press.

WALLACE, A. F. C. 1961. *Culture and personality.* New York: Random House.

WHITE, R. H. 1959. Motivation reconsidered: The concept of competence. *Psychological Review.* 66:297–333.

WITTGENSTEIN, L. 1953. *Philosophical investigations.* New York: Macmillan.

YANKELOVICH, D., AND BARRETT, W. 1971. *Ego and instinct.* New York: Random House.

Name Index

A

Abraham, 156
Adelson, J., 196
Adler, A., 57, 64, 67, 70, 71
Ainsworth, M. D. S., 179, 189
Allen, V. L., 187
Allport, G. W., 3, 10, 11, 19, 95, 96, 97, 98,
    99, 100, 101, 102, 103, 104, 105, 106,
    107, 108, 109, 110, 111, 112, 113, 114,
    115, 120, 122, 132, 144, 158, 160, 164,
    171, 190, 202
Amundsen, R., 103, 105
Ardrey, R., 179
Aristotle, 4, 12, 18, 87, 94, 127, 201
Augustine, 15

B

Bakunin, M., 146
Baldwin, J. M., 14
Bannister, D., 115
Barker, R. G., 7
Barrett, W., 185, 186
Barron, F., 201
Barth, J., 188

Baumrind, D., 184
Beethoven, L. van, 109
Berger, P. L., 139, 144, 156
Bernheim, H., 5
Binswanger, L., 146, 148, 149, 150
Bogart, H., 9
Bowlby, J., 54 179, 189
Brett, G. S., 12
Brücke, E., 21
Buddha, 74
Burckhardt, J., 56, 58, 146

C

Campbell, D. G., 195
Camus, A., 4, 138, 151, 160, 161, 192, 205
Carus, C. G., 11, 56
Cattell, R. B., 6
Charcot, J., 5
Chomsky, N., 115
Christ, 74
Churchill, W., 26
Clausen, J., 13
Coleridge, S. T., 89
Coles, R., 165, 166, 179
Comte, A., 204

Subject Index

Role *(cont.)*
    defined, 187–88, 196
    role structure, 196, 197, 199, 200, 202
Root ideas, 1, 9, 93, 112, 113, 127
    defined, 9–19, 53, 93

S

Secondary process thought, 27
Self-awareness, 51, 71, 72, 73, 91, 109, 126,
    138, 152, 153, 154, 155, 156, 157, 159,
    160, 161, 162, 199
Self-concept, 1, 40–41, 70, 73, 74, 76, 83–86,
    94, 97, 104, 112, 117–21, 134–37, 144,
    152–55, 161, 166–78, 193–96, 200, 201
    as archetype, 58, 60
    defined, 14–16
Self-deception *(see* Self-awareness)
Self-esteem, 16, 83, 102, 168, 170
Sentiment, 82, 83, 91–92, 97, 104, 105, 110,
    117–18
    defined, 82
    of self-regard, 83–85, 87, 88, 92, 102–103,
    183
Social class, 138
Socialization, 1, 43–50, 70, 75, 81, 83–86, 94,
    105, 106, 117–21, 126, 134–37, 144,
    155–57, 166–78, 184, 196–99
    defined, 13–14

Superego, 41–52, 88, 92, 154, 182, 185, 200

T

Trait, 6, 100, 111
Transcendence, 150, 152, 153, 155, 161
Types:
    body, 5
    character, 37–38, 50
    Jungian, 68
    personality, 5

U

Umwelt, 148, 149, 152
Unconscious, 1, 21–35, 41, 42, 48, 51, 54,
    57, 69, 71, 72, 73, 74, 75, 78–79, 88–
    89, 90, 106, 107, 123–24, 126, 137–40,
    152–55, 178, 179–81, 199–200
    collective, 57, 58, 59, 60, 69, 72, 180
    defined, 11–12
    personal, 57, 58, 63, 180
    sociological, 137–38, 180

W

Will to power, 151, 152, 160
Will to truth, 151